The Appropriated Voice

The Appropriated Voice

Narrative Authority in Conrad, Forster, and Woolf

Bette London

ANN ARBOR
THE UNIVERSITY OF MICHIGAN PRESS

Published in the United States of America by
The University of Michigan Press
Manufactured in the United States of America

1993   1992   1991   1990   4   3   2   1

Library of Congress Cataloging-in-Publication Data

London, Bette Lynn.
   The appropriated voice : narrative authority in Conrad, Forster,
and Woolf / Bette London.
      p.   cm.
   Includes bibliographical references
   ISBN 0-472-10160-9 ✓
   1. English fiction—20th century—History and criticism.
2. Modernism (Literature)—Great Britain.   3. Conrad, Joseph,
1857–1924.   Heart of darkness.   4. Forster, E. M. (Edward Morgan),
1879–1970.   Passage to India.   5. Woolf, Virginia, 1882–1941.   To
the lighthouse.   6. Authority in literature.   7. Sex role in
literature.   8. Narration (Rhetoric)   I. Title.
PR888.M63L66   1990
823'.91209—dc20   89-48925
                                                              CIP

For my parents, Clara and Oscar London

Acknowledgments

It seems especially appropriate for a book entitled *The Appropriated Voice* to acknowledge here—with gratitude—some of the many people whose voices have supported, challenged, and sustained my own. Frederick Crews's enthusiastic engagement, relentless humor, and unflagging commitment saw this project through its earliest manifestation, and he has generously continued to support my work even as my voice has take off in directions he might not wish to own. Alex Zwerdling offered subtle and incisive readings of an earlier version of this work, and his continued intellectual support has been sustaining. I have received helpful suggestions on both earlier and later versions of this work from Robert Alter, Bruce Johnson, and Richard Pearce.

The University of Rochester has provided both personal and institutional support for this project. A University of Rochester Mellon Faculty Fellowship provided the release time necessary for completion of the manuscript. My colleagues in both the English Department and the Susan B. Anthony Center for Women's Studies have created a challenging and intellectually stimulating environment that has fostered dramatic and ongoing changes in my thinking. James Longenbach generously read several chapters of this book and offered astute criticisms as well as timely and much appreciated support. I am grateful both for his friendship and for a sense of our different but shared intellectual project. Constance Penley has provided continued intellectual support for and encouragement of my work in feminism, and her own work has helped me to constantly rethink and refine my own feminist positions. In their own work as well as their responses to mine, other colleagues in the Susan B. Anthony Center—in particular, Bonnie Smith and Sharon Willis—have continued to remind me of the possibilities and contradictions in feminist theory and criticism.

Part of chapter 2 appeared in *Criticism* 31 (Summer 1989) (copyright © 1989 Wayne State University Press). A version of chapter 5 was delivered to the Susan B. Anthony Center faculty research seminar, and I am grateful for many helpful suggestions from that audience.

LeAnn Fields, my editor at the University of Michigan Press, has enthusiastically supported and efficiently handled my manuscript through every stage of its passage into book, making my dealings with the Press not only painless but actually pleasurable. Robin Sherlock contributed conscientious and imaginative research aid and has expertly assisted in every stage of the manuscript preparation; generously giving of her time and herself, she has given much more to this book than can be summed up under the title of research assistant.

Finally, I wish to thank Thomas Hahn, whose intellectual and emotional companionship have made this book possible; who has read and re-read this book (in all its stages) with rigor, patience, and generosity; who, by his own example, has pushed me to think harder and more complexly about critical matters; who has nourished all my voices and voices I didn't know were in me; and whose commitment has often kept me going, helping me to find my voice and to appropriate it.

Contents

Chapter 1

The Appropriated Voice

Modernism is dominant but dead.

—Jürgen Habermas

In the postmortems performed on the canon of modernist literature and art, a familiar picture of modernism reemerges—of modernism conceived in terms of authentic self-expression, original production, and aesthetic autonomy. This modernism finds its fullest articulation in the concept of voice as the locus of unique, personal identity, and in particular, the projection of the artist's voice, as Fredric Jameson argues, as "a personal, private style, as unmistakable as your fingerprint, as incomparable as your own body." Style, as voice, proclaims its allegiance to the individualized body and individualistic personality, so that, in Jameson's words, "the modernist aesthetic" becomes "organically linked to the conception of a unique self and private identity."[1] Whether invoked as nostalgia for lost presence or as subject of a postmodern critique, this vision of modernism reinscribes modernism's own self-proclaimed aesthetic; it reinscribes what Perry Meisel has called "the myth of the modern," a myth itself in need of questioning.[2]

Yet what should be clear from our postmodern perspective is that modernism is neither a monolithic nor an unproblematic entity; like the cultural productions of our present age, it participates in and responds to a crisis in cultural authority and narrative legitimacy. Its contradictions are performed in its representations and reproduced in the conditions of our reading. In an age of mechanical reproduction

*like
Benjamin*

that has both canonized the "modern classics" and distributed them
in multimedia packagings, we cannot recover their originality; we
cannot read them innocently. Yet the particular determinants of our
own cultural positioning situate us advantageously for the interrogation of modernism's self-definitions. Approaching a modernism that
has already been institutionalized, we can perhaps best reopen its
practice by exploiting the position we occupy, by, what I would like
to call, "reading interestedly."

Such an undertaking redirects our attention to the assumptions
that govern our practices of reading. Foremost among these, as Walter Ong stipulates, are assumptions about speaking subjects and their
audiences: "About any work of literature, it is legitimate to ask who is
saying what to whom. To treat any work exhaustively, this question
must always ultimately be asked. Without addressing oneself to this
question, it would appear impossible to judge the value of any utterance . . . ."[3] Yet as Foucault has argued, such "disinterested" questions may predetermine the judgments they empower, foreclosing
the field of literary meaning. Foucault's own strategic shift from the
question "Who really spoke?" (with its embedded logic of privileged
subjectivity) to the question "What difference does it make who is
speaking?" seeks to unleash an alternate line of questioning. A re-
focused inquiry might ask, Who empowers or authorizes our discourse? How does discourse position subjects? How does our speech
come to be?[4] Attention to these questions begins to address the interests excluded from "exhaustive" critical treatments; and it begins to
expose the interests served by keeping such questions suppressed.

Turning away from emphasis on speakers to the conditions of
our speech, an interested reading of modern fiction might uncover its
politics of transparency: the ideological underpinnings of its claims to
aesthetic immediacy and political disinterestedness. For the disinterested posture we have valued in these modern works—and in
their most authoritative readings—remains blind to its own informing ideologies. In the case of the early modernist writers I consider
here—Conrad, Forster, Woolf—it produces readings bound to refor-
mulate the authors' liberal humanist intentions and their claims to
aesthetic self-sufficiency. Reading with attention to our own difference, however, to our own positions of interest, we might contest
these very things; we might shift modernism's ruling paradigms,
relocating its sites of literary, narrative, and cultural interest.

To the extent that postmodernism (re)constructs modernism as its foil, modernism, as we experience it in our literary artifacts, remains closed to postmodernism's textual strategies and political critique; it remains the property of a dominant critical culture that has elaborated and institutionalized modernist assumptions in its own methodologies.[5] Jameson's representation of the modernist project, for example, though not uncritical of its interest in individual identity, reproduces critical orthodoxies. It reads uncannily like Albert J. Guerard's celebration of the great writer's voice, a hallmark for him of Conradian achievement: ". . . most agree that there is something recognisable in every great writer's voice. Can we approximate something similar to the voiceprint which, it appears, will soon be accepted as evidence in courts of law?"[6] Identifying this voice through "characteristic movements of mind," Guerard classifies its manifestations by degrees of authenticity, distinguishing "[a]n even more truly Conradian voice" from its lesser varieties.[7] If postmodernism calls into question this voice of self-identity, exposing its realization as a modernist fantasy, it does not challenge the assumption that terms like *authentic voice* are the ones through which modernism is conceived.

What I want to argue in this study, however, is that modernism's ruling constructs must themselves be read problematically, and that they are problematized *within* modernism—within the modernism we are empowered to perceive. I choose voice for my focus because of its peculiar centrality to modernism's textual productions and literary history and to the more recent theoretical challenges to modernism's canonical authority. In this larger context, voice itself is in question—the subject of contested meaning: organic center of the text, agent of aesthetic unity, site of a personal presence, instrument of ideology, effect of mechanical reproduction, product of political technologies. My title, *The Appropriated Voice*, marks the convergence, or collision, of these competing understandings. Echoing the title of Barbara Hardy's well-known book *The Appropriate Form* (1964), it also records its distance from and indebtedness to formalist predecessors.

The shift from a rhetoric of decorum to one of power struggle—from appropriateness to appropriation—and from the boundedness of form to voice's potential indeterminateness traces a critical movement reflected in the trajectory of my own thinking. This work represents, then, in part, the appropriation of my own voice by current critical vocabularies; but it represents as well my desire to appropriate

the insights of contemporary theories to produce new readings of precisely those modernist texts (*Heart of Darkness, A Passage to India, To
the Lighthouse*) one might assume we have already read exhaustively.
This study, then, also affirms an abiding interest in canonical texts
and in creating a space for their continued re-readings. In challenging
the terms by which these texts have presented themselves—the terms
by which they have generally been understood—I do not have in
mind some programmatic alternative, some version of what the novels *should* be. Rather, my interest is in making their appropriations
(the ones they represent, facilitate, and perform) the subject of our
critical inquiry. For the texts remain of interest for the ways they
articulate and negotiate the cultural configurations of their own contemporary scene as well as for the ways they have been spoken over
time and the ways, even today, they continue to speak.

The term *appropriation* has been foregrounded in the discourses
of postmodernism—as the condition of aesthetic practice and the
mechanism of political authority. As such it stands in opposition to
what Rosalind Kraus has called modernism's "discourse of originality."[8] As Douglas Crimp has argued, the arts of appropriation
herald a new (aesthetic) ideology: "The fiction of the creating subject
gives way to the frank confiscation, quotation, excerptation, accumu-
lation and repetition of already existing images."[9] On the political
front, the work of cultural criticism (e.g., Edward Said, Homi Bhabha)
has unveiled the appropriative structures that underwrite the construction of the colonial subject in Western narrative and political
economies; at the same time, much feminist theory has focused on
the appropriation of "woman" by (masculine) discursive practices
that deny women independent speech. The exclusion of these
"other" voices is sustained by a critical enterprise that places its value
on the representation of authentic experience and textual originality.[10] Yet as theories of cultural suppression suggest, it is in appropriation itself that we might locate the site of resistance to political
hegemony—in, for example, the discourses of mimicry, parody, and
pastiche. Displaying the quotations, imitations, accumulations, im-
positions, and confiscations that make them up, these discourses
speak through and against positions of appropriatedness.

These discourses of appropriation constitute the subject of the
present study; suppressed by a critical insistence on modernism's cult

of originality, they constitute what might be called modernism's *other* ideology: its performance of its own political and aesthetic complicities; its display of its own second-handedness.[11] Promoting its own difference from modernist mythologies, postmodernism has abetted this suppression; yet its insights make it possible to perceive the counter-discourses at play in modernism. Put another way, postmodernism can be seen to focus the ways modernism both participates in and resists its narratives of mastery. If the question, "Who really spoke?" governs the modernist project, it is a question that, within modernist productions, is already implicated in its own critique. For in modernist texts, the question cannot be answered by naming a speaker or measuring the authenticity of his speech. Rather, the question turns back upon—and into question—its own conditions of meaning: the autonomy of the subject, the category of authenticity, the parameters of speech.

Integrity of voice, I want to argue, is not the modern novel's given—or even its supreme achievement; it is the question the novel sets itself. For the fiction of the early twentieth century, voice represents less a locus of authority than authority's problematic. More generally in the period, and particularly in the novels I have selected for scrutiny, voice represents the site of a struggle articulated on a number of fronts: between competing voices, competing individualities; between political power (conceived in the broadest way) and individual autonomy; between artistic innovation and narrative's conventional authorities. Whether the novelist deploys first-person narrators (Conrad), a vestigial form of omniscience (Forster), or a depersonalized voice that obliterates itself (Woolf), voice, at this moment, becomes the thing the novel must construct. Understood as constructed, the production of voice prompts a new set of queries: What is the basis for any voice's authority? How can voices be distin- guished? To what extent can voice be considered a personal and personalizing property?

The three works I have highlighted stand as representative responses to a perceived crisis in narrative and cultural authority. Different as their approaches may be, they share in a profound challenge to the easy identification of voice with the substance of individuality; they share in an interrogation of the very grounds by which voice (in the novel) can be understood to exist. Exploring voice as both the subject of representation (marker of character identities) and as the representation of the narrative's workings (the place of the absent author), they each pose voice as a riddle: a thing that is and is not one's own. Inscribing this riddle across aesthetic and political domains, the novels stage the construction of voice as a narrative and cultural event. My readings pursue the mechanisms of this staging: the specific narrative conditions under which one's voice can be appropriated by other voices and the constraints (political and other) that impinge upon the voice's autonomy. While explicating the way the problem of voice produces distinctive and challenging narrative effects, these readings also raise larger questions about the operation of narrative in a cultural context.

In particular, they explore, at the level of represented content and of representation itself, the implication of these texts in contemporary discourses of race, gender, class, and nationality. They reveal the text's often unwitting participation in the very ideologies it critiques—whether through acts of conciliation or collaboration or through confinement to oppositional strategies. While colonialism figures prominently for Conrad and Forster as the novel's site of contest, as does sexual identity for Woolf, the essays that follow seek to complicate this formulation by reconsidering the spaces in these novels inhabited by the narrative. Such a study reveals the self-contradictory positions the narrative occupies and the intersection it demarcates between competing ideologies. My readings thus reflect ideological crossings and conflicts. In Conrad, for example, the trail of voice that insinuates itself through the novel's colonial context leads to a consideration of the construction of gender as constitutive of the speaking subject of the narrative. In Forster, the racial and sexual politics that conspire in Adela's charge against Aziz are transposed onto and replayed in the "feminized" voice of the narrative—a voice at odds with and centered upon its own "Englishness." In Woolf, voice itself (whether masculine or feminine) participates in and produces a kind of domestic imperialism, implicating narrative in positions of sexual power, class privilege, aesthetic conformity, and social authority.

At the same time, these novels all speak their desire for an unappropriated voice—a voice unmediated by compromising accents. In this respect, *Heart of Darkness* stands as an almost formulaic text; for the desire for pure voice is thematized in Kurtz and structures Marlow's quest. Perhaps less self-consciously, it structures the search, in Forster, for an untainted passage to India and in Woolf, for an authentic subjectivity. That such quests inevitably lead to failure cannot, as many critics would like to have it, leave unchallenged the structuring desire itself. For we now stand in a position to disentangle modernism's desires—its explicit ideology—from the performance of its texts. Attention to performance, however, shifts critical paradigms; it places mediation—or what I prefer to call appropriation—at the heart of modernism's darkness. The impossibility of an unmediated voice rests, in this revaluation, not on modernism's discovery of the abyss as the limit of its challenges but on its discovery that even the abyss has already been appropriated by representation. In this light, *A Passage to India* can be read as a parable. For if the novel answers the desire for authentic experience with the caves' resounding "Ouboum!", this utterance represents not some unmediated voice exploding sense and meaning but rather voice's echo—the emblem of its inevitable secondariness.

These novels, then, move not toward the increasing purification of voice but toward the recognition of voice's fictionality—its constructedness. As site of appropriation, voice operates simultaneously in aesthetic and political terrain, arenas artificially separated by traditional critical categories. But formalist assumptions—among them the assumption that form constitutes the most significant and distinctive feature of literary modernism—have tended to sustain this separate spheres mentality. The result has been the production of a modernism that either excludes politics from its purview or relegates the political to its "proper," nontextual place. The large body of critical readings, for example, that seek to situate modernist texts in their social and historical place tend to operate within a "content" or "context" paradigm; introducing the political through circumstantial evidence, they complement rather than dislodge the text's formal preeminence. Yet if modernist practice calls attention to the text's aesthetic makeup, such attention to material production can also bring cultural modes of production into view, exposing the ideological components of the aesthetic. The narrative crisis, for example, signaled by a withdrawal from omniscience, produces political as well as aesthetic consequences. For the need to rethink voice fundamen-

tally—to find a ground and position from which to speak—answers
to more than a simple problem of artistic agency.

If the political and aesthetic constructions of voice, then, run
parallel paths in the practice of modern fiction, they are paths that
sometimes meet and whose meetings invite further scrutiny. Consequently, my concern here with cultural determinations involves less a
reconstruction of external historical realities than a reconsideration of
the places *in* narrative through which culture speaks: the places
where narrative speaks about culture, but even more where it speaks
culture through the reproduction of its mechanisms and tropes. The
intersection, in voice, of the political and aesthetic produces unsettling narrative effects, pressing against the formal containments of
narrative to produce texts of shifting shape and disrupted coherence.
But the uneasiness these novels occasion—occasion by the very ques-
tionableness of the voices they present—may be, I want to argue, a
primary source of their compelling interest. One consequence, then,
of a study such as this would be to reconsider the terms of pleasure
that novels offer us.

The problem of voice I have isolated in these texts participates in
and reflects the larger project of modernism. Jacques Derrida, of
course, has made voice a center of his decentering critique of modern
Western philosophy; and Vincent Pecora, in a recent essay on Conrad, returns to Schopenhauer and Nietzsche to uncover in the philosophical roots of early modernism anticipations of deconstructive understandings of voice and its textual strategies: "Indeed, it would
appear that the problem of voice—both literary and human—is absolutely central to the whole phenomenon commonly called modernism
in Western literature."[12] My own study pursues a different genealogy, investigating this "central phenomenon" through the insights of
those who, while clearly influenced by deconstruction, have turned
their attention to the voice's cultural (social, sexual, political) structurings. In my individual chapters, I have tried to suggest the wider
implications of my emphases through references to other works by
these authors and through reference to a variety of other literary and
nonliterary texts. Thus I read Forster's novel against his Indian letters, journals, and essays to suggest the complexities of his position
as a cultured subject, bound up with historically available discourses
on race, class, and nationality. And I read both Conrad and Forster

against the insights of recent revisionary work in cultural ethnography; for in their representations of other cultures, they occupy positions being defined, in the course of this period, by the development of the discipline of "modern" anthropology. The exposure—in ethnographic studies—of the textual construction of other cultures and of the fiction of cultural relativism offers a provocative critique not only of earlier anthropological writings but of (contemporaneous) literary texts premised on receptivity to other cultures and authorial objectivity. Finally, I read Woolf's narrative postures against current French feminist theories of the feminine, and against her own pronouncements (in letters, diaries, lectures, and essays) of a feminist and modernist aesthetic. Taking off, for example, from an extended reading of "Mr. Bennett and Mrs. Brown," I consider the ways the problematics of voice are embedded in the very definitions of literary modernism. In this respect, Woolf provides a fitting conclusion to this study, for her works make explicit—in their very narrative difficulty— a set of concerns about voice that Conrad and Forster treat, for the most part, less self-consciously.

*   *   *

> What difference does it make who is speaking?
> —Michel Foucault, "What Is an Author?"

Concluding an essay that radically challenges traditional, humanist notions of authorship, Foucault's question stands as the ultimate statement of an informed indifference. In a "culture in which fiction would not be limited by the figure of the author"—as it has been in our own culture, Foucault argues, since the eighteenth century—the question "Who is speaking?" would no longer be significant.[13] But for us, occupying some uncertain place between these ways of thinking, the question, "What difference does it make who is speaking?" does not clearly read rhetorically. And perhaps, as Andreas Huyssen suggests, it may no longer be the most effective ground for a radical critique: "To reject the validity of the question Who is writing? or Who is speaking? is simply no longer a radical position in 1984."[14] Foucault's question, in fact, taken out of context, invites a double reading: a reading attentive to the significance of differences *in* speakers and to the significance of the difference, from speakers, *of* speech. In the remainder of this chapter, I would like to consider the implications for my own study of these two possible readings.

As the subtitle of this book suggests, my concern with the question of voice is intimately tied to the question of authority and to individual authors. And as my recourse to biographical materials intimates, it *does* make a difference that Joseph Conrad, E. M. Forster, or Virginia Woolf speaks. Their personal investments in the integrity of voice are readily documented: Conrad, as belated British citizen, acutely sensitive to slips and mispronunciations of an alien tongue; Forster, as self-proclaimed denationalized citizen, seeking a voice uncompromised by the ubiquitous British public school; Woolf, as fictional founder of the Society of Outsiders, refusing the privileges and prerogatives of masculine authority. We assume such investments fuel the obsessive concerns of their narratives and give them their specificity; such an assumption, at least, satisfies our desire for a "personal voice" that would preserve fiction's—and criticism's—humanity. Moreover, especially in the case of Woolf, interest in "the author" has produced a dramatic critical and cultural resurgence of interest in what that author has produced.

Yet as the above formulations should suggest, the author's voice, as I understand it, lacks a single, authoritative identity, existing in all the variableness of private self-constructions, collective critical fictions, and popular public mythologies. Identifying this voice (whether conceived as that of an historical personage or critical construct) does not stabilize the meanings of the text, although it may lend a peculiar poignancy to the gap between presumed authorial desire and textual effect. Thus in the case of Conrad, Forster, and Woolf, their texts yield abundant evidence of their infiltration by the very voices they set themselves to abandon or suppress. Like the texts, the author is subject to discursive instability, defined, in any given context, by the voice(s) with the strongest proprietary claims. The difference that the designation of an author's voice allows in our understanding of a text, then, is not a difference from the condition of appropriation but an entry into a potentially different set of appropriations that, given our canonization of authors, carries a particular historical weight.

In part, then, what I am suggesting is the way the author's voice—and the author him- or herself—becomes a public property, a situation implicit in the publication, and sometimes even writing, of the author's "private" letters and diaries. Thus with the wealth of Woolf materials made available in the last ten to fifteen years, Woolf has become what a theatrical production of 1985 nearly made her: "a one-woman show," a self-contained culture industry. As a *New Yorker* cartoon forecast with its fantasy of "The Virginia Woolf Book Shop" (partitioned by subject, "Her Friends," "The Fiction," "The Criticism"), the possibilities for self-proliferation seem limitless. Certainly, on the critical marketplace, the premium on Woolf studies has run so high as to have potentially exhausted itself; for years now, experts have been declaring a glut, while critical productions continue to appear with predictable regularity. And as feminist criticism, in particular, has brought Woolf renewed centrality, her "person" has been alternately traduced, enshrined, and reconstituted—so much so that we must ask, Whose Woolf is being circulated and reproduced?

The question, no less pressing for Conrad and Forster, remains the fundamental one: Who is speaking here? In the name of the author, what voices meet? The relatively recent centenary celebrations of the births of Forster and Woolf, with their attendant volumes of critical essays—along with earlier commemorations and recent revaluations of Conrad—bring this problem to the fore. They also introduce the added questions of a critical politics: Who decides what one can and cannot say about an author? Who authorizes "the enduring voice" of the great writer such volumes work to produce? Again, Woolf proves a particularly dramatic case, staging these questions quite literally. For with Leonard Woolf's scrupulously edited edition of *A Writer's Diary* (1953), Quentin Bell's authorized biography (1972), and the more recent release of the unabridged diaries, edited by Bell's wife, Anne Olivier Bell, the voice of Virginia Woolf has emerged as a family production—and not without occasioning considerable controversy.[15] Moreover, with Leonard Woolf applying his imprimatur to works of literary criticism, such personal authority more directly enters the academy: "Mr Leaska's analysis and interpretation of *To the Lighthouse*, to which I have been asked to write this foreword, are the most illuminating study of Virginia Woolf's novels which I have read—indeed, the only work comparable with it for critical illumination is the monumental study by Professor Guiguet."[16] The controversy occasioned by such controlling powers has therefore surrounded not only the nature of the biographical presentation of Woolf but also the type of interpretations sanctioned by the literary establishment and even the accessibility of Woolf's texts. Jane Marcus, for example, makes the issue of appropriation quite explicit, prefacing one of her most recent books with a brief overview of feminist critics' struggle, in the last decade, to lay claim to Woolf: "Our quarrels with Quentin Bell and the Literary Estate may be seen as a test case for feminist scholarship, a kind of custody battle over her reputation."[17] Even where particular interests cannot be so readily identified, critical formulations reflect controlling beliefs.

The rhetoric of adulation, for example, that informs so much of our critical industry—tribute, celebration, commemoration, homage—constructs the voice of the author according to specific ideologies: as implicitly stable and as sufficiently expansive and humane enough to accommodate great diversity. In other words, the author, like his or her texts, partakes of the qualities of "the classic"—the classic, as Frank Kermode defines it: possessing both "intrinsic qualities that endure" and "an openness to accommodation which keeps [it] alive under endlessly varying dispositions."[18] With respect to the texts and authors I consider here, I would like to modify this definition, locating the classic stature of the "modern masters" and "masterpieces" in their capacity for appropriation.[19] Such a formulation of the process reads less benevolently than Kermode's and points to different stakes. It points, potentially, to what cannot be accommodated to the fiction of liberality—to meanings too incompatible with each other to maintain the illusion of unity; to readings radically resistant to an ideology of honoring or even of diversity; to critiques of the author's canonical stature or cultural authority. In the academic debates surrounding colonialism and feminism, for example—debates that remain politically and emotionally charged—these authors and texts have been appropriated by all sides. But the competing critical voices cannot be easily reconciled; engaged in a struggle for meaning, ownership, and authority, they call into question the integrity of authorship—the possibility of a single voice, however expansive, we can rely upon.

In part, then, I have chosen these writers for the center of my study precisely because they have already been the subject of so much and such varied response—because they and their works proclaim, so dramatically, the appropriations by which they have survived.[20] The very success and endurance of the literary texts have prompted us to reinvent the authors repeatedly, so that the recent emergence of the Polish Conrad, the homosexual Forster, and the feminist Woolf represents only these figures' latest avatars. But, ironically, that same condition leaves the author dispossessed; in the proliferation of voices laying claim to *Heart of Darkness*, *A Passage to India*, and *To the Lighthouse*, the authority of their authors has been radically dislocated or displaced, a condition strikingly apparent in the cultural transformation of these texts into "modern monuments."[21] Translated into films, disseminated through their most quotable lines, circulated as the subject of popular cartoons, these texts have become cultural artifacts, if not cultural clichés. In their postmodern manifestations, however, their monumental status invites fracturing. For they now clearly speak without authors and with questionable authority, a condition that returns us to the fractured authority and "already read" quality of the "originals." In looking closely at some of these popular appropriations, I want to make clear at the outset that, as Jonathan Dollimore argues in a different context, "such appropriations [are] not a perversion of true literary reception, they [are] its reception." As Dollimore further suggests, the "sociopolitical effects of literature are in part achieved in and through the practice of appropriation."[22]

Another *New Yorker* cartoon illustrates this phenomenon. In a scene that clearly represents an amusement park "Jungle Ride," Disneyesque creatures fill a formulaic tropical landscape. In the foreground, alongside the tour boat, a crocodile sits placidly, its face fixed in a giant smile. As the boat enters "the interior," a hippo wades playfully in the approaching waters, while a gorilla greets the boat from the branches of an overarching tree and a snake smiles down on the adventurers from a winding vine. In the boat, tourists with sunglasses, cameras, balloons, madras shirts, and boater hats observe, with their backs to us, the unfolding scene. In the front right-hand corner of the boat, one tourist, his concerned face unnaturally white, looks off to the side, directing our gaze to a concealed figure that meets his eye. Emerging from the edge of the jungle, stepping out from behind a tree, the figure—a picture of distress—looks the classic marooned castaway; he speaks crazedly to the passers-by. The caption reads, "'Kurtz is dead.'"

"Kurtz is dead."

Drawing by Stevenson; © 1980 The New Yorker Magazine, Inc.

Like most jokes, this one depends upon our simultaneous recognition and misrecognition of what we see, a situation reinforced by the fact that the telltale line, "Kurtz is dead," quotes its source inaccurately. That source, of course, is never named directly; but it is assumed to be so deeply embedded in our cultural memory that any educated reader would be struck by the absurdity of the cartoon's textual and contextual incongruities. On the first level, then, the joke reads at the expense of our present cultural positioning, making us complicit in its "inappropriate" appropriation of a literary masterpiece. The cartoon could be the perfect gloss for the Habermas quotation at the chapter's start, "Modernism is dominant but dead"—dead by virtue of its very familiarity, emptied of any subversive power it might once have had. With its "dread beasts" comfortably contained, the cartoon dramatizes—and caricatures—the "domestication" Lionel Trilling feared when, over twenty years ago, he recorded his doubts about the teaching of modern literature. Writing of his students, he explained: "I asked them to look into the Abyss, and, both dutifully and gladly, they have looked into the Abyss, and the Abyss has greeted them with the grave courtesy of all objects of serious study, saying: 'Interesting, am I not? And *exciting*, if you consider how deep I am and what dread beasts lie at my bottom. Have it well in mind that a knowledge of me contributes materially to your being whole, or well-rounded, men.' "[23] That Trilling considered *Heart of Darkness* "the paradigmatic literary expression of the modern concern with authenticity"[24] only adds to our appreciation of the cartoon's ironies, with "Joseph Conrad's great short novel" now the scene of a commercial, mass culture fantasy constructed entirely of the fake and artificial: manufactured experience, simulated thrills, and expressly fabricated settings.

The cartoon, moreover, domesticates Conrad's voice in other ways; in effect, it sanitizes one of the novel's most well-remembered lines: "Mistah Kurtz—he dead." Taken out of context and restored to orthographic and grammatical regularity, the line loses its problematic authority. For in the original context, the words are spoken by "the manager's boy" in "a tone of scathing contempt."[25] The significance of the line—as any reader knows—lies less in the fact it announces than in the conditions of its pronouncement; in other words, it matters—critically—who speaks. The situation of the speaker confers a moral meaning on the words, or, depending on how you read them, a moral ambiguity: decisive indictment of Kurtz and/or ironic tribute to his overbearing life. Moreover, politicized readings of the novel have made the line the site of racial controversy; as one of the few examples in the text in which African natives speak, it has become a test of Conrad's cross-cultural understanding. Chinua Achebe offers the most damning critique: "As for the announcement of Mr. Kurtz's death by the 'insolent black head in the doorway,' what better or more appropriate *finis* could be written to the horror story of that wayward child of civilization who wilfully had given his soul to the powers of darkness and 'taken a high seat amongst the devils of the land' than the proclamation of his physical death by the forces he had joined?"[26]

Achebe's criticisms point to a story Conrad elides: a story that might restore "the boy's" voice and give him a claim to his own history. At the same time, it unearths a story traditional criticism has deemphasized: a tale of exploitation and appropriation played out in the voice of the native, with his imperfect imitation of the conqueror's speech. This "untold" story makes visible the price exacted by the novel's metaphysic, for the presence of Kurtz's voice that the novel insists upon exists at the expense of the other voices it silences or destroys. For Achebe, Conrad's representational practices merely re-inscribe the political appropriations the narrative superficially criticizes. Transposed into the fantasy world of the cartoon, however, these problems seem to disappear. The questionable scene now exists without the history and politics that render it problematic. But it exists only through the rules of literary recognition that compromise its aesthetic autonomy and innocence. In its supreme appropriation of cultural authority, the cartoon thus brings to the surface the novelistic appropriations it would seem to override.

The cartoon, then, reads only superficially at our expense; its representation of the "great novel" proves less absurd than it initially seemed. For the textual reconstruction opens to view new interpretive possibilities. It exposes the challenges to aesthetic autonomy already inscribed in the text: the ways, for example, the novel reads like the late nineteenth-century equivalent of a "jungle ride," pieced together out of the staple materials of contemporary adventure stories, travelogues, missionary diaries, and explorer's accounts. It points to the novel's narrative dependence on and deployment of popular mythologies. Taking its words out of Conrad's mouth, it foregrounds the disembodied and re-embodied voices that haunt Conrad's tale, redirecting our attention to one of the novel's central concerns: the appropriated voice. For the novel intimates what the cartoon spells out: the impossibility of original utterance or authentic speech; the fiction of voice as its own authority. Demystifying the speaking subject, the novel defuses, even as it engages, the question, Who speaks?

Apocalypse Now, *Heart of Darkness*'s most notorious offshoot, highlights a similar problem. In perhaps the most maligned feature of the film "adaptation," the movie constructs a voice for Kurtz—the voice the novel fails to supply. It is as if the film had to assert what the novel implicitly denies—that *Kurtz* speaks at all.[27] The paramount failure of Kurtz's monologue speaks less to Marlon Brando's acting, Francis Ford Coppola's directing, or its own improvised writing than to the film's attempt to present this patent construction as a voice of profound originality.[28] Wittingly or not, the movie exposes the insignificance of individual speech. The same problem occurs in the novel in every attempt to represent Kurtz's utterances, reminding us that the intrigue of Kurtz's voice depends upon its fictionality. The movie's "lapse" thus returns us to the fiction's construction of and dependence upon unrepresentability. It returns us to the novel's own representation of compromised authority.

What is striking in the critical reception of the film are the conventional literary assumptions that underwrite the reviewers' judgments: assumptions about the authority of voice and the uses to which literature can legitimately be put. Thus another recurring complaint about the movie locates its problem in the character of Willard/Marlow, the assumption being that if Kurtz cannot speak authentically, Marlow, in the novel at least, certainly can. In this reading, Willard is seen to lack Marlow's verbal authority. But the problem of Willard's voice is the problem of Kurtz's—seen from the other side: the problem of the under- as opposed to overdramatized. Comparing the movie's "Marlow" unfavorably to the novel's, the film critics simplify what the novel problematizes: voice itself. Neither Willard nor Marlow can supply Kurtz's lack. For even in the novel, Marlow's voice is not a stable guide. Its authority must be constructed in the contested space of the narrative, and thus it is always in process—never fully realized. What the movie refuses us in its narrative voice—stability, coherence, self-sufficiency, moral authority, psychological density—clues us in to the questionable assumptions that shape our reading.

The movie's flagrant, and uncredited, appropriation of Conrad's text, moreover, offers a peculiar access to the novel's textual strategies: its construction of its narrative as literary and cultural pastiche. Thus the movie's "pulp overtones"—the "studied business with dossiers and tapes; the comic-strip-inset closeup of a photograph being passed from hand to hand; the B-movie readings of lines derived from Conrad . . . and of lines that could only come from a B-movie" all have their analogues in the novel itself, in the "trash-adventure-fiction" that haunts Conrad's novel as much as Coppola's film.[29] Written with the audience of *Blackwood's* in mind, the novel skirts the high-art/low-art line, mixing verbal registers and blurring generic boundaries. Discrediting Coppola's appropriation—his "cannibalization" of Conrad—much criticism of the film has fallen back upon a myth of Conrad's textual purity, of a recoverable voice of unproblematic authority.[30] But in its desire for an "unappropriated Conrad," such criticism articulates an impossible fantasy. For what the movie underlines is that our Conrad comes to us dismembered: already a composite of prosaic passages and famous Conrad lines, of cinematic descendants and critical scaffoldings, of academic endorsements and cultural familiarity.

Coppola's dismemberment and deployment of *Heart of Darkness* assume the text's status as a kind of public property. Overproduced, overtaught, overanthologized, its meaning inevitably emerges in the process of being contextually revised. No novel of Forster—or for that matter, Woolf—exerts such a hold on our collective cultural memory. For both Forster and Woolf—though in widely different ways— author, not text, constitutes the object of communal interest. Even where a text appears to be in question, the integrity of the author turns out to be the central stake. Debates over David Lean's *A Passage to India* (1985), for example, have focused on the place of Forster's voice in the film/text and on the status of the novel as the author's personal property. Interestingly enough, these arguments repeat, almost verbatim, the controversies surrounding the initial publication of the book—with "Forster" now replacing "India" as the subject of contest. Transposed into these terms, the argument becomes whether *Forster*'s Indians or Anglo-Indians were really "like that"—the way Lean represents them: as clowns, villains, fools, and caricatures. For the most part, devaluations of the movie have tended to valorize the novel's representational practices and to valorize Forster as superior cultural critic. But arguments on both sides remain bound by the criterion of faithfulness to the original—to Forster, himself, as much as his text. They thus echo Forster's own concerns about translation into film: "Nothing would have survived of the original except my name."[31]

The debates over the film read almost like battles over copyright, the right to speak in Forster's name. Noel Annan, quite literally, represents the history of the film in these terms: as a series of intrigues by which Lean "charmed" the dons of King's College, Cambridge (the executors of Forster's literary estate), into approving the dishonorable script (unfaithful to Forster, disrespectful of his audience) Lean himself authored and substituted for the "authorized" screenplay by Santha Rama Rau.[32] Annan's charges have not in fact been verified. Frank Kermode recalls that Annan was not present at the meeting in question; that Lean had submitted his script in advance; that the dons were not fully persuaded by Lean's paraded knowledge. While Lean certainly knew *A Passage to India* very well, Kermode admits, he did not, as Lean himself claimed and Annan verified, know the book "by heart."[33] Nonetheless, the assumptions that inform Annan's judgment—and Kermode's final remark—echo in several critiques, with the impetus behind many commentaries on the film remaining the question of Forster's controlling interest in the film and posthumous approval. Thus Stanley Kauffmann praises the film for "honoring" Forster, in spite of the fact that Forster never wished to see it filmed, while Salman Rushdie derides the film for dishonoring the wishes of the dead.[34]

Criticisms of Lean have focused on his appropriativeness—his desire to replace Forster, to remake Forster in his own image: literally, to produce *David Lean*'s "A Passage to India." Santha Rama Rau, in her stage adaptation of the novel, apologetically acknowledged her own top billing: "I do remember the shock of seeing the posters which announced: A PASSAGE TO INDIA by SANTHA RAMA RAU and in tiny letters underneath, Based on a novel by E. M. Forster."[35] In contrast, Lean has baldly acknowledged his desire to "correct" or "improve" Forster. Implicitly accepting a conventional view of Forster as a "miniaturist of the heart," Lean has been quite open about his own more grandiose effort: to make the British movie about India "to which all others are trailers,"[36] to do what "nobody" has yet "succeeded in"—"putting India on the screen."[37] To a large extent, this posture constitutes the transgression the critics will not allow: Lean's assertion of his own adaptation's primacy. Put most baldly, the criticism comes down to this: "But no artifice could have rescued a director for whom the original just wasn't good enough."[38]

Such wranglings over Forster's authority anticipate the curious turn of events that have made Forster, in the film industry at least, one of the hottest properties of the 1980s. The more "reverential" adaptations of Forster by Merchant-Ivory make explicit the standards of literary accountability by which *Passage* has been judged. Joking about their refusal to do a Hollywood spinoff, *A Room with a View, Part II*, Ismail Merchant jokingly explained, "We'll only do it if you can resurrect Forster to write the book."[39] Intended as a light— perhaps even predictable—joke, Merchant's offhand comment points to the serious investments of an author-centered industry. Like the criticisms of Lean, it assumes the author's stable and determining presence, a stability belied by Forster's own self-conscious positionings of himself. For as *A Passage to India* demonstrates, in Forster's productions, the subject of authority is much more vexed and the autonomy of the aesthetic realm is subject to repeated challenges. Lean's excesses, in fact, point to the voices of cultural imperialism that always threaten to infect Forster's text—to the appropriative posture inscribed in the conditions of his narrative. They suggest the passages Forster does not so much avoid as negotiate: epic impulses ("putting India on the screen"), cross-cultural posturing (Indians presented as Englishmen in blackface), cultural stereotyping, narrative rationalizations and balancings.

Curiously, much of the evidence marshaled against Lean has its direct analogue in Forster's biography. One of the remarks by Lean, for example, that Rushdie singles out as particularly egregious, reads remarkably like statements sprinkled throughout Forster's Indian diaries and letters: "As for Aziz, there's a hell of a lot of Indian in him. They're marvellous people but maddening sometimes, you know. . . . He's a goose. But he's warm and you like him awfully."[40] Compare, for example, this statement from *The Hill of Devi*, "It's so typical of the Oriental who makes a howling mess over one thing and does another with perfect success and grace" or this description of the Rajah of Dewas, ". . . he was charming, he was lovable, it was impossible to resist him or India."[41] Similarly, Lean's desire to make his film less "anti-English, anti-Raj," to "keep the balance more" coincides at least with Forster's stated intent, the premium he placed on being "fair." "I don't like Anglo-Indians as a class," Forster once explained. "I tried to suppress this and be fair to them, but my lack of sympathy came through."[42] Even Lean's celebrated extravagance ("the caves in India not being imposing enough," Pauline Kael complains, "he dynamited and made his own"[43]) can be seen as taking Forster's literary license to its extreme; for finding the caves "not all that remarkable," Forster admits, he "improved" them when he put them in his book.[44]

I do not mean, especially, to defend Lean or to align him with Forster's "true" intent; but I want to suggest what may be problematic about salvaging Forster at Lean's expense. For the desire to fix Forster's voice (the desire reflected in Lean's critics) itself serves certain interests that require further inquiry—interests that would, for the most part, preserve Forster's traditional place in the critical establishment: as man of morals and manners, as modest genius, as subtle craftsman of small gems, as benign critic of empire. Even attempts to cast Forster as radical cultural critic tend to fall back on one of two lines: historical relativism (he was an enlightened man for his time) or representational transparency (his simple story presents unproblematic political lines). Either way he remains an untroubling presence: a kind of cultural curiosity.

Yet for me what remains most troubling about Forster's novel— and what constitutes its greatest interest—is its resistance to being placed. The contradictory currents it articulates on both the political and aesthetic fronts make it difficult to determine whether the critics' cherished decorum—the mark of artistic autonomy—is something the novel embraces or violates. For the novel's voices prove neither unitary nor stable, existing in a continual state of struggle and realignment. And what seems most radically in question is the author's stabilizing presence. Ironically enough, Lean's film may be most illuminating for the way it has focused these questions—not so much in its own performance but in the responses it has generated. For the film has engaged its audiences in precisely the type of proprietary struggles Forster's narrative plays out—plays out as its own conscious and unconscious colonialist legacy. What Lean's production has foregrounded is the way Forster's text—and Forster as text— operates as a battleground for cultural authority. Like the film, the novel enacts a complicated relation to the prescribed and prescripted, to the possibility of originality. And like the film, it compels the question, In whose name does it speak?

Spoken for by almost every conceivable interest, Woolf—as public figure—presents a more evidently problematic case. The portrait of her that emerges in the popular marketplace is, to say the least, contradictory, in part because the perception of Woolf's biographical accessibility is so often countered by a sense of her texts' formidable opacity. Thus unlike Conrad or Forster, her popular stature seems only loosely connected to any of her specific writings. A televised version of *To the Lighthouse*, for example, could not generate the interest sparked by competing print versions of her biography or even by Edna O'Brien's *Virginia*—a play whose title alone promised biographical intimacy. Presenting, in *Newsweek*'s words, "the many faces and voices" of Virginia Woolf, the play, like other successful stories of her life, could be annexed to the approved Woolfian iconography: "the genius who was haunted and finally hunted down by madness."[45]

No comparable appeal attaches to "popular" renditions of Woolf's books. For as John Leonard's review of the PBS production of *To the Lighthouse* suggests, Woolf's fiction and mass media remain incompatible terms: "Imagine a television program that makes you think for two hours. Imagine one that made me reread Virginia Woolf."[46] Obviously, the print explosion that has catapulted Woolf into household fame has not necessarily challenged the complementary myths of Woolf's fiction as notoriously unreadable. A UPI photograph, reprinted in the *Virginia Woolf Miscellany* (Fall 1987) in a section headed "No Comment" makes the point graphically. A photograph of beauty pageant contestants clad in bathing suits, posed for the camera, smiling and waving vapidly, bears the headline: "Miss USA: Only Seven More Viewing Days." The accompanying text reads: "With the Miss USA contest only seven days away—February 17— photo-journalists and investigative reporters from all over the country are gathering in Albuquerque, N.M., to study the pageant participants engaging in moments of spontaneous fun. This photograph was taken just after the Virginia Woolf–reading comprehension competition, one of many events by which each candidate is judged."

The jibe at the pageant participants deploys Woolf's "high-brow" reputation in a predictable way; reinforcing stereotypical conceptions of the effete novelist, it mocks Woolf as well. But read either way, its ridicule lacks real sting. On its own terms, the photo-text has little interest except as a crude rendition of popular thinking. Yet the unlikely pairing of Virginia Woolf and beauty pageants uncovers a disturbing—and clearly unintended—set of possibilities. For paraded before us in every possible guise, Woolf has become a prized viewing object for cultivated eyes. Her photograph appears with unparalleled regularity—blazoned on tee-shirts, book jackets, and the walls of homes and offices—making Woolf the educated person's most respected "pin-up girl." Posed, packaged, and presented in countless memoirs and "documentary" narratives, Woolf maintains her spectacular hold on the general public through the unabated interventions of the publishing world.

This marketing of Woolf has kept her straddling incompatible realms: the most academic of authors; the most readily recognized. Hence the peculiar adaptability of Woolf to a "comic book" series, for a book entitled *Virginia Woolf for Beginners* speaks pointedly both to Woolf's mass appeal and to her notorious difficulty. But as the back cover of that book makes clear, in keeping with other contemporary mythologizing, the book's subject is not Woolf's fiction but her self: "Many years (and biographies!) after her death, Virginia Woolf remains a contradiction and an enigma. Finally—the definitive documentary comic book on the life and times of the most confusing and fascinating literary woman of the century."[47] Trading on the vast Woolf industry, the book declares its own self-contradictory place: trivializing and exalting Woolf simultaneously; perpetuating the biographical controversies it purportedly decides; participating in the critical exploitation it claims to rectify. Introducing "The cast," "The settings," and "The plot" for its unique biography, the book's abstract proclaims the creation of a new fictional entity: "Virginia Woolf"—a text that rivals and replaces Woolf's works as the site of contested meanings.

Such popular appropriations mark a cultural extreme where, in the reconstruction of the author, the novelist no longer speaks. But even in academic circles, fashionable interest in Woolf has often privileged biography in an attempt to recover Woolf's voice, her "true" authority. Describing the panel participants at the Woolf Centenary Symposium in Texas as they listened to Woolf's voice on a BBC tape, Jane Marcus offers an account of the incident that pushes this position to its literal extreme. She records the shock of the audience in hearing a voice remarkably different from the "hesitant hysterical voice" Woolf's biographers had led them to expect:

> Two features stand out on this tape—the authoritative self-confident commanding tone of the born leader and public speaker, and the rhythmical musical range from low to high of

the writer who loves the sound of words. They roll off her tongue in accents betraying her class, of course, but also in liquid syllables suggesting a bubbling spring of laughter counterpointing her cool control. The voice is so sure of itself, so eminently sane and healthy that it banishes for ever the biographer's hysterical invalid.[48]

Marcus's account posits this voice as a final authority, definitively resolving biographical and critical complexities. Although she remarks, parenthetically, the demurral of English working-class women from the representation of Woolf's voice she articulates, Marcus seems unaware of her own mythologizing, of her own critical projections. But like the biographers she condemns, she appropriates Woolf's voice for her own ends. Her story remains no more than a compelling fable of the desire for authenticity.

Commenting on the papers from a centenary conference conducted on the other side of the Atlantic, Eric Warner presents his different sense of the authentic Woolf: "Her current notoriety stems in part from her being used for all manner of partisan purposes, many of which would probably have alarmed and dismayed her, and which have only an adventitious connection with the profounder, more enduring part of her work."[49] Yet as the context of Warner's remarks reveals, Woolf's endurance as an object of academic study has been bolstered by that partisan popularity, and as his own formulation suggests, it is sustained by the critic's proprietary claims: the claim to speak on Woolf's behalf or in her name. Moreover, the "enduring part of her work" does not constitute some unconstructed and impartial reality; rather, as the volumes of criticism on Woolf demonstrate, it must be defended, reconstructed, and legitimated in continuing contests over critical authority.

In all of this, Woolf's case is, of course, not unique, although the partisan voices that would claim her perhaps speak more self-consciously than in the other cases I have considered here. But when Ian Watt can declare *Heart of Darkness* "the most powerful literary indictment of imperialism"[50] while Chinua Achebe calls for a universal condemnation of the novel as a racist text, the possibilities for partisan positions seem abundantly clear. And when Alan Wilde can observe in 1981, "The lesson of the criticism of the last fifteen years or so seems to me to be that, thematically considered, *A Passage to India* can be made to yield totally opposed and equally valid interpretations,"[51] while four years later critics of Lean's movie present the novel's meaning as thematically fixed, we can see the problematic convergence of academic authority and popular prejudice. In the reception of these works—and perhaps especially in their case—the antithetical voices of art and politics, of the academy and publicity, repeatedly intersect. The popular appropriations of these novelists merely bring into dramatic relief the questions of voice that have shaped the history of our readings of their novelistic achievements. The history of the reception of these writers and books is the history of the uses they have been made to serve and the voices through which they have come to speak; as I hope to demonstrate, it is a history already dramatized in the texts themselves. The starting point for my study of these novels is also, then, the particular heritage they leave.

Joseph Conrad

Chapter 2

Only a Voice/Only a Lie:
The Novel as Polygraph

... I never could invent an effective lie—a lie that would sell,
and last, and be admirable.
    —Joseph Conrad, Letter to R. B. Cunninghame Graham

Early in *Heart of Darkness*, Marlow recounts his arrival at the Central
Station, where he is greeted by the news of his steamship's loss. The
boat lies "at the bottom of the river," sunk, presumably, in a pre-
cipitous "rescue mission" initiated and "unfortunately" aborted just
two days before. Marlow records in considerable detail (and without
much explicit commentary) the general manager's explanation of the
"affair." While Marlow pretends to uncertainty—"I did not see the
real significance of that wreck at once. I fancy I see it now, but I am
not sure—not at all"[1]—even the most naive reader of the novel can
be trained to read in this interview the unmistakable signs of the
manager's lie.[2] A type of polygraphic printout, Marlow's narrative
registers the verbal and nonverbal divagations that mark the manager's departure from the truthful line: his preemptive presentation
("He began to speak as soon as he saw me"), his tendency to monologue ("he paid no attention to my explanations"), his insistent repetitions ("the situation was 'very grave, very grave'"), his fidgets and
jerks (the broken sealing wax), his sudden starts and stops (23).

When, at the end of his narrative, Marlow recounts his own
celebrated lie, the melodramatic flourishes that invade his discourse
function as narrative analogues to these signifying marks. They signal, as the critics have been quick to note, a departure—even a falling

29

off,—from a presumably coherent narrative line.³ They strike the note of inauthenticity the scene has been orchestrated to announce. While nature fails to register Marlow's transgressive act (the heavens do not fall), the text transcribes the violent fluctuations of his recorded voice, graphing shades of difference across its discursive field. A subtle instrument of detection, it maps the truth value of Marlow's tale. Read as polygraph, however, the novel betrays not only the single lie Marlow acknowledges, but the multiple lies that underwrite and interrupt his narrative account. Ironically, these lies place Marlow in the manager's camp. A keeper of the darkness, Marlow treats his own audience to a display of managerial arts: voicing their questions, answering questions that have not been asked, anticipating objections, forestalling critique. Like the manager, he participes in a preemptive rhetoric that transforms collegial conversation into controlling monologue.⁴

I introduce the anachronism of the polygraph quite deliberately, for it strikingly focuses some of the novel's central concerns—in particular, its insistent and complex convergence of voice, identity, and lies.⁵ Though postdating the novel by many years, the polygraph's technology fulfills an impulse *Heart of Darkness* gestures at, taking up the question of identity where phrenology leaves off—providing, as it were, an X ray of the *inside* of the mind. The polygraph thus performs a practice the narrative enacts: it renders visible, in the alienist-doctor's infamous words, "the changes [that] take place inside" (11). And where Conrad's aesthetic privileges vision—"My task is . . . above all to make you see"—the polygraph answers to this need; like narrative discourse, it makes voice accessible to sight, and consequently, something one can "read."⁶

Conrad's own documented fascination with technology thus finds its way, circuitously, into this "scientifically interesting" tale.⁷ In a letter written only months before the inception of *Heart of Darkness*, Conrad expatiated on his first exposure to radiology, to "*the secret of the universe*," to "*the vibrations that make up me.*"⁸ Commenting on "*the nonexistence of, so called, matter*," he anticipates what might be called the technology of identity—the technology lie detection exploits; noting that "*all matter* being only that thing of inconceivable tenuity through which the various vibrations of waves (electricity, heat, sound, light, etc.) are propagated," he represents individuality as scientifically conceived, the waves, in turn, "giving birth to our sensations—then emotions—then thought." This philosophy informs *Heart of Darkness*'s portrait of Kurtz—a model of immateriality, a vehicle for "the various vibrations" to pass through. Kurtz's "secret," the novel suggests, may be that he is not only no more than a voice, but that he is a voice only technically: a field of horizontal sound waves. Generally read as some type of quest for "the secret of the universe," *Heart of Darkness*, in its entirety, can also be seen to engage this philosophy: in its aesthetic practices and in its own troubled meditation on individuality.

A "pretechnological" work, *Heart of Darkness* explores the paradoxes of such advanced technology. Voice identification, for example, posits voice simultaneously as that which is most essentially individuated (a verbal fingerprint) and that which is most radically constructed, reducible to its constituent figures and tropes, literally, to the sound waves that make it up. In the polygraphic encounter, the determination of unique identity inevitably invokes the specter of reproducibility. Deconstructing voice, the polygraph presumes a stable vocal pattern against which difference can be assessed. Conrad's novel works through similar effects. Using the polygraph as model, then, I propose to interrogate the novel's construction of voice, and in particular, its construction of difference as the condition for determining a voice's veracity.[9]

From the beginning, the narrative depends upon the perception of differences that cannot readily be seen—the irreducible moral distinction, for example, between spots of red on a map and similar spots of yellow, orange, blue, or green. Or, as in Marlow's opening lines, it depends upon the perception of an invisible continuity: "'And this also,' said Marlow suddenly, 'has been one of the dark places of the earth'" (5). Marlow's voice intrudes itself upon the ship's silence to re-mark the parameters of cultural identity. It is against this grid, he insists, that Kurtz's ultimate difference must be seen—difference from the shipboard audience, from the crass colonialists, from ordinary madmen, from *anything* the ordinary mind can conceive. Kurtz's difference constitutes Marlow's truth and the novel's originality. This difference, affirmed in the novel's final scene, makes the novel, in Conrad's words, "something quite on another plane than an anecdote of a man who went mad in the Centre of

Africa,"[10] something more than "an incoherent bogie tale."[11] Only a
voice, however, Kurtz is constituted as precisely that which cannot be
seen: "Do you see him? Do you see the story? Do you see anything?"
(27). As measure of the story's readability, Kurtz fixes voice as the
locus of narrative authority.[12]

Similarly, Marlow's voice determines his credibility. While he
offers his visible self as an anchor to reality ("Of course in this you
fellows see more than I could then. You see me, whom you know."),
his voice is the only thing his audience can "see": "For a long time
already he, sitting apart, had been no more to us than a voice" (28).
And it is the *difference* of his voice (Marlow does not spin typical
seamen's yarns) that constitutes Marlow as a knowable entity: "His
remark did not seem at all surprising. It was just like Marlow" (5). Yet
Marlow establishes his identity *within* the tale as a departure from this
known. Speaking of his Continental relatives he admits, "I am sorry
to own I began to worry them. This was already a fresh departure for
me" (8). As he expects his audience to confirm, this departure undermines his very identity: "Then—would you believe it?—I tried the
women. I, Charlie Marlow, set the women to work—to get a job."
Here, as elsewhere in the text, "departure" signals duplicity—on the
polygraphic chart, a deviation from the standard line. Plotting his
Congo journey—"I felt somehow I must get there by hook or by
crook"—Marlow constructs himself as lie; his actual departure graphically registers this sense of imposture as a moment "of startled pause,
before this commonplace affair" (13). Once launched, Marlow cannot
escape this fabricated identity. The product of misrepresentation,
Marlow finds his voice falsified. Moreover, in "allowing" the common perception that he speaks with Kurtz's authority, Marlow further implicates himself in this duplicity at every stage of his journey.

The initial Continental episode provides the pre-text of Marlow's
narrative ("yet to understand the effect of it on me you ought to know
how I got out there"); and it sets in motion the novel's double trajectory where difference (departure) signals both duplicity and integrity.
It reveals, moreover, the paradoxical construction of Marlow's narrative authority: insisting on his own difference from himself, he repeatedly invokes "the shade of the original Marlow" as proof of his
tale's veracity. He invokes this shade, moreover, as proof of his own
commitment to truth: "*You know* I hate, detest, and can't bear a lie"

(27, emphasis mine).[13] No exponent of photographic realism, Marlow substantiates his tale through the testimony of his own voice rather than, as it were, "The Testimony of the Kodak."[14] In the horrific episodes Marlow recounts, his audience must confirm "the horror" of his experience by measuring Marlow's departures from himself rather than the excesses he perceives.

Introducing the "grove of death," for example, the first station on his tour of atrocities, Marlow offers himself as testimonial. "You know I am not particularly tender" (16), he interjects, and later elaborates, "I've seen the devil of violence, and the devil of greed, and the devil of hot desire; but, by all the stars! these were strong, lusty, red-eyed devils, that swayed and drove men—men, I tell you" (17). While Marlow's awakened sensibilities bear witness to the unspeakable things he has seen, his spectacular descriptions collapse into the stylized portraits of allegory: ". . . it seemed to me I had stepped into the gloomy circle of some Inferno" (17); ". . . all about others were scattered in every pose of contorted collapse, as in some picture of a massacre or pestilence" (18). Framing the atrocities—placing them in an aesthetic context—Marlow reserves his "tenderness" for himself. As in the preceding outburst, this tenderness appears as narrative excess: the dislodging of the *story*'s frame via interjections ("You know"), exclamations ("by all the stars!"), repetitions ("devil . . . devil"; "men—men"), and direct address ("I tell you"). The scene's horror thus inscribes itself not in *what* it represents but in the *narrative* spectacle of Marlow's excitability.

This same type of narrative display marks other scenes of atrocity, most notably Marlow's midnight meeting with Kurtz. In this much elided account, Marlow's disordered speech assumes the climactic place in the narrative. For at the moment of crisis—the moment of the confrontation itself—the record of Marlow's struggle with Kurtz gives way to the performance of a more immediate contest over dramatic credibility. The tension of the original encounter registers in the increasing desperation with which Marlow addresses his present audience: ". . . you understand," "And, don't you see," "Believe me or not," ". . . by Heavens! I tell you, it had gone mad" (67–68). The madness of Marlow's text, however, becomes the spectacle his audience sees. Broken by interjections ("Confound the man!" "—but what's the good?" "Soul!"), fluctuating wildly between self-justification and report, jumping fitfully between times and thoughts, the passage proves a concentrated study of discontinuity. A narrative out of control, it occupies almost as much space as the narrative it disrupts: the record of Marlow's rescue mission. Marlow concludes this section by declaring the insanity of Kurtz's soul, insisting on its tangible reality: "I saw it—I heard it. I saw the inconceivable mystery of a soul that knew no restraint, no faith, and no fear, yet struggling blindly with itself" (68). Yet within the narrative, Kurtz's struggle, like Marlow's, remains a telling oversight. Marlow's voice substitutes for and displaces the sight and sound of Kurtz.

In the larger field the novel graphs, Kurtz constitutes "the horror" the narrative overwrites. He figures as a marker of difference both within the plot of Marlow's story and in the plotting of Marlow's voice. It is Kurtz's difference—"the lone white man turning his back suddenly on the headquarters, on relief, on thoughts of home" (32)— that enables Marlow, long before he meets him, "to see Kurtz for the first time." And it is the differences in Marlow's voice (its marks of disorder and excitability) that signal Kurtz's intermittent presence in the text. In both cases, however, these are differences Marlow constructs, as Marlow's interchangeable figures for Kurtz suggest: the emissary of light and progress, the high priest of diabolical excess, the man who "pronounced a judgment upon the adventures of his soul" (71). In Marlow's voice, Kurtz accommodates himself to the shifting structures of credibility. For Marlow, then, Kurtz is indeed a "remarkable man"—one who can be marked in whatever form the services of difference demand.

In this reading, Kurtz stands in the place of "the lie"—or at least, as the marker of the constructed nature of truth. His significance resides in his capacity to represent difference, however ephemeral that difference may be. Marlow's investment in difference determines the peculiar form of his loyalty: he lies so as to affirm Kurtz's truth— to confirm his last words, "The horror! The horror!" as "a final burst of sincerity" (68). But Marlow's loyalty is less to Kurtz than to Kurtz's functionality. Fixing Kurtz as the man who "had something to say," Marlow represents this construction as Kurtz's essential identity. Lying, he constructs, as it were, his own difference, to set Kurtz in relief. For just as Marlow's "deathbed" silence retroactively empowers Kurtz's cryptic words ("I was within a hair's-breadth of the last opportunity for pronouncement, and I found with humiliation that probably I would have nothing to say. This is the reason why I affirm that Kurtz was a remarkable man" [72]), his lie to the Intended procures Kurtz's status as the teller of dark truths.

What I want to argue, however, is that Marlow lies about Kurtz to (re)construct his own narrative as truth—to stabilize the play of differences his narrative enacts. Discrediting the Intended, Marlow bolsters his own credibility, ensuring his position as the one authorized reader of Kurtz's life. The sole possessor of Kurtz's last words, Marlow controls the meaning and circulation of Kurtz's voice. More important perhaps, Marlow's lie validates his larger discourse, producing a retroactive "source" for its irregularities; with Marlow's interview with the Intended as master code, the frequent signs of disturbance that infiltrate the text can be re-read as traces of *the* lie the narrative ultimately unearths.[15]

Certainly, this lie figures prominently in moments of narrative distress—moments when the narrative breaks down and turns in upon itself: "'I laid the ghost of his gifts at last with a lie,' he began suddenly. 'Girl! What? Did I mention a girl?'" (49). But as I have tried to demonstrate, such disruptive patterns figure prominently in numerous passages throughout the text, so much so as to call into question their function as differentiating codes. Linked to Kurtz's problematic presence and to the believability of Marlow's tale, these moments of disturbance lack a single base. Moreover, they challenge precisely what Marlow's lie affirms: the meaning of "the horror," the truth of Kurtz's words. They suggest what the novel's final scene conceals: that lies—as marks of difference—may be the narrative's operative mode.

Read as "fresh departure," the lie to the Intended confirms Marlow's established identity: "You know I hate, detest, and can't bear a lie." It testifies to Marlow's essential truthfulness and to the truth of the experience he recounts—an experience so horrible as to propel him from his standard line. But read in the context I have been suggesting—as part of a pervasive pattern of meandering—the lie *establishes* this prior claim, writing over contradictory evidence. It reveals the way the narrative deploys difference to construct Marlow's identification with truth—an identification already rendered suspect by the repetitive overstatement of Marlow's differentiating claims ("hate," "detest," "can't bear").

As polygraph, Marlow's narrative produces what Peter Brooks

has called "an unreadable report."[16] For Marlow's voice, despite its
omnipresence, proves difficult to read. It witnesses so many departures as to call into question its stable identity, as to call into question
its base of truth. Its differentiating marks read ambiguously, signaling
either the tale's unique origins (what puts it off the chart) or its absence of uniqueness (the absence Marlow's voice fills). The production of a "readable" lie at the novel's close speaks to the desire for
polygraphic proof—for clear demarcations and controllable difference. But what the narrative detects is the process of construction
itself: the construction of the lie (articulated step by step) but even
more, the construction of truth that the lie abets.

*   *   *

> The "Dark Continent" is neither dark nor unexplorable.
> —Hélène Cixous

The problematic truth value of Conrad's tale involves more than Marlow's individual authority; it involves the cultural practices and codes
that constitute his identity—in particular, the myths of race and gender that subtend his discourse. Freud conflated these myths when he
formulated feminine sexuality as "the dark continent"; and it is
Freud's formulation Cixous challenges.[17] But in *Heart of Darkness*,
Conrad was already deploying darkness along these dual tracks to
uphold the inscrutable center of his work.

At first glance, gender might seem to be beside the point, given
its lack of visibility. The novel's masculine codes operate, for the most
part, silently and unself-consciously. But the reproduction of gender
hierarchies enforces the novel's invisible ideology. The suppression
of the feminine—a non-event, in narrative terms—sustains the masculine worlds of the novel's dual plots (the telling of the tale and the
events told about). As the novel's final scene suggests, Marlow pur-
chases his truth at woman's expense, founding masculine authority
upon the discredited feminine.[18]

This last scene replays the one that marks the story's start: the
production of woman as "whited sepulchre." For like the Intended,
Marlow's aunt stands as a hollow monument, harboring death and
duplicity; she stands as the object of Marlow's offhand remark, "It's
queer how out of touch with truth women are" (12). In this initiating

scene, Marlow constructs the place of the feminine as "a blank space," a space of domestic monotony, locating it "in a room that most soothingly looked just as you would expect a lady's drawing-room to look" (12), a place of "quiet chats" and "decent" cups of tea. In Marlow's configuration, woman occupies the place of lack, emptied of even the darkness of feminine sexuality. In the context of the ensuing narrative, the blankness of the feminine constitutes the stable ground upon which masculine adventure can be mapped, the sameness that sets masculine difference in relief. Relegating women to "a world of their own" (12), Marlow writes them out of the narrative, out of existence itself; the ultimate embodiment of marginality, they frame masculine truth and reality.

The displacement of women onto the narrative peripheries naturalizes their association with absence: the absence of truth, the absence of life, the absence of mystery. Their absence supports the construction of "the dark continent" as the locus of these things: a place of "wild vitality," the site of what is "natural and true," the point of "contact with reality." Moreover, their absence supports the projection onto Africa of the "dark continent" of female sexuality—sexuality imaged in the "uncontrollable desire" of "a wild and gorgeous apparition of a woman," a woman "savage and superb," and in the feminized landscape she reflects, "the colossal body of the fecund and mysterious life" with its "own tenebrous and passionate soul" (62). In the narrative iconography, Africa occupies the place of seduction, the enigma of femininity: "There it is before you—smiling, frowning, inviting, grand, mean, insipid, or savage, and always mute with an air of whispering, Come and find out" (13). The narrative maps onto Africa what civilization lacks.

The construction of Africa as the locus of sexuality reinforces the novel's restrictive gender ideology; it works to bar women from the text, denying them a place as narrative subject or even as object of the narrative quest. While the native woman would seem to escape this constrictive framework, she remains positioned in the narrative as the ideological counterpart—and opposite—of white, European womanhood, and hence outside the category "woman." This exclusive definition reflects political realities: the appropriation of gender to racial ideologies.[19] The narrative's production, then, of the second dark continent (female sexuality) repeats the formation of the first, where "a place of darkness" fills the "blank space" a boy hankers after and dreams about (8). In the mapping of this new representational field, "the woman," like Africa, drops out, giving way to the fiction of "impenetrable darkness" that the image projects (female sexuality, darkest Africa).

In the novel's representational matrix, the suppression of women underwrites its cultural myths. And these myths, in turn, consolidate the gendered fictions upon which they are based. Identified with the "lie" of civilization (imaged as feminine obliviousness), women are denied access to the "truth" of savagery (imaged as female sexuality)—a truth grounded on the lie it refutes. The novel's competing definitions of the feminine thus uphold a single system of exclusion. Displaced on both sides, women are denied access to their own sexual/textual identity; they remain constrained to the margins of masculine imaginings. The masculine production of feminine identity works in the interests of the dominant ideology, naturalizing the displacement it constructs. Marlow's representation, for example, of women's "natural" duplicity ("It's queer how out of touch with truth women are"), renders *woman* and *lie* interchangeable, preparing for the substitution the final scene effects, where Marlow's lie supplants the woman that it names. Interrupting himself in the middle of his tale, Marlow shifts from one term to the other in the catching of a breath. It is as if the very word *lie* triggers its equivalent, calls forth a variant of *woman*: "'I laid the ghost of his gifts at last with a lie,' he began suddenly. 'Girl! What? Did I mention a girl? Oh, she is out of it—completely. They—the women I mean—are out of it—should be out of it'" (49).

In the world of Marlow's desire, women and lies have no place; as agents of corruption, they must be kept out of that world, expunged from the text. But as the passage makes clear, women are "out of it" because Marlow's narrative can only figure them that way: "Oh, she had to be out of it" (49). Women's expulsion from the world of dark truths does not so much protect women's position as preserve masculine constructs; for women's absence constitutes a condition of narrative coherence—the foundation of masculine authority. Woman's unauthorized presence at the center of the text, as Marlow's digression displays, threatens narrative itself: it collapses inside and outside, story and frame, speech and silence, past and present.

The production of narrative thus colludes with ideology to keep women in their place. Moreover, the nonrepresentation of women promotes the novel's myth of inscrutability, functioning as both a cause and effect of its ruling construct: the unexplorable heart of darkness. The novel's embedded sexual politics protects this construct from too much scrutiny, from an investigation of its claims to essential truthfulness. For the narrative must conceal the cultural "lies" it sustains. Dependent upon unexamined assumptions, themselves culturally suspect, the novel, in its representation of sex and gender, supports dubious cultural claims; it participates in and promotes a racial as well as gender ideology the narrative represents as transparent and "self-evident."

In contrast to gender, however, Conrad's racial attitudes have been the subject of considerable critical scrutiny, particularly since Chinua Achebe's famous 1975 attack, where he declared "this simple truth": "that Conrad was a bloody racist."[20] Achebe's remark reminds us of the contextual nature of truth—that truth and lie are culturally conceived. As the polygraphic model suggests, they depend upon a process of differentiation—upon departures from the base of a constructed identity. As Achebe explains, turning his investigation to cross-cultural interchange, we do not detect as lies remarks that conform to our dominant ideology, to our culturally constructed identity: ". . . white racism against Africa is such a normal way of thinking that its manifestations go completely undetected" (Achebe, 9).

Achebe's own critique foregrounds a single aspect of a complex ideology; like Conrad's defenders, Achebe offsets only the differences his frame of reference trains him to see. Detailing the distortions mapped by the novel's registers of race, he reads gender univocally. Yet the very features that inform Achebe's racial critique—the dehumanization of the Africans, the refusal "to confer language on the 'rudimentary souls'" (Achebe, 6)—mark the novel's representations of women as well. For these other "rudimentary souls," denied even the distinction of a name (the aunt, the Intended), also speak only to convict themselves, to confirm "how out of touch with truth women are." Similarly, the narrative's projection of Africa as "a place of negations" (Achebe, 2), as "'the other world,' the antithesis of Europe" (Achebe, 3) coincides with its construction of the feminine as the foil to masculinity. In saying this, however, and in my own critique of Conrad's gender ideology, I do not mean to add sexism to

Conrad's other crimes; I am not particularly interested in pursuing
the particular manifestations of the racism or sexism of author, narrator, or text. Such arguments, it seems to me, too easily resolve complex questions of political accountability, overlooking or oversimplify-
ing the complicitous relationship between narrative and ideology—a
relationship no writer escapes. What interests me, then—and where
these issues intersect—is the way the narrative enacts the construction of cultural identity: the construction of the white male speaking
subject as narrative authority.

In this context, Achebe's criticisms, however radical, participate
in ruling cultural paradigms; maintaining the absolute distinction between subjective experience and objective reality, they flatten out the
complexities of subjectivity. Ultimately, these objections come down
to a question of authenticity—this is not what Africans are *really*
like—a question that can be turned back on itself by the other side.
Thus Cedric Watts answers Achebe by defending the authenticity of
Conrad's *subjective* response: ". . . Conrad is offering an entirely plau-
sible rendering of the responses of a British traveller of c.1890 to the
strange and bewildering experiences offered by the Congo. The passage is patently justified on realistic grounds."[21] In a move reminiscent of Conrad himself, Watts upholds "truth to experience" as the
ultimate and irreducible criterion of literary worth. What I want to
argue, however—and what I believe the novel amply demonstrates—
is that plausibility is itself continuously constructed on the narrative
and cultural stage; neither "truth" nor "experience" can be considered absolute. Authenticity thus stands as a problem posed by the
novel—a problem that contributes to its constellation of meanings—
and not as the novel's unproblematic base.

The questions that concern me can perhaps best be addressed by
recent revisionary work in ethnography—work that challenges the
celebrated objectivity of the anthropologist as observer-participant.
James Clifford, a leading figure in this field, has proposed reading
Heart of Darkness as a paradigm for ethnographic subjectivity, with
Conrad/Marlow occupying the ethnographer's place.[22] In the ethnographic encounter, Clifford argues, experience is never innocent; it
is always mediated through the agency of the text—the texts eth-
nographers write and the prior texts that shape the cultural configurations they perceive. *Heart of Darkness* rehearses this dual event, with
Marlow reproducing Conrad's doubled authority: the authority of

experience and the authority of authorship. Both types of authority, the novel suggests, are textually produced.

Conrad himself frequently offered "truth to his sensations" as the core of his aesthetic philosophy; in a letter of 1902 to William Blackwood, he opposed "action" to artfulness, promoting the former as the anchor of his "modern" literary mode: ". . . action observed, felt and interpreted with an absolute truth to my sensations (which are the basis of art in literature)—action of human beings that will bleed to a prick, and are moving in a visible world."[23] But as his own textual allusion suggests (*Merchant of Venice*, 3.1), the experience of immediacy is itself mediate. *Heart of Darkness*, moreover, complicates Conrad's professed aesthetic, making the truth of Marlow's sensations contested narrative ground. And it makes action a dubious authority, for the text represents not action but acting, with its cast of two-dimensional figures dancing before a phantasmagorical screen. Drawing upon a vast repository of texts, the novel collapses original experience into literary pastiche.

The novel's cultural representations further complicate artistic authority, highlighting the problem of textual complicity. Such a problem was not foreign to Conrad's understanding. Writing of his Malaysian tales—and answering charges of inaccuracy—Conrad betrayed his textual base: ". . . all the details about the little characteristic acts and customs which they hold up as proof I have taken out (to be safe) from undoubted sources—dull, wise books." But he admits, "I never did set up as an authority on Malaysia."[24] In *Heart of Darkness*, however, where Conrad has stronger claims to personal authority and expertise, the recorded experience is no less textually suffused. As Patrick Brantlinger has demonstrated, confirming Achebe's complaints, the novel's rendition of Africa bears striking similarities to popular travelers' tales—to the best-selling accounts of nineteenth-century explorers and missionaries.[25] Such affinities testify to something more than literary influences and borrowings; they suggest the way ideology determines not only what an observer writes, but what a "first-hand" observer sees. As Brantlinger notes, "The more that Europeans dominated Africans, the more 'savage' Africans came to seem."[26] Romanticizing such conventional tropes as primitive savagery, *Heart of Darkness* recuperates the myth of darkness that upholds the dominant ideology.

"In both novels and ethnographies," Clifford writes, "the self as

author stages the diverse discourses and scenes of a believable
world."[27] In *Heart of Darkness*, a novel-ethnography, we see this staging in the ongoing production of the text we read—a text that corre-
sponds to the two ethnographic encounters the novel presents: Marlow let loose in Africa and Marlow aboard the anchored ship. To
control these situations, Marlow, as author, produces pre-texts of
plausibility. In the first case, he reinvents Victorian mythology, constructing Africa as text: "the dark continent." In the second, he reinvents himself, constructing "Marlow, the narrator" as the voice of
cultural authority. The result is a hybrid text in which resistance to
conventional cultural practices (resistance that produces a text of un-
believability) is grafted onto reproductions of the dominant ideology.

The foregrounding of Marlow's struggles with his audience—
struggles over plausibility—opens to investigation the novel's construction of authenticity. For the stake of these narrative struggles
turns out to be experience itself—experience conceived not as the
exclusive property of its "author" but as something authorized con-
tractually. In the context of these encounters, the truth of Marlow's
experience depends upon communal belief—upon making his audience see. The project, of course, invokes Conrad's own much
quoted pronouncement of the artistic enterprise, inviting a reading of
Marlow as practitioner of applied Conradian philosophy: "My task
which I am trying to achieve is, by the power of the written word to
make you hear, to make you feel—it is, before all, to make you *see*."[28]
But Marlow resituates this project against a backdrop of colonialism,
bringing into focus a disturbing set of analogies. For Marlow's task
proves nothing less than the manipulation of reality, the restructur-
ing of experience: to *make* his audience hear what *he* hears, feel what
he feels, see what *he* sees.

The novel thus situates the production of plausibility at the intersection of ethnographic self-fashioning, colonial coercion, and artistic
autonomy. Marlow's prefatory remarks inaugurate these incongru-
ous couplings. Appealing to the imagination of his audience, Marlow
enlists their endorsement of his unconventional claims; he invites
them to reconstruct England as a place of darkness, the site of Roman
conquest: "Imagine the feelings of a commander," "Imagine him
here," "Or think of a decent young citizen in a toga," "Imagine the
growing regrets" (5, 6). The passage sets the stage for Marlow's

"proper" story, introducing the script it will re-present as its own subtext, retold in the life of Kurtz: "Imagine the growing regrets, the longing to escape, the powerless disgust, the surrender, the hate." But the passage also establishes the terms of Marlow's audience interchange, and here the text is the same as in the preceding anecdote: coerced consent.[29] For it rapidly becomes clear that Marlow's "Imagine's" are not so much invitations as commands; the act of narration constitutes the audience as a collective yes-man, invoked only to confirm preimposed structures of reality. Grounding the text in colonial genealogies, the passage performs the originary moment of colonial authority.

To read the narrative as colonial paradigm is, of course, to read partially: to read the novel against itself. It is to read Marlow's narrating persona against his narrated self, to read his displaced performance of colonial power against his powerful topical critique. Such double reading discloses the text's hybridity—the countertext it intimates in the narrative interstices. It reveals, for example, the way Marlow's narrative practices salvage the premise his story puts to the side: the construction of an idealized British imperialism, backed up and redeemed by "the idea." Edited out of the story (the narrative breaks off at the mere mention of "the idea"), this recuperated colonial ethic reenters in the margins of the text—reenters in the terms of Marlow's narrative address.[30]

Homi Bhabha has astutely analyzed the mechanics of colonial power in terms of "the English book"; he traces an insistently repeated "scene in the cultural writings of English colonialism" in which a book, implanted in an alien culture, attempts to enforce colonial ideology by exploiting difference to produce cultural and linguistic homogeneity.[31] The discovery of the English book becomes, in his reading, the originary moment of colonial authority. Reversing this scenario, *Heart of Darkness* maintains the structures of power such scenes unveil, with Marlow imposing the book of his un-English experience onto his English audience.[32] Dominating his audience, Marlow deploys what Bhabha has called "the most artful technologies of colonial power" (Bhabha, 148) to ensure his unimpeachable authority. He participates in coercive rhetoric: appropriating the voice of his audience, foreclosing independent interpretive lines, delimiting discursive possibilities, naturalizing ideology. In what stands as a classic colonial maneuver, Marlow passes off his founding assumptions as established communal belief: "The fascination of the abomination— *you know*" (6, emphasis mine).

Yet as Bhabha suggests, the exercise of colonial power turns in upon itself; the self-reflexiveness of Marlow's text can be understood, in part, then, as a colonial side effect. For the conditions that produce discursive domination outline the grounds of potential intervention as well. According to Bhabha, the authoritative moment "the book" represents "gives rise to a series of *questions of authority*," estranging the book itself, "the familiar symbol of English 'national' authority" (Bhabha, 155). Marlow's representation of himself as text produces this dual effect: establishing and challenging his authority simultaneously. It reveals the constructed nature of his national identity—an identity destabilized by the enactment of its structuring in narrative exchange. Staging a scene of mastery, Marlow's encounters with his audience invoke the very thing they suppress: the countertext of vulnerability.

A particular example may help clarify this argument. As "colonial" agent, Marlow's authoritative position depends upon his Englishness and his masculinity—the very qualities his manly interchanges confirm. For Marlow's aggressive encounters with his audience align him on the side of superior power, imaged as masculinity. Yet the very self-consciousness of these assertions sets the unexamined content of his story in relief, exposing Marlow's "backsliding" as subject of the tale. His performance of masculine authority puts into question what the narrative conceals: Marlow's identification with the position of the feminine or Other in the events his narrative records. Such identification is, of course, neither fully conscious nor complete; it exists as a function of textual grafting. Marlow virulently discredits the world of women, while the life of the natives remains beyond his conceptual reach. But differentiating himself from the male, European colonial regime, Marlow lacks other positions from which to speak. Narrative itself, his story suggests, demands this crisis of authority.

Marlow's narrative reenacts the cultural construction of femininity: the transformation of a place of origins into a place of ends, of the source of life into the locus of death. For in relation to Kurtz, Marlow undergoes just such an adjustment—an adjustment from Kurtz's creator to Kurtz's text. Marlow's story initially posits Kurtz as

Marlow's intent: his journey's meaning, purpose, object, end. But the demands of narrative reverse this project, making Marlow Kurtz's chosen—what Kurtz intends. Kurtz's first words to Marlow, "I am glad" (61), position Marlow in this respect. Belonging to Kurtz's party, Marlow appears as the fulfillment of Kurtz's desire, what Kurtz has been waiting for. In the context of the story's resolution, Marlow's arrival enables Kurtz to die, a function reinforced by Marlow's later entry, as if on cue ("'I am lying here in the dark waiting for death'" [70], Kurtz announces tremulously), to witness Kurtz's last words. Giving life to Kurtz, then, Marlow also gives him death; and in the logic of Marlow's narrative, the two become the same event.

Marlow's narrative would seem to track the acquisition of feminine identity, for it puts Marlow in the feminine place—literally, the place of Kurtz's Intended. Bound to Kurtz, Marlow doubles for the prospective bride; he usurps her place as Kurtz's chosen—the one chosen to hear his confidences, witness his death, preserve his memory, be his scribe. Fulfilling classic feminine paradigms, he even struggles for Kurtz's soul, recalling it to the path of virtue, "'You will be lost,' I said—'utterly lost'" (67), and "converting" it, in his narrative testament at least, to the moral life. Like the Intended, he effaces his own ordeal—almost sacrifices his own life—to make his existence a monument to Kurtz: a living memory, an eternal echo of his voice.

Summing up Kurtz, Marlow explains, ". . . he had one devoted friend at least, and he had conquered one soul in the world that was neither rudimentary nor tainted with self-seeking. No; I can't forget him" (51). In the passage's less than certain identifications, Marlow seems to exclude himself; but in his devotion to Kurtz, Marlow could fill either slot (the devoted friend, presumably played by the Russian, or the conquered soul, cast as the Intended's lot). The two parts could even be the same, for the text's ambiguity highlights the merging of identities Kurtz sets in play. Remembering Kurtz, Marlow numbers himself among his conquests; for conquest turns out to be the only relationship Kurtz admits. Marlow's final interview with the Intended, where he doubles her every word, ironically points to the position they share. In this scene of rivalry, Marlow and the woman compete for the Intended's place: the right to know Kurtz best. Embattled with each other, they struggle for the status of Kurtz's most enduring conquest.

Marlow's account of his climactic meeting with Kurtz can be seen to set the stage for such a reading. For in it, Marlow registers a masculine protest against his enforced dependency—against his (feminine) relational position to Kurtz's absolute authority. The scene encapsulates Marlow's reconstructed role: to wait on Kurtz. Invoking his own audience, Marlow protests his position of powerlessness and passivity: "And, don't you see, the terror of the position was not in being knocked on the head—though I had a very lively sense of that danger too—but in this, that I had to deal with a being to whom I could not appeal in the name of anything high or low. I had, even like the niggers, to invoke him—himself—his own exalted and incredible degradation" (67). The real terror of this situation, as Marlow presents it, thus turns out to be *Marlow*'s loss of his sexual and racial identity.

Marlow's colonial postures allow him to construct a more favorable position for himself, to overwrite in the narrative present the text of his past vulnerability. But as with other simple reversals, the two texts remain interlocked. Destined to repeat the story of Kurtz, Marlow reinscribes the limiting conditions of his own authority. For in Marlow's relationship to his audience, he takes up the place of Kurtz, inserting himself—his voice—as his audience's "fate." Like Kurtz, he establishes himself as an irrefutable authority; marked off by experiences that cannot be shared, Marlow remains his story's ultimate point of reference, its only source of appeal. To comprehend that story, his audience must invoke Marlow—Marlow himself; they must invoke what he repeatedly reminds them of, that "me, whom you know." Marlow's narrative aggression thus unveils an exhibition of self-referentiality. The performance puts his audience in Marlow's former place: the place of the feminine—to watch and to wait, to hang on "the man's" words. As the frame narrator reveals, Marlow too has his conquests and Marlow too has his scribe: "The others might have been asleep, but I was awake. I listened, I listened on the watch for the sentence, for the word, that would give me the clue to the faint uneasiness inspired by this narrative that seemed to shape itself without human lips in the heavy night-air of the river" (28).

Constructing himself in Kurtz's image, Marlow fulfills the colonial imperative Kurtz both travesties and enacts. He participates in what Henry Staten has called, in psychoanalytic terms, Kurtz's "sadistic project of mastery," the epitome of the colonial design: "the desire to force by violence a response from an unmoved and indifferent nature which is imaged as female."[33] Badgering his audience, as he does periodically, Marlow assaults their indifference, subjecting them to violent verbal harangues. And as I intend to argue, he does so by implicitly projecting them as female, or at least by challenging their masculinity. Making his voice the instrument of power and the locus of all conflict, Marlow perfects his impression of Kurtz, weeding out all but the essential, "A voice! A voice!"

Marlow's wranglings with his audience pinpoint areas of narrative stress. Provoking a response—even one of hostility—Marlow asserts his Kurtz-like capacity for multiple conquests: "'Try to be civil, Marlow,' growled a voice, and I knew there was at least one listener awake besides myself" (34). To the devotion of the frame narrator, Marlow can add another voice's forced recognition of his existence. Such recognition reaffirms Marlow's masculinity—demonstrating its coercive power, while deflecting the narrative from Marlow's lapses in manliness. Restaged as narrative contest, Marlow's representations of personal "weakness" emerge as displays of narrative prowess. For moments *in* the narrative that betray Marlow's contested masculinity frequently inaugurate narrative commentaries that reclaim Marlow's voice for the dominant ideology.

These narrative transactions interrogate problematic positions of cultural identification, positions that collapse or transgress gender and racial codes. Marlow's assertion, for example, of "remote kinship" with the "wild and passionate uproar" of frenzied natives leaping and howling on the shore launches a defense of "true" manhood: "Let the fool gape and shudder—the man knows, and can look on without a wink. But he must at least be as much of a man as these on the shore. He must meet that truth with his own true stuff—with his own inborn strength" (37). In the course of this analysis, manhood as admission of otherness ("if you were man enough you would admit to yourself that there was in you just the faintest trace of a response") melds into manhood as the power to resist (what one does with one's "own inborn strength"). Provoking a response to his own passionate outburst, Marlow defends his manhood from both sides. For with the guttural response he presumably elicits—"Who's that grunting? You wonder I didn't go ashore for a howl and a dance?"—Marlow takes firm control of his rhetorical ground, demolishing his questioner. A real man, he argues, would be tempted by the uproar; a real man would withstand temptation because he has a proper set of priorities to bolster his strength of mind. In the situation Marlow orchestrates, his detractor puts his own manhood doubly at risk: by failing to admit responsiveness to Marlow's sentiments and by failing to resist—as his uncouth interruption demonstrates—passionate entanglement.

In a move his narrative interchange enacts, Marlow attributes his own achieved manhood to his voice: "An appeal to me in this fiendish row—is there? Very well; I hear; I admit, but I have a voice too, and for good or evil mine is the speech that cannot be silenced." Situating his voice between his audience and his experience, Marlow reconstructs the crisis he narrates, but this time with the native element wiped out. For in engaging his audience, Marlow pits his manhood against theirs; in doing so, he puts the natives aside, reconstituting manhood as the exclusive property of *white* men. Establishing his voice, then, in an act of dominance, Marlow suppresses both his own audience and the natives themselves. He carves out for himself a position of colonial authority—a position that rapidly involves him in acts of cultural complicity. For Marlow must choose his common ground, and he chooses racial solidarity. Effectively exploding the notion of native manhood, Marlow covers the rift between himself and his audience. He seals the exclusion his narrative performs by offering up *his* "savage" fireman as an object of communal ridicule: "He was there below me, and, upon my word, to look at him was as edifying as seeing a dog in a parody of breeches and a feather hat, walking on his hind legs" (37).

Marlow's most prolonged tussle with his audience works through similar manipulations of positions of identity. Following upon Marlow's account of his moment of maximum unmanliness, the passage pursues the interrogation of manhood the earlier exchange introduced.[34] Describing his own response to Kurtz's presumed death, Marlow collapses in upon himself savage unrestraint and feminine susceptibility; he admits to "a startling extravagance of emotion, even such as I had noticed in the howling sorrow of these savages in the bush" (48). As in earlier instances, however, Marlow's admission launches a counter-attack, an attack facilitated by the audience response he is able to extract: "Why do you sigh in this beastly way, somebody? Absurd? Well, absurd. Good Lord! mustn't a man ever— Here, give me some tobacco" (48). Marlow's peremptory demand shifts the narrative ground to the gruff world of masculine community. Having secured a position there, he takes on his audience's objection, making it the mark of *their* lack—their inadequacy: "You can't understand. How could you?—with solid pavement under your feet, surrounded by kind neighbours ready to cheer you or to fall on you, stepping delicately between the butcher and the policeman, in the holy terror of scandal and gallows and lunatic asylums—how can you imagine what particular region of the first ages *a man's* untrammelled feet may take him" (50, emphasis mine).

Marlow's reconstruction of the domain of masculinity positions his audience in woman's place: excluded from knowledge, truth, and adventure—excluded from even imaginative entry into man's terrain. In the scenario Marlow articulates, his audience inhabits the familiar realm of domesticity, coded as feminine by marks of comfort, kindness, shelter, and delicacy—a bounded world contained by domestic detail (the butcher) and domestic discipline (the policeman). Discoursing on the "true stuff" of masculinity, Marlow consolidates this gendered positioning: "These little things make all the great difference. When they are gone you must fall back upon your own innate strength, upon your own capacity for faithfulness" (50). Binding his audience to these little things (two good addresses, kind neighbors, the local policeman), Marlow definitively excludes them from the trials of masculinity.

The dual transgression that initiates Marlow's tirade provokes a pointed defense of *one* of its poles: Marlow's manhood. As in the earlier instance, Marlow's claim of emotional kinship to savage howlings drops out in the ensuing demonstration of masculine superiority. It reemerges, at the end of the passage, as a dying man's claim on him: "a claim of distant kinship affirmed in a supreme moment" (52). Reclaimed in the interest of masculine codes, the helmsman's death stands as a supreme moment of male bonding—the bonding between Marlow and his audience. For Marlow positions that death in a world they know: "Perhaps you will think it passing strange this regret for a savage who was no more account than a grain of sand in a black Sahara" (51–52). He explains his regret in terms his audience can understand: the contractual claims of partnership. And he accommodates that partnership to the unequal positions colonialism commands: "It was a kind of partnership. He steered for me—I had to look after him, I worried about his deficiencies" (52). Relegated to culturally determined slots—instrumentality and lack—the helmsman's body becomes the site of recaptured communal belief. A sacri-

fice to colonial authority, it delineates the common ground Marlow
and his audience occupy.

As these passages demonstrate, Marlow's voice betrays the problematic conditions of its own construction, the paradoxes of all colonial authority. In articulating a text of mastery, Marlow repeatedly
inscribes threats to his own authority: in the area of intervention his
audience represents—an intervention he himself provokes—and in
the prior texts upon which his authoritative postures depend. For the
inscription of an audience opens a space for reading differently—for
re-readings, displacements, and misreadings the author cannot control; Marlow's exercises in intimidation thus turn our gaze back on his
vulnerability.[35] The reconstructions of authority these passages effect
do not, then, operate monolithically; rather, they function to expose
the fables of identity by which the voice of cultural authority is
achieved. In Marlow's case this means writing out or writing over the
traces of otherness imprinted on his voice; suppressing or displacing
identifications with the feminine and non-white, Marlow produces a
voice that conforms to colonial ideology, that conforms to the voice
his culture writes for him.

The "official" reading of *Heart of Darkness* posits Marlow's narrative as a journey into self: the discovery of his voice and identity.[36]
But such a reading seeks meaning in the "kernel" the narrative contains; it pursues the trope of internal discovery the first narrator disclaims in Marlow's name. My own approach redirects attention outside, to the meaning constructed externally in Marlow's framing
"asides." In the margins of the text, a different trope of identity ap-
plies, where voice is not so much discovered—or uncovered—as im-
posed from on high. Recording the stress points of this acquired
voice, the narrative registers the lies that support cultural authority—
that promote the illusion of an autonomous identity. It registers the
lie of voice itself. For Marlow's voice does not exist autonomously; it
is constructed before our very eyes.

*   *   *

A voice! A voice!

—Joseph Conrad, *Heart of Darkness*

The novel's insistence on voice—Kurtz's, Marlow's—poses a set of
problems for interpretation: the problem of "real presence," of cul-

tural autonomy, of individual authority, of distinguishability. Moreover, there remains the problem of the voices the novel does not
name—the voice of the narrator who transmits the story and the
voice of the author imperfectly aligned with his designated spokes-
men. Held up as the novel's ultimate standard of truth, voice remains
a contested subject. The very insistence on its presence—"A voice! A
voice!"—produces a characteristic double effect, elevating voice to a
position of narrative preeminence where, by virtue of those same
repetitions (the phrase recurs insistently), voice itself is rendered suspect. Simultaneously privileged and problematic, voice can be read as
the question the novel interrogates, the focus for a network of overlapping critical concerns.[37]

Marlow's narrative situates Kurtz's voice as its origin and end—
as something preexistent to be found. He posits this voice as something external to himself and distinguishable from the other voices
(white and black) he presents as mere background sound. In the
mapping of Marlow's desire, Kurtz fulfills the conditions for Marlow's preferred narrative form—dialogue. For Marlow plots his journey as a movement toward talk: ". . . that was exactly what I had
been looking forward to—a talk with Kurtz" (48). The narrative, however, works to displace Marlow's empirical demands. Kurtz's voice,
when the narrative presents it, cannot sustain his claims. The structure the narrative performs reverses the one Marlow outlines; it represents voice as manufactured—something constructed, not found.

If Marlow imagines Kurtz as voice, it is probably because voice
would seem to represent the irreducible essence of individual identity. In a world of visual illusions—the colonial shadow dance—voice
at least promises some solidity. But Kurtz's voice lacks substance and
originality. Kurtz says nothing striking; rather, he says nothing strikingly. As Marlow admits, describing his famous talk with Kurtz,
"They were common everyday words—the familiar, vague sounds
exchanged on every waking day of life" (67). It is Marlow who en-
dows Kurtz's words with impressive force, who, like the Russian,
attributes to Kurtz's voice the power to make him see—"see things":
"They had behind them, *to my mind*, the terrific suggestiveness of
words heard in dreams, of phrases spoken in nightmares" (67, emphasis mine). Kurtz's voice, by itself, produces only formulaic
utterances—familiar phrases, melodramatic clichés, textbook eloquence. Consequently, even the Russian's defense of Kurtz's origi-

nality cannot escape ironic re-reading: "You ought to have heard him recite poetry—his own too it was, he told me. Poetry!" (65). The Russian vouches for Kurtz solely on the basis of Kurtz's authority ("he told me")—authority not beyond questioning. Moreover, even if Kurtz's poetry proved "his own" originally, in the figure of recitation the Russian introduces, we sense the potential of that poetry for repetitive re-readings. Reciting rather than originating, endlessly rehearsing some great speech, Kurtz's voice partakes of secondariness; it sounds no truer than the voices Marlow sets it against.

Kurtz's voice, moreover, lacks proprietary markers that stamp it as his own. In the catalog of his possessions, "My Intended, my ivory, my station, my river, my—" (49), "my voice" does not appear; disconnected from his body, his voice does not belong to him. An appropriating mechanism that takes everything into itself, Kurtz's voice proves eminently appropriatable. As his journalist "colleague" affirms, Kurtz's voice could be made to serve any end ("'What party?' . . . 'Any party'" [74]). Distinguished by his voice, Kurtz "speaks" by being spoken for and spoken through. The Russian, for example, speaks Kurtz—and nothing but Kurtz: "The man filled his life, occupied his thoughts, swayed his emotions" (57). In Marlow's narrative recital, the Russian stands in for the absent Kurtz, representing him vocally. Shadowy himself, Kurtz inhabits the harlequin's voice. When we hear Kurtz speak in his own person, his voice has a disconcerting effect, "as if the words had been torn out of him by a supernatural power" (68–69), as if the forest had expelled and drawn in its breath (61). Marlow stresses this voice's dehumanized elements, its distinctness from its human subject: "A voice! A voice! It was grave, profound, vibrating, while the man did not seem capable of a whisper" (61). He points to its purely mechanical effects, its "volume of tone" and clarity of expression: ". . . it sounded to me far off and yet loud, like a hail through a speaking-trumpet" (66). An instrument of the wilderness, Kurtz's voice becomes a chamber for other voices to pass through, echoing and amplifying the voices it self-projects: "I think [the wilderness] had whispered to him things about himself which he did not know, things of which he had no conception till he took counsel with this great solitude—and the whisper had proved irresistibly fascinating. It echoed loudly within him because he was hollow at the core" (59). No more than a voice, Kurtz turns out to be not even that; Marlow represents him as no more than a vocal box.

Significantly, in Marlow's first sight of Kurtz, he does not hear Kurtz speak. Kurtz appears, rather, as a kind of speaking machine, enacting the motions of speech in the absence of the real thing: "I could not hear a sound, but through my glasses I saw the thin arm extended commandingly, the lower jaw moving, the eyes of that apparition shining darkly far in its bony head that nodded with grotesque jerks" (60). When Kurtz's voice does reach him, it is a voice out of sync with its visual markings: "A deep voice reached me faintly. He must have been shouting" (61). The scene encapsulates a central feature of Marlow's metaphysic, where voice appears, above all, as something that one sees. Its presence is reconstructed from visual clues or, as in Marlow's preceding narrative, from visual imaginings. A voice with nothing behind it, Kurtz functions synesthetically: an optical illusion projected onto the novel's aural circuits.

Conceived as reconstruction (as the recovery of Kurtz's voice), the narrative conceals the workings of its art—its construction of the very voice it tracks. It conceals the fact that Kurtz is only a voice in Marlow's head—a voice he constructs and deploys for his own ends. The "real presence" of Kurtz (the subject of Marlow's insistent claims, "A voice! A voice!") can be read, then, as another lie the narrative charts, a fiction it must sustain. For Kurtz's voice lies behind Marlow's, forming its narrative base. The mere hint of its lack of substance threatens narrative collapse: "A voice. He was very little more than a voice. And I heard—him—it—this voice—other voices—all of them were so little more than voices—and the memory of that time itself lingers around me, impalpable, like a dying vibration of one immense jabber, silly, atrocious, sordid, savage, or simply mean, without any kind of sense. Voices, voices—even the girl herself—now—" (49).

Marlow's meditation robs Kurtz's voice of integrity—of personal presence, individuality, distinctiveness. Collapsing voice into voices, it produces voice in the abstract: a conglomeration of random sound waves, an "immense jabber" without sense. Kurtz's voice, like all the others, remains a "dying vibration" in Marlow's head, giving the lie to Marlow's insistence on its unique palpability. But Marlow, quite literally, gives the lie to his own insight, interjecting that lie, as he does here, at every crisis point: "'I laid the ghost of his gifts at last with a lie,' he began suddenly." Sacrificing Kurtz and the Intended, sacrificing his own integrity, Marlow lies to keep Kurtz's voice intact. For the "presence" of Kurtz's voice keeps Marlow's voice out of sight, covering the constructed identity (Marlow) to which it gives life.

I have argued in the previous section that Marlow's voice does not exist independently; it is the product of a negotiation of the cultural coordinates of race, gender, and nationality. Seen in another light, it is the product of narrative itself; and narrative, in many ways, constitutes the novel's self-conscious subject. In the larger frame of *Heart of Darkness*, Marlow's voice exists as the problem the first narrator sets: the condition of everything we see. With that narrator in focus, we might ask, Whose voice is it anyway? Who speaks Marlow? And who does Marlow speak? Such a reading, however, opens the possibility of a chain reaction effect, in which first Marlow's, then the narrator's, and then Conrad's voices would come under scrutiny as the critic illuminates these narratives of decreasing visibility. Traced back through a chain of readers and critical authorities, the process threatens infinite regress.

Heart of Darkness, however, resists neat concentric rings; in nearly a century of critical responses, there has been no consensus about the boundaries of its voices or the authority with which they speak. The familiar critical construction "Conrad/Marlow" speaks to this dilemma, as does the alternative insistence on their separability. Attempts to "place" the frame narrator in relation to Conrad or Marlow come up against similar problems of decidability. Repeatedly offered as the key to interpretation, irony has failed to adjudicate these competing claims. For the novel's irony participates in the instability of its voices; dependent upon a proper reading of voice, ironic certainty falters in the face of unreadable reports. The problematics of voice exists, then, as the novel's legacy—as a series of questions to be investigated, not settled definitively. Replaying the problem posed by Kurtz, the novel explores the limits and possibilities of voice. It offers voice itself as its most unsettling effect—voice dislocated from the stabilizing constructs of personal identity.

The novel's overlapping voices complicate its delineation of character. Marlow's voice, for example, seen as distinctly his, exists as a process of differentiation—a process that repeatedly collapses into exhibitions of affinity: affinity with Kurtz, with the Russian harlequin, with the Company's manager, with the Intended, and with the frame narrator. Marlow's entire text might be read as one of Kurtz's "splendid monologues": a verbal production that absorbs everything into itself. In terms of the narrative, it is the closest thing to Kurtz's voice we perceive. But with Kurtz as its obsessive subject, Marlow's monologue renders problematic the identity of the "self" it speaks. In relation to Marlow, however, all of the characters speak problematically; the distinctiveness of their voices often exists only technically—a function of linguistic markers, of quotation marks that distinguish formulaically named identities. Without these markers, these voices and Marlow's often sound disturbingly the same.

As has been frequently noticed, Marlow shares the Russian harlequin's position to Kurtz; they speak of Kurtz in one voice, with "mingled eagerness and reluctance to speak" (57). With different degrees of self-consciousness, they voice their texts of idolatry. And as the frame narrator makes clear, they share narrative techniques; for Marlow describes the Russian's story in terms that echo the narrator's account of Marlow's own words: "There was no sign on the face of nature of this amazing tale that was not so much told as suggested to me in desolate exclamations, completed by shrugs, in interrupted phrases, in hints ending in deep sighs" (57). Less obviously, Marlow speaks in the manager's mode, applying "a seal" to his words "to make the meaning of the commonest phrase appear absolutely inscrutable" (22). Projecting his voice "as though it had been a door opening into a darkness he had in his keeping," Marlow, like the manager, inspires uneasiness. He places *his* audience in the position in which the manager puts him: "You fancied you had seen things—but the seal was on" (22).

These affinities extend, in Marlow's echoes of the Intended, across gender lines; they threaten, throughout the narrative, to cross over demarcations of race. Turning our gaze upon the spectacle of narration, they invoke the shadowy presence of Conrad himself. But they do not cohere in some newly achieved ironic understanding of Marlow's identity. Extending in all directions, they call into question the possibility of any boundaries, of any voice's distinguishability. They attribute to voice a kind of narrative free agency—agency independent of any informing identity. Collapsing inside and outside, the replication of voices deconstructs the narrating subject itself.

Heart of Darkness presents a split subject of narration that might be rendered schematically as the split between writing and speech: this split produces the overwritten text of the first narrator, inscribed with signifying marks of "literariness," and the spoken text of Marlow, imprinted with marks of orality. Marlow's narrative comes into being as the site of this fissure—the place of inscription of a second "I." But the textual trappings of Marlow's colloquial utterance—its deployment of generic codes for melodrama, mystery, suspense, romance—reduce the gap between the voices of these two narrating presences. Moreover, the first narrator's intrusions into Marlow's text track his adoption of Marlow's accents and tones; his final words, with their iterative reference to "the heart of an immense darkness," situate Marlow's voice *inside* this narrator's literary mode.

The narrating subject, then, seems neither clearly one nor two; and it proves difficult to determine whose voice controls whose. Thus when Marlow resumes his story after a narrative aside, "'. . . Yes—I let him run on,' Marlow began again" (28), the line completes the first narrator's description of his response to Marlow's storytelling. Momentarily, the two voices collapse into one, until the naming of Marlow fixes the subject of speech. The space of double reading, however, calls into question Marlow's narrative authority; it reveals its dependency on the sufferance of his audience. Bringing to the surface the situation of the text, it re-marks Marlow's voice as the possession of the first narrator. If Marlow's narrative constructs the first narrator in his own image, the novel does not exclude the possibility of the reverse being true. The novel's asymmetrical frame, represented by a few scant lines at the end, reads ambiguously: a sign that Marlow has taken over the first narrator's voice—that he has indeed conquered his audience—or a reminder that Marlow's voice exists at the first narrator's whim, dependent upon that other voice for its transmission.

The introduction of Conrad does not resolve these problems of authority, for Conrad's presence figures indiscriminately. The tracking of intertextual allusions to Conrad's autobiographical writings— as in Marlow's childhood fantasy about the map of Africa (*A Personal Record*) or his representation of the primeval world of adventure, a world without benefit of neighbor or policeman ("Familiar Preface")— does not secure Conrad's presence behind Marlow.[38] For Conrad also speaks behind the first narrator, who establishes this link in the opening of his narrative: "Between us there was, as I have already said somewhere, the bond of the sea" (3). The location of this "somewhere" identifies the "I" as the "author" of *Youth* and of Conrad's letters.[39] Pushed far enough, the possibilities for identification seem limitless. Conrad's voice, for example, also echoes in Kurtz, a fellow author of double texts. And it echoes not only in the folds of Kurtz's magnificent eloquence, but in the pragmatic purity of Kurtz's infamous footnote, "Exterminate all the brutes." In a letter to Cunninghame Graham, written just after the first installment of *Heart of Darkness* had appeared, Conrad admitted "respect" for extreme anarchists: "'I hope for general extermination'. Very well. It's justifiable and, moreover, it is plain. One compromises with words."[40] The anarchists' sentiments echo in the novel in a context that particularizes and reverses the power politics of the scenario Conrad describes here, where the anarchists' target is clearly European civilization itself. But the attraction Conrad acknowledges in the uncomplicated logic of the anarchists' stance—and the distrust he voices for the power of words—complicates our reading of Kurtz's revealing scrawl. For the uncanny echoes that unite these texts press Conrad's voice in directions from which the novel clearly veers.

In *Heart of Darkness*'s textual labyrinth, the trail of allusions crosses itself. "Conrad" enters as yet another fragmented voice, displaced over the surface of the text. "He" does not attach himself to any single identity. A voice without substance, Conrad exists like the rest: "—him—it—this voice—other voices—" (49). A product of the voices it represents, *Heart of Darkness* appears as an unmotivated text: a text without clear, authorizing intent. As Vincent Pecora suggests, the novel defies articulate intentions: "Conrad has represented the impossibility of capturing intentions—including his own—without equivocation by means of a narrative that questions the integrity, authenticity, coherence, and truth of every voice that speaks, or speaks *in*, this novel."[41] In an Author's Note appended to one edition of the text, Conrad explained his aesthetic purpose; but the suggestive terms he activates immediately complicate the professed elucidation, echoing as they do Marlow's moment of maximum confusion: "That sombre theme had to be given a sinister resonance, a tonality of its own, a continued vibration that, I hoped, would hang in the air and dwell on the ear after the last note had been struck."[42] Like the wilderness it names, *Heart of Darkness* answers to the demands of those who traverse its bounds, providing the enclosed space through which voices can be heard. Holding voice before our eyes, the novel strips voice of everything we commonly know it by: all marks of individuation, all signs of proprietorship. The narrative pushes toward the mere projection of voice—voice with nothing behind it. As such, voice embodies the abstract of the novel's adventure plot: the penetration of the silence of the heart of darkness. But the act of reading reconstructs voice as identity; it participates in the construction of narrative authority. Redrawing the boundaries between voices that mark them as distinct entities, it reclaims voice as familiar narrative and cultural property. The act of reading thus participates in the "lies" that make voice readable—the very lies reading itself detects. The problematics of voice, then, becomes the drama that reading replays; reading voice, we read the central paradox *Heart of Darkness* proclaims.

E. M. Forster

Chapter 3

The Voices of Politics

> For the book is not really about politics, though it is the political
> aspect of it that caught the general public and made it sell. It's
> about something wider than politics, about the search of the
> human race for a more lasting home, about the universe as
> embodied in the Indian earth and the Indian sky, about the
> horror lurking in the Marabar Caves and the release symbolized
> by the birth of Krishna. It is—or rather desires to be—
> philosophic and poetic, and that is why when I had finished it I
> took its title, "Passage to India", from a famous poem of Walt
> Whitman's.
>
> —E.M. Forster, "Three Countries"

The voices of politics resound in *A Passage to India* beyond the author's intent; they resound, the novel suggests, because voice cannot
exist without a political edge. Politics, to put it crudely, "sells." This is
as much a condition for the characters caught in the economy of
empire as it is for the novel itself. Desire, as Forster here acknowledges, can govern only intentions, not effects ("It is—or rather desires to be—philosophic and poetic"). Between desire and effect, politics persists in the realm of borrowed speech—speech that cannot
escape its genealogy of cultural and literary forms. Forster's act of
poetic entitlement (a kind of literary theft) does not, then, determine
the novel we read. His comments notwithstanding, *Passage* has been
alternately blamed for its failure to represent political realities in an
adequate fashion and applauded for its success in presenting "something wider than politics"; and it has been scrupulously combed to
document every instance, however indirect, of the contemporary political scene.[1]

What I would like to suggest, however, is that politics defines the novel at the heart of its apolitical domain: what might be called the theater of discourse. For, as I will argue, the novel stages its cross-cultural encounters through theatrical means. But in the novel's closet drama, discourse replaces action and voices the novel's un-voiced political themes. In locating the novel's political arena in the discursive realm, I am bringing together what have, in the Forster scholarship, remained largely separate strains: the exploration of speech and silence, generally conceived as metaphysical theme, and the identification of the historical and political events that underwrite the novel's representation of the colonial regime.[2] Following the in-sights of recent works of cultural criticism, my own approach calls into question the assumptions that sustain this separation of the "lit-erary" and "political" domains—the very separation Forster so elo-quently defends. I begin with the premise that discourse—language, writing, speech—is itself a historical event and its production and circulation a political reality of considerable force. I work from an understanding of ideology that teaches suspiciousness of the insis-tent apolitical claim: "For the book is not really about politics . . . ." As *A Passage to India* illustrates, even the most metaphysical concerns (the "true" subject of the book, Forster contends) have a political base, not only because the privileging of metaphysics is itself political but because its representations require a voice that must find its artic-ulation in culturally coded economies of writing or speech.

Representation, then, can never be transparent, whatever its in-tent. And in a novel centrally concerned with the process of cultural representation, we might do well to investigate the structures upon which the representational process is based. Current critiques of the practice of ethnography have called attention to the rhetorical fea-tures that inform and determine the way culture is inscribed. As James Clifford writes, "Literary processes—metaphor, figuration, narrative—affect the ways cultural phenomena are registered, from the first jotted 'observations,' to the completed book, to the ways these configurations 'make sense' in determined acts of reading."[3] A kind of ethnographic account (what Clifford calls a "true fiction") in novel form, *A Passage to India* records the constructions and transla-tions of a culture (India) that resists the "determined acts of reading" its interpreters impose. The reading of the writing of India becomes the novel's subject in a kind of infinite regress, with the British writing an identity based upon the reading of an India they invent, while the Indians read this British "writing" and reconstruct themselves. Moreover, in the novel's representational matrix, the colonial officials compete with their subjects for the status of ethnographic "case."

For Forster, then, who both represents the ethnographer's position in his novel (witness, for example, Adela Quested, figuratively jotting down her field notes) and who himself assumes the anthropologist's "objective" guise, the literary maintains a double hold: it is the condition of ethnographic inscription and the novelist's own particular mode. In the first instance, it marks a crucial link between the seemingly disinterested efforts at cultural understanding (as variously represented by Aziz, Fielding, Adela, and Mrs. Moore) and the expressly political exercises of cultural control (as represented by the powers that constitute the colonial regime): the two modes of discourse share a common narrative and rhetorical base. In the second instance, the literary marks the limits of Forster's own cross-cultural enterprise: the novel's overt refusal to "make sense" of India is belied, at least in part, by its own imposition of narrative coherence and form.[4]

What such self-reflexive anthropology (itself the subject of considerable debate) reminds us is that writing is a form of power on the cultural stage and language a mechanism of control. Allegories of interpretation fashion even "scientific" thought and other "objective" discursive modes. Borrowing, then, from the anthropologists' own literary forays, I propose to consider the narrative practices and rhetorical tropes by which authority is constituted in the colonial situation the novel represents. I am particularly interested in those discursive moments where neither political power nor literary fashioning is explicitly at play. For my argument rests upon the contention that discourse determines meaning in ways that exceed any individual's intent.

I do not here rehearse the specific political and historical events upon which Forster structures his work, events whose influence on the narrative have already been ably documented in some detail. I do not mean to deny their considerable weight, but I am interested in embedded political structures of a different kind—structures that sometimes parallel, sometimes contradict, what we commonly under-

stand to be the novel's ideological frame. The mechanisms of power
that concern me are those registered in the individual voice: imitation, distortion, suppression, appropriation. These mechanisms operate, to some extent, independent of the content of the utterance
itself, and they sometimes work at cross-purposes to the author's
intent. I do not, however, mean to reduce all politics to a question of
representational form, but rather to suggest that the politics of discourse represents an important and insufficiently acknowledged
component of the novel's political economy. I recognize that my approach, by emphasizing underlying narrative structures, risks dis-
solving all distinctions (between Muslim and Hindu, between colonial officials of various sorts, between Britishers in official and
unofficial roles), exposing my own complicity in the totalizing structures of Western thinking. But I would argue that the neutralizing of
distinctions is one of the effects of hegemonic power the novel represents and that the deployment of power through narrative remains of
particular significance given the novel's implicit claims to stand outside politics. The texts of inequality, domination, and exclusion this
approach unveils can thus extend our understanding of the workings
of a political power base, bringing it into the personal voice and into
the artistic practices that have traditionally defined liberal humanism's positions of resistance.

*   *   *

A Passage to India presents its central drama as a power struggle between competing voices: between, in its broadest reach, English and
Indian discourse, and between idiolects within each dominant voice.
But it is a power struggle that has already been won. For the novel
represents, in its verbal excavations, the conditions of power that
reduce all voices to one. As Talal Asad has demonstrated in another
context, in competition between "unequal languages," the "weaker"
is almost always forcibly transformed, for translation generally operates in one direction alone.[5] In the terms the novel articulates, this
means not only the suppression of native languages, but, within the
English-speaking community, the absorption or appropriation of he-
retical modes of discourse. The novel's display of heterogeneous utterances merely conceals, for the moment, the monolithic edifice it

presents, in which soliloquies of power displace the dialogic mode on the novel's representational stage. The novel thus demonstrates that the "dialogue" between cultures Forster desires must remain an unrealizable goal, for even the artist's dialogic imagination must adjust itself to the monological imperative of colonialism. In the politics of the text, the individual voice thus becomes the contested zone.

Seen in this light, the story performs an allegory of rhetorical consolidation and retrenchment; it dramatizes and enacts the curtailment of narrative possibilities demanded by a colonial regime. Hence the sameness of its plots and the theatricality of its means. Those characters committed to the possibility of cultural interchange, as disclosed in the opening chapters' carefully staged vignettes, follow their own circuitous paths to a common disillusionment. Those who attempt to speak "in a different voice" (Aziz, Fielding, Adela, Mrs. Moore), to remain observer-participants outside the political domain, discover the impossibility of speaking in a voice of one's own, the impossibility of maintaining "ethnographic" disinterestedness.[6] For the novel's dramatic structure works to disclose the intransigence of culturally bound discourse—discourse that marks the interests served by such a neutral stance. And the novel's final "act" reveals what its fictions of autonomy conceal: in the colonial theater, even exchanges between noncombatants are always marked politically.[7] Making voice the site of such markings, the novel replays its melodramatic possibilities in a different register. In this reading of the novel's tale of intimacy and betrayal, the absent "villain," one might claim, lurks in the echo chambers of the voice.

The locus of authority—and the site of possible transgression— voice can be articulated only within existing power structures, and it operates differentially along the axes of race, nationality, and gender. Thus voice inevitably speaks its political position, even when it speaks only to reveal itself an echo.[8] For the Westernized Muslims, for example, living on the edge of the government zone, an apolitical position does not signify when politics dominates their private conversation and appropriates not only their language but the intonations of their speech. Even in objecting to the British, these Indians declare their annexation, for their discourse belongs to the rulers they reject. What the master tongue articulates, and thus allows them to say, determines the desires they express as well as the expression of their sentiments. "They all become exactly the same, not worse, not better," Hamidullah remarks of the English. "I give any Englishman two years, be he Turton or Burton. It is only the difference of a letter" (11). When these sentiments reappear in the voice of Ronny Heaslop at the English club, we recognize the "original" source the Indians echo: "But whether the native swaggers or cringes, there's always something behind every remark he makes, always something, and if nothing else he's trying to increase his izzat—in plain Anglo-Saxon, to score" (33). When the Indians qualify their judgments, the marked echoes remain. "But of course all this is exceptional," Hamidullah adds. "The exception does not prove the rule" (12). "Of course there are exceptions," Ronny concludes.[9]

Aziz may temporarily withdraw from such conversations, but the mimetic conventions that inform them underwrite his daily life, from the dress he wears to the words he speaks to the surgery he performs. He can stand outside politics only by tacitly admitting his absorption into the colonial forms. Thus Aziz rebukes Fielding for his freedom of speech, adopting a characteristically English position, "the protector who knows the dangers of India and is admonitory" and characteristically English tones; a kind of cultural informant, he represents his country and compatriots in terms that fit a British mold: "You can't be too careful in every way, Mr. Fielding; whatever you say or do in this damned country there is always some envious fellow on the lookout. You may be surprised to know that there were at least three spies sitting here when you came to enquire" (120).[10] In the ultimate gesture of colonial absorption, Aziz speaks of India as a monolithic culture to which he does not belong. Ironically, his speech forestalls the intimate dialogue he desires by acting as instrument for the censorious British voice. Even to himself, however, Aziz argues against such open converse, and he argues on essentially political grounds: "That frankness of speech in the presence of Ram Chand Rafi and Co. was dangerous and inelegant. It served no useful end" (122). Aziz's "conversion" at the end of the novel makes explicit the politicization he cannot avoid. He does not so much discover politics as discover his "side." And he does not so much find his voice—or lose it—as exercise "his" voice under new rubrics: "Clear out, all you Turtons and Burtons. We wanted to know you ten years back—now it's too late. If we see you and sit on your committees, it's for political

reasons, don't you make any mistake" (321). Having declared his
national allegiance, Aziz articulates the desires his new allegiance
requires: to "drive every blasted Englishman into the sea" (322).

As for the British, their mere presence in India bespeaks their
political part; their personal pronouncements, however varied, inevitably participate in the power of a ruling class. Their discourse demonstrates what Edward Said calls "positional superiority," even if it
avoids superiority of other sorts.[11] Fielding, who claims that he cannot get his mind on to politics, quite literally offers his position ("I
needed a job"; "I got in first"; "I'm delighted to be here too—that's
my answer, there's my only excuse") as a substitute for the obligatory
political response: "England holds India for her good" (112). Unwill-
ing to mouth the lines his culture dictates, he nonetheless speaks
from a position that takes its own values as an unquestionable base;
like the other Anglo-Indians, he does not shape his discourse with
the "mental conventions" of an Indian audience in mind. His bleak,
definite words "wound" their ears and "paralyse" their minds (112).

Similarly, Adela's experiments in unorthodox discourse are compromised by the power of command: "Miss Quested now had her
desired opportunity; friendly Indians were before her, and she tried
to make them talk, but she failed" (43). Desiring dialogue, Adela
dominates the verbal field; and, as at the picnic, finding herself alone
with Indians, she does not have much to say. She can converse only
with her kind. Ultimately, Adela has no place in India except what
her position confers; it is by virtue of her engagement to Ronny that
she ensures her presence in the country and establishes the ground
from which she speaks. Yet one of the first consequences of her new
position is the censorship it entails—censorship that works to enforce
race and gender solidarity. Speaking to Aziz of the Anglo-Indian
mentality, she withholds the full force of her words: "'I can't avoid
the label. What I do hope to avoid is the mentality. Women like—'
She stopped, not quite liking to mention names; she would boldly
have said 'Mrs. Turton and Mrs. Callendar' a fortnight ago" (145).

Even Mrs. Moore, who exhibits the greatest democracy of discourse, speaks through the authority of the Christian god: "God has
put us on earth to love our neighbours and to show it, and He is
omnipresent, even in India, to see how we are succeeding" (51). Her
voice is not entirely her own. "She must needs pronounce his name

frequently" (52), the narrative explains; ". . . something made her go on" (51). In her discourse, original utterance and quoted scripture blend, with no discernible line: "Good will and more good will and more good will. Though I speak with the tongues of . . . " (52). Though she speaks in the tongue of an elderly English woman, she assumes the position and authority of God.

The unmarked quotation (I Corinthians 13), with the incomplete transcription of its words, clears a space for appropriation. The biblical source reads: "Though I speak with the tongues of men and angels, and have not charity, I am become as sounding brass, or a tinkling cymbal."[12] And much of the novel works to play a series of substitutions upon the elliptically represented terms. The line from I Corinthians, elusively tied to its source, provides a paradigm for the novel's political economy in which there is no unappropriated voice. All speech turns out to be in "the tongues" of others, with the Indians' English voices only the most explicit case.

Anglo-Indian discourse, for example, is a self-imitative form. As Ronny's experience demonstrates, apprenticeship for a sahib means learning to speak conventionalized words, to acquire "the qualified bray of the callow official" (81). As both Adela and Mrs. Moore discover, the price of his acceptance is the surrender of his voice. His previously cited lines, for example, represent the epitome of appropriated discourse: "When he said 'of course there are exceptions' he was quoting Mr. Turton, while 'increasing the izzat' was Major Callendar's own" (33). Even Fielding, who cannot learn the accepted tongue (among the English, "he appeared to inspire confidence until he spoke" [62]), nonetheless speaks by a definable code. Like Mrs. Moore he speaks for good will, "good will plus culture and intelligence" (62); like Adela, he asserts "the sanctity of personal relationships" and the efficacy of a "thorough talk." Like them, he speaks in a language he does not invent. And language dwarfs its speakers, recreating them in its own image, locking them within its own constraints. The myth of original, apolitical utterance is thus dispelled by the implicatedness of discourse. In the novel's political theater, there can be no uncommitted parts.

The novel's representation of voice in a theatrical context makes explicit the way voice is constructed according to discernible conventions and codes; moreover, it illuminates the conditions of its deployment within a controlled environment. The picnic at the Marabar, the novel's most elaborately staged event, reveals the limits, in this context, of impromptu performance, of speech out of part. As managing director, Aziz provides costumes, character actors, sideshows, machinery, and props; the narrative even offers a stage direction, "Various pointless jests" (138). But for the principal participants, the event remains an unscripted act; in the absence of the authority of an English man, Aziz "plans" an exercise in improvisation: "My idea is to plan everything without consulting you; but you, Mrs. Moore, or Miss Quested, you are at any moment to make alterations if you wish, even if it means giving up the caves" (139). The very premise of such an enterprise, in the Anglo-Indian situation, dooms it from the start.

For improvisation is always improvisation of powerlessness, at least in Indian hands.[13] The promise of flexibility and imaginative sympathy that improvisation opens up discloses the reality of relationships that are rigidly fixed: the inevitable scenario of a subject people paying deference to the powerful elect. Thus when Adela sees a snake, Aziz "helps" her identification along: ". . . yes, a black cobra, very venomous, who had reared himself up to watch the passing of the elephant" (140). Adela, however, prefers to see through Anglo-Indian eyes; looking through Ronny's field glasses, she finds the withered stump of a tree. Unable to enter the discourse of improvisation, her voice follows her eye: "So she said, 'It isn't a snake.'" For Adela, as for the other Anglo-Indians, speech must constitute either truth or lie; although she desires to escape the mentality of Anglo-India, it does not occur to her to sacrifice the authority of the word. The villagers, valuing politeness over precision, will not allow Adela to contradict herself; they will not abandon the snake she has planted in their minds. Aziz, improvising again, negotiates a middle ground: "Aziz admitted that it looked like a tree through the glasses, but insisted that it was a black cobra really, and improvised some rubbish about protective mimicry" (141). The passage represents, the narrative suggests, "a confusion about a snake which was never cleared up" (140). But the confusion does not so much attach to the snake's identity as to the nature of competing discursive modes.

Aziz's explanation, "protective mimicry," is enacted in his very words, in the appropriated scientific terms. He does not expect his statement to be believed as truth (presumably, even he recognizes it as "rubbish"), but he expects to be heard. Yet in the theater of empire, improvisation is vigorously disallowed. Indian mimicry is accepted as an insignia of subjugation, but British mimicry remains a contradiction in terms. While the very base of imperial authority is mimetic ("making England in India"), its power depends upon disguising this effect. The British will not even admit the provisional logic that the appellation Anglo-India visibly displays. The British improvise power, then, by denying improvisation as an operative term. Conflating script and scripture, they claim for all their utterances the authority of the written word.

Thus when Adela "improvises" an explanation for her experience in the caves, she does not recognize the act as such; she is given a text ("assault by an Indian"), the oldest story around, to which she makes her experience conform. But in the logic of empire, the superimposed effect (the story Adela tells) assumes the privilege of cause. For Adela to recognize the conditions of improvisation—to acknowledge her own story as improvised, as she seems to do at the trial—is to subvert the political machine. Among the Anglo-Indians, it is to make herself unheard: "I didn't catch that answer" (229), the Superintendent declares when Adela departs from her carefully rehearsed testimony. In what appears to Anglo-India as inexplicable improvisation, Adela explodes "the flimsy framework of the court" (231). But even this explosion, as I will argue later, is contained within the staged ceremonies of recuperated British ideals.

Improvisation forms a common ground where England and India coinhabit but do not meet, for only one party admits the performance at all. When the Indians improvise among themselves—exaggerate, impersonate, distort, invent—they aim for a histrionic effect; neither actor nor audience is duped, for they understand the act's theatrical terms. But when the Indians improvise for the English, the performance falls flat, for the audience judges by a different set of rules. When, for example, Aziz covers up for Adela, explaining away her departure from the caves, the logic of evidence reads "guilt." But the performance was meant to protect his guest: "He was inaccurate because he desired to honour her, and—facts being entangled—he had to arrange them in her vicinity, as one tidies the ground after extracting a weed" (158). When the English improvise for the Indians, they

protect only themselves. Presenting a united front after the "catastrophe" of the caves, they expect to be taken at their word: "People
drove into the club with studious calm—the jog-trot of country folk
between green hedgerows, for the natives must not suspect that they
were agitated" (180). Forgetting the fictional origin of their performance, they come to believe their own facade. In improvisation,
then, there can be no converse, for the English and Indians proceed
from opposite understandings of the term. Where the Indians act self-
consciously, mimicking "characters" and indulging in extravagant
forms of discourse, the English do not act out of character at all; as in
their performance of *Cousin Kate*, they "reproduce their own attitude
to life upon the stage," dressing up "as the middle-class English
people they actually were" (40).

The novel presents the political situation as a theater of self-
impersonation, with the British imposing the standards to which all
performances must adhere. The metaphor is one other chroniclers of
empire share: George Orwell, for example, in "Shooting an Elephant"
and Leonard Woolf in *Growing*, the memoirs of his years in Ceylon.
Looking back on his experience, Woolf recalls, "For seven years, excited and yet slightly and cynically amused, I watched myself playing
a part in an exciting play on a brightly coloured stage or dreaming a
wonderfully vivid and exciting dream."[14] In such a situation, the
Indians essentially have two choices if they want an opportunity to be
heard: to impersonate the English or to impersonate an English-based
Indian stereotype—what the English believe Indians are. Any performance that deviates from the script is declared nonexistent or simply
reinterpreted along these lines.[15] Under the conditions of power the
novel represents, then, the Indians are denied even a "self" to impersonate, and they are denied an autonomous voice.

But the British are presented as equally constrained, compelled
to enact self-imposed stereotypes. "A sahib has got to act like a sahib," Orwell self-reflexively observes.[16] Writing of his Anglo-Indian
associates, Leonard Woolf ponders the origin of their facade: "The
white people were also in many ways astonishingly like characters in
a Kipling story. I could never make up my mind whether Kipling had
moulded his characters accurately in the image of Anglo-Indian society or whether we were moulding our characters accurately in the
image of a Kipling story."[17] *Passage* would seem to confirm the theory

of a textual base, where experience is molded by literature and not the other way around. For within the novel's fictional reality, the English character unfolds itself in the prefabricated forms of vaudeville melodrama and third-rate novels of adventure and romance. Forster himself acknowledged the representational bind. Describing his early efforts to compose *A Passage to India*, he observed: "I began it in 1912, and then came the war. I took it with me when I returned to India in 1921, but found what I had written wasn't India at all. It was like sticking a photograph on a picture. However, I couldn't *write* it when I was in India. When I got away, I could get on with it."[18] Forster's text constitutes a copy of a copy, a fiction dependent upon the absence of the original term.

Adela's experience in the caves brings to the surface the theatricality that governs colonial discourse—and that supports its sexual politics—not only in her own melodramatic rendering of it but in Anglo-India's personal and political response. The "exalted emotion" she generates reads like a catalog of literary clichés: the unselfish devotion ("What can we do for our sister?" [179–80]), the ennobling sorrow ("She is my own darling girl" [180]), the regrets ("Why don't one think more of other people?" [180]), the self-accusations ("To refuse, and then give in under pressure. That is what I did, my sons, that is what I did" [185]). The discrete actors speak here in a single voice, and when political considerations supplant Adela's private tragedy, the stage language remains the same: "They had started speaking of 'women and children'—that phrase that exempts the male from sanity when it has been repeated a few times" (183). In their eyes, the "chilly and half-known features of Miss Quested" vanish to be replaced by "all that is sweetest and warmest in the private life" (183).

The Anglo-Indians exercise power by a form of narrative control. In their moment of crisis, they stage a drama, but unlike Aziz, they leave no space for *extempore* effects. With the script already written, they need only cast the characters and rehearse their lines. Predictably, they cast themselves in all the desirable roles: hero, victim, martyr, loyal friend. And they invest these roles with the fervor of their own frustrated aims, reserving the lead performances for white men: "Miss Quested was only a victim, but young Heaslop was a martyr; he was the recipient of all the evil intended against them by the country they had tried to serve; he was bearing the sahib's cross" (185). Demanding absolute submission to their collective fiction, the Anglo-Indian authorities impress even the less-favored actors with the inevitability of their control. Aziz, cast as villain, plays the part, "acting the criminal" as soon as he is apprised of the plot: he "lies" about evidence, tries to run away, sobs and breaks down at his arrest. Similarly, given a choice between the only available roles, "to avenge the girl" or "save the man" (165), Fielding accepts the apostate's part; there is no option to join a different play.

The ensuing performance, enacted as one long dress rehearsal for the trial's opening day, displays the mechanisms by which colonial power works: narrative foreclosure and rhetorical control. Such control, moreover, demands the silencing of women and their surrender to male authority. As the Collector's advice to the Anglo-Indian women suggests, the most effective way to ensure narrative conformity is to reduce, as radically as possible, the opportunities for (women's) speech: "Don't go out more than you can help, don't go into the city, don't talk before your servants. That's all" (181). In the proper functioning of the colonial machine, the Collector seems to suggest, a perfectly adjusted organism would be silent, to appropriate the narrator's terms. Where speech is unavoidable, rhetorical restraints solidify the orthodox line. Internalizing an unvoiced prohibition, the Anglo-Indians agree to censor certain words. Neither Adela nor Aziz is mentioned by name: ". . . she, like Aziz, was always referred to by a periphrasis" (182). The practice limits interpretive options and polices dialogue, for the allowable terms are all of a kind. The name, Aziz, for example, "had become synonymous with the power of evil. He was 'the prisoner,' 'the person in question,' 'the defence'" (202).

Such rhetorical procedures control unauthorized readings and, in some cases, create the desired text. When Fielding questions Turton about the source of the charges against Aziz, the Collector will not speak Adela's name: "'Miss Derek and—the victim herself. . . .' He nearly broke down, unable to repeat the girl's name" (163). The emotion that prevents his proper identification, however, seems as much an effect of his own euphemism as its cause. Adela may achieve the stature of "victim" by virtue of the Collector's appellation, the sentence suggests, and not the other way around.[19] Turton's politic formulation, moreover, evades the question of origins that prompted the response, obscuring the fact that Adela does *not* actually originate the charge. Miss Derek reads the cause into the effect, and Anglo-India authorizes the reconstruction the interpolation affirms: "Miss Quested couldn't stand the Indian driver, cried, 'Keep him away'—and it was that that put our friend on the track of what had happened" (168). Adela's original authority is thus subordinated to the official story Anglo-India chooses to endorse.

Ironically, then, it is Adela's charge against Aziz rather than her experience in the caves that subjects her to a "rape." For the charge puts her in Anglo-Indian hands, where she is examined under glass and spoon-fed her words. Or perhaps, more accurately, a "proper" voice is extracted from her. The episode thus marks a progressive silencing of Adela. For Adela's illness, with its hysterical symptoms, fixes her gender position and restricts her vocal independence. When, for example, Adela breaks the code of silence, mentioning Aziz by name—"Aziz . . . have I made a mistake?" (202)—Ronny's melodramatic recoil forecloses the subversive narrative line: "A shiver like impending death passed over Ronny" (203). And when, at her trial, Adela withdraws the charges, the Anglo-Indian community insists on *their* more authoritative knowledge of the event. For her voice, like her body, has become Anglo-Indian property. Momentarily, they consider pursuing the prosecution, upholding the terms of Adela's sworn deposition against her impossible-sounding spoken words.

In fact, in Anglo-Indian eyes, Adela never really has a voice at all, for they cannot recognize a voice governed by competing narrative demands. As woman, Adela remains "another bad case," an actor who panics under pressure and forgets her lines. Years after the event, they continue to proclaim, "That Marabar case which broke down because the poor girl couldn't face giving her evidence—that was another bad case" (261). Their judgment replicates the local newspaper's critique of Miss Derek's performance in *Cousin Kate*: "Miss Derek, though she charmingly looked her part, lacked the necessary experience, and occasionally forgot her words" (40). Although the Anglo-Indian community resents this Indian criticism of Miss Derek, calling it "the sort of thing no white man could have written," they judge Adela in nearly identical terms. In the eyes of Anglo-India,

Adela's identity is conferred entirely by her part: ". . . it was her position not her character that moved them; she was the English girl who had had the terrible experience, and for whom too much could not be done" (211). When she fails to perform convincingly, as far as they are concerned, she ceases to exist. So thorough is their disavowal of her that Adela, after the trial, finds herself dependent on the one "renegade" from the community for even a place to sleep.

Although the Anglo-Indians do not credit Adela's "new" story, they feel compelled to suppress the threat she poses to their autocratic narrative stance. The fiction of empire cannot withstand much inquiry into origins, since it premises itself on eternal omnipresence: a condition of authority without locatable origin or end, something "clamped down, in *saecula saeculorum*," as George Orwell contends.[20] To investigate origins is to bring imperial power into the provisional realm, to reveal it as a human construct and not an unalterable act of God. And it is to reveal the shaky logic at its core, for the purported cause of colonial power, "England holds India for her good," postdates its effect, the presence of England in India as a political force.

Fielding, perhaps even more than Adela, exposes these contradictions when he chooses what at first seems an autonomous narrative line: "He was still after facts, though the herd had decided on emotion" (165). In refusing the ready-made speeches, he reveals the inadequacy of the Anglo-Indian master plot; he suggests the possibility of other scripts, and consequently, the status of the colonial performance as a theatrical act. This, finally, is the heresy with which he is charged. When Turton asks Fielding to apologize to Ronny Heaslop, and Fielding replies, "Are you speaking to me officially, sir?" he is asking the one question that is not allowed. In the world Anglo-India creates, *all* discourse is official, for the Anglo-Indians are always on stage. But the performance can work only if its status is denied. "Feelings like these are the normal by-product of imperialism; ask any Anglo-Indian official if you can catch him off duty," George Orwell writes, implying, by definition, that no such official could be found.[21]

The response to Fielding's defection marks his greater threat, his greater power to project a convincing voice. Where Adela merely falters, from the Anglo-Indian perspective, Fielding has been "bought." Referring to him with pointed irony as "the one righteous Englishman in a horde of tyrants," the English essentially denational-

ize Fielding, writing him out of their ranks. Yet Fielding's "alternative" discourse is not un-English; rather, it is English in the extreme,
upholding as it does the sacred values of reason and truth. It thus
threatens the English voice by revealing that voice's defection from its
own ideals: "Nothing enrages Anglo-India more than the lantern of
reason if it is exhibited for one moment after its extinction is decreed"
(165). Bearing "the lantern of reason," Fielding becomes a British
cliché, a mouthpiece for the rationalistic creed: "Great is information,
and she shall prevail" (191). His tone resounds in Adela's shallow
faith: "God who saves the King will surely support the police" (211).

Although Fielding and Adela depart from the standard repertoire, verbally, they never really switch sides. In a sense, they "out-
British" their associates, returning British discourse to the letter of its
law. Adela's recantation, for example, is voiced in preeminently English terms, "to tell the truth and nothing but the truth" (227). Far
from repudiating logic and reason, she takes them to an extreme in
her visionary topography of cause and effect: "The court, the place of
question, awaited her reply. But she could not give it until Aziz
entered the place of answer" (228).[22] The trial, then, that marks, in
one sense, the temporary defeat of Anglo-India, is in another sense a
victory for British discourse. For the trial is conducted in the field of
speech and entirely on British terms. Aziz's vindication results not
from the power of a competing discourse but from the successful
operation of the British machine.

Staged as a series of set pieces, the trial consists, in its basic
structure, of a sequential monologue, undisturbed by the color of
the speaker's skin. For even the most politicized Indians recognize
the need to ventriloquize, recognize that British values constitute the
only terms of appeal. Thus Hamidullah knows he must defend Aziz
on Western lines: ". . . he prated of 'policy' and 'evidence' in a way
that saddened the Englishman" (173). The pleader at the trial, Mah-
moud Ali, speaks with "ponderous and ill-judged irony" (220), testimony of his unsuccessful verbal effort to achieve a convincing British
effect. And "the eminent barrister from Calcutta" (220) speaks "in an
Oxford voice" (221). In a trial conducted on the British model and
adjudicated under Western eyes, the Indians can have no authentic
voice. Officially, they speak in borrowed tones; unofficially, they
have no voice at all. A more "authentic" utterance surfaces only in the

occasional unauthorized interruption: the challenging of McBryde's theory of Oriental Pathology ("Even when the lady is so uglier than the gentleman" [219]) and the chanting of Mrs. Moore's name ("Esmiss Esmoor"). But these remain anonymous utterances—distortions of the master tongue—for which English remains the linguistic base.

For the British, the trial topples their central performers, but reinscribes the underlying principles of their script: the absolute authority of the word, the correspondence of voice and deed. The trial does not fundamentally challenge Anglo-Indian discourse; it saves it from its own excess, returning it to the first principles upon which it depends. Moreover, in reinstating the non-conformers, Fielding, Adela, Mrs. Moore, the trial gives them a voice *within* the dominant discourse. It brings them from the sidelines onto the center stage. Before the trial each suffers a disorder of speech and the forcible transformation of his or her words. Fielding is literally silenced within his own community, cut off from all converse with his kind; he is represented in their circles only through the distorted utterance rumor repeats. Mrs. Moore, after her experience in the caves, jumbles scripts and lines, speaking rarely, mostly to herself, in garbled monologue. Adela, like a broken record, endlessly repeats the same lines, "rehearsing" her "terrible adventure" in "an odd, mincing way" (212).

For each the trial serves as a "restorative" act. Fielding receives the imprimatur of the Lieutenant-Governor, who legitimizes his "subversive" discourse, declaring it "the broad, the sensible, the only possible charitable view" (258).[23] Mrs. Moore is momentarily restored to life. Indianized in the voice of the crowd, she "speaks" at the trial, where otherwise she would have no legal rights. "She is not here, and consequently she can say nothing" (226), the Magistrate explains. Mrs. Moore's "silent" testimony constitutes her most intelligible speech since her breakdown in the caves. Adela, on the witness stand, recovers her voice. "Flat" and "unattractive" (229), the voice is nonetheless her own; the distorted intonations of her rehearsed speech ("odd" and "mincing") give way to characteristically "hard prosaic tones" (230). Renouncing her own people, she places herself in their camp; for her "confession" marks her as the mastermind, however unintentional, in an elaborate power play. Tainted by a common discourse, she finds she can no longer condemn the English women she once scorned. At the very moment they disown her, she makes herself one of them. Of Mrs. Turton, she observes to Fielding, "Do you find her preposterous? I used to. I don't now" (246).

The trial marks the limits of the novel's theater of discourse. Having "spoken out," Fielding and Adela find themselves *inside* the play, the creations of their own speech acts: "When they agreed, 'I want to go on living a bit,' or, 'I don't believe in God,' the words were followed by a curious backwash as though the universe had displaced itself to fill up a tiny void, or as though they had seen their own gestures from an immense height—dwarfs talking, shaking hands and assuring each other that they stood on the same footing of in-sight" (264–65). Early in the novel, Fielding observes his guests, "A scene from a play, thought Fielding, who now saw them from the distance across the garden grouped among the blue pillars of his beautiful hall" (77). But like Adela, he discovers there is no "safe" vantage point in the wings; not even the audience occupies neutral ground. For the audience does not really exist; it consists of players at one remove from the central stage. Those who begin by "examining life" end by "being examined by it" (244–45). Thus Fielding and Ad-ela can occupy the position of audience only to observe their own participation in the colonial charade.

Appropriating all the novel's voices, then, colonial discourse per-forms to an empty house. The novel's most devastating critique of imperialism may be to represent precisely this state: the social and political status quo.[24] For the novel reveals the inevitable dominance of the master discourse even as it replicates its hollow tones. It offers no political solutions, but it registers a protest from within the domi-nant voice—a protest against the very determinateness of discourse it cannot help but represent. The final section of the novel suggests Forster's effort to widen the stage, to present a voice so absolutely "other" it cannot be absorbed. The "Temple" section of the novel even begins with a kind of program note to orient the reader to the curtain's rising on a radically changed setting and scene: "Some hundreds of miles westward of the Marabar Hills, and two years later in time, Professor Narayan Godbole stands in the presence of God" (283).

The extravagant Hindu ceremony presented in this section sup-plants the "Caves" section's spectacle of the court. But less com-prehensible to the novel's audience, the "Temple's" event is nonethe-less staged, bounded by the novel's own discourse. The narrative practices that produce this interlude limit the "otherness" it can represent. As the following chapter will argue, the drama of appropriation that constitutes so much of the novel's subject is replayed, most particularly in this section, in the narrative voice. Moreover, as the novel moves toward its conclusion, the alien setting becomes the backdrop for a more familiar scene: the final "dialogue" between Fielding and Aziz. The "spirit" of Hinduism, an intimation of metaphysical depths, gives way to the novel's political "frieze." Unable to escape their positions, Fielding and Aziz embrace the parts they are prescribed to play. As they shout political slogans, their words cannot connect. The actors are no more than voices, the mouthpieces of a discourse that is preordained. Fielding's impromptu question, "Why can't we be friends now?" is suppressed by the exigencies of a script that proclaims, "No not yet," "No not there" (322).

*   *   *

When *A Passage to India* was first published, story has it, civil servants outward bound for India, seeing themselves caricatured there, threw their copies overboard, declaring that "Anglo-Indian Society was no longer 'like that'."[25] This theatrical performance dramatizes most fully the conditions the novel reflects where the audience is inevitably a part of the play. But a study of the novel's reception reveals the constitutive part its audience has always played in the creation of the text. From the beginning, national allegiances and political ties created a double response—a response centered upon questions of representational authenticity. "The author's pictures are faithful and vivid. That is particularly the case in regard to the Anglo-Indian characters he has created," St. Nihal Singh wrote at the time of publication. "They are not even good caricatures," an Anglo-Indian reader complained, ". . . most of what he knows about [Anglo-Indians], their ways and their catchwords, and has put into his book, he has picked up from the stale gossip of Indians."[26]

The rhetoric that informs these oppositional judgments reveals the assumptions that they share: that the novel can be judged by standards of ethnography. The comments rehearse a debate familiar to cultural anthropology—the value of representations based on experience versus those derived from other texts. And the literary conclusions coincide with those of classical anthropology: presentations filtered through texts constitute bad literature as they do bad ethnography. To free the novel from its textual heritage is presented, by one reviewer, as the mark of highest praise; it is to remove the novel from the literary arena and grant it scientific objectivity. Thus an English woman writes, "The Indians in this book are not, as in all other Anglo-Indian novels, deplorable but unavoidable pieces of the scenery. They are not cast for the roles of simple villains and clowns. They are men with different conventions from Englishmen—how different has never been revealed before."[27] Arguing a more overtly political position, and essentially taking the opposite side, Nirad Chaudhuri upholds these standards of authenticity: "Aziz would not have been allowed to cross my threshold, not to speak of being taken as an equal"; "Godbole is not an exponent of Hinduism, he is a clown."[28]

What these judgments have in common is a belief in the absolute distinction between literature and culture, between text and experience, between aesthetic fiction and political truth. But like the characters in the novel, the critics observe from an interested position and create a text in the way they see. What I have tried to argue in my reading of the novel is the lesson of revisionist anthropology: the collapsing of these central dichotomies. For within the novel's field of representation, "experience" is always textually construed—filtered through prior fictional models and textualized in the narrative and rhetorical determinants that enable it to be transmitted, translated, and even understood. As Clifford and others have argued, culture must be written before it can be read; moreover, writing culture means writing texts—whether it be in the scientific, political, or literary domain. In the critical debates surrounding the novel, the text occupies the place of the "other culture" that is constituted in the readings that give it shape.

What should be clear from the sampling of responses I have offered is that the contours of the novel are molded by the political preconceptions its readers bring to the text and the particular "languages" they speak. In the most glaring instance of this phenomenon, one reviewer literally rewrites the plot of the novel to conform to his notion of "political reality." Unable to countenance a white woman having sexual fantasies about an Indian, he observes, "My private theory is as follows. The 'hallucination' was not Adela's but Aziz's."[29] This radical rewriting of the text remains, however, only the most glaring example of a process in which all readers engage. It is no less true for those who find in the novel the ultimate expression of fair play. For to say that Forster presents his material "without the faintest intimation of prejudice for one side or another"[30] is to read through a particular, politicized point of view. It is to valorize the principle of fairness and to define fairness in a very specific, if not contradictory way: ". . . I have never known so accurate, so penetrating, and so sympathetic an account of the divergent characters and lives as this. It is sympathetic with both sides."[31] A compendium of objectivity, accuracy, and sympathy, this "special kind of fairness"[32] forecloses other interpretive possibilities for cultural interchange.[33] It makes possible the type of literary praise we now read with cultural embarrassment, as in Rose Macaulay's paean to the novel's truthfulness: "He can make even these brown men live."[34]

The "apolitical" positions that cite the novel's fairness do not, then, so much escape politics as keep their politics disguised. The assessment of the novel's fairness has, moreover, been the subject of considerable debate. In the face of much celebration of the novel, one contemporary critic felt compelled to offer the missing view, to describe "how the book strikes an Anglo-Indian"; fifty years later, V. A. Shahane collected a volume of essays to present "the Indian" side: "One of the basic reasons for this volume is the need to project the Indian image. It is my belief that the essays by the Indian writers presented here bear the indelible stamp of 'Indianness' which may seem refreshing in the context of the purely western response to Forster's great masterpiece."[35]

For these commentators, the novel was a recognized political event, a view echoed in many contemporary accounts. "It is a political document of the first importance," Rebecca West claimed. It is a warning to "the Dyers and the O'Dwyers of India, and to those who keep up the political repute of these people in this country," another reviewer noted. The novel is an "event of imperial significance," yet another reader observed.[36] These statements point to the fact that our political perspectives are largely textually produced and our knowledge of other cultures the result of what we read. The history of *A Passage to India* further testifies to the overlap of the literary and politi-

cal domains. A set book for the Indian Civil Service, the novel became
a filter through which to view the imperial regime. Nirad Chaudhuri
claims that *A Passage to India* "has possibly been an even greater
influence in British imperial politics than in English literature." For
him, the politics of the novel are determined by the ways it can be put
to use: "Mr. Forster's novel became a powerful weapon in the hands
of the anti-imperialists, and was made to contribute its share to the
disappearance of British rule in India."[37] More modestly Forster
claimed, "It had some political influence—it caused people to think of
the link between India and Britain and to doubt if that link was
altogether of a healthy nature. The influence (political) was not intended; I was interested in the story and the characters. But I wel-
comed it."[38]

Writing in 1962, Frederick Crews remarked, "Forster's present
reputation, so far as one can judge, has been affected by ideological
considerations as much as by artistic ones"[39]—a judgment the preceding survey of the criticism would confirm. Crews's remark signals
a shift in critical terms. But, I would argue, the conditions Crews
articulates continue to operate today. Much of the praise of the
novel's aesthetic achievement in the past twenty-five years has been
no less motivated by ideological concerns, whether they be the special place accorded aesthetic virtues or an implicit conviction of the
novel's enlightened political line. The valuation of the novel, however, that characterizes much of this recent response presumes a clear
distinction between political and literary terms; it thus denies the
inescapably political nature of the novel's own discourse. In the extensive studies of Forster's aesthetic achievement—characters, plot,
imagery, metaphysics, even mysticism—the underlying assumption
seems to be that politics is something great literature transcends.
Thus in a foreword to G. K. Das's study of Forster's Indian sources,
John Beer concludes,". . . his long account of the matter recalls us to
the fact that Forster's basic preoccupations always extended far beyond politics."[40] And for John Colmer, writing a centenary essay on
Forster in 1979, politics has at best a dubious place; it belongs, and
then only questionably, to those most oppressed by the political situation the novel represents. "It is perhaps natural for Indian writers
to be especially critical of Forster's alleged political deficiencies," Col-

mer concedes, but in general political "statements" do not belong to the novelistic realm.[41]

With renewed critical interest in ideology and literature, the emphasis in Forster studies has begun to undergo another shift. Overt political considerations have reemerged in the discussion of Forster—but it is politics conceived in a wider way. To connect the novel's aesthetics to its political base, as my own study does, is thus to reflect yet another turn in the politics of literary response. It is to suggest that every reading of the novel enacts a political event and that politics informs the novel's aesthetic terms and effects. If, as I have suggested, the voices of politics resound in the novel, it is, then, not only because the novel represents voice as a political construct but because the novel reverberates with the politicized voices its readers contribute to the text they continually reconceive.

Chapter 4

The Politics of Voice

If our children stop in India they get to talk *chit chit* (?) and it is
such a stigma—we are disgraced.
—Passenger aboard "City of Birmingham,"
E. M. Forster, *Indian Journal: 1912–13*

For E. M. Forster, traveling to India for the first time, this remark by a
fellow traveler epitomized the quintessentially British attitude he was
to strive so hard to disavow. It marks the imperialist's fear of contagion, of a dangerous slippage in identity, and it marks the site of
anxiety—the privileged voice. Contact with the natives, the English
woman suggests, breeds infection—infection in the sentence, a disorder of speech. Broken English ("'Chi-chi,'" a footnote to Forster's
journal tells us, "is the modern spelling of 'cheechee,'" "a disparag-
ing term applied to half-castes or Eurasians because of their 'hybrid
minced English'") becomes the somatic sign by which we read the
undermining disease. Contiguity, it would seem, necessitates imitation, and by imitation we are undone. For if English children, by
association with Indians, can lose their Englishness, then their parents, by associative extension, will bear the marks of their disgrace.
At the heart of such anxiety lies a tremendous fear of the power of
mimicry to erase difference and destabilize identity. Yet, ironically,
the model the English fear their children will emulate is not a native
original but an already edited text, a corrupted version of speech
already English. The English fear of "going native"—of regression to
a primitive prototype—thus translates into the fear that their children
will become Indianized versions of themselves.[1]

84

Because proximity is dangerous, the systematization of racial supremacy attempts to ensure that the mimetic impulse is not a recipro-
cal act, that it operates, in its own terms, only from the ground up.
Yet as the anecdote illustrates, fears of contagion are not so easily
allayed. Moreover, such fears operate in more than one way: for
Forster the real danger is that constant exposure to the *English* might
contaminate his own voice. In the diary entry where the anecdote
appears, for example, he is careful to mark the speech as other than
his own—to bracket it as quotation, to gloss it with implicit irony, and
to call into orthographic question, at least, the most offensive phrase
("*chit chit* [?]"), as if to reinforce the fact that such expressions are
unfamiliar to his tongue.

Yet Forster's distancing strategies may finally be no more successful than the English strategies he condemns. For if the British
created a myth of racial supremacy to prevent identification with the
other, Forster created a myth of denationalization to prevent identification with his kind. Of Malcolm Darling's residence in India, he
wrote, "It is interesting to see how the place transformed him. When
he arrived, he had the feeling of racial superiority which was usual
among Englishmen at the time. In a few months he lost it, and it
never returned" (*HD*, 22). And of himself, after a second trip to India,
he wrote in 1922, "In some ways I am denationalised more than is
convenient."[2] Yet Forster's Indian writings repeatedly show that culturally conditioned feelings of superiority can never be completely
erased. A European, as Edward Said suggests, can never be an
Oriental—only an Orientalist.[3] The overlay of objectivity merely disguises the representational distortions of any cultural discourse. Forster, in other places, acknowledged this inescapable fact; after completing *A Passage to India* and noting its success, selling "like
hotcakes," to quote his very English words, Forster wrote, "How
dreary fair-mindedness is! Having tried to practise it for four hundred
pages, I now realize that it is only a British form of unfairness. Next
time I shall order a suit of Khaddar and be done."[4]

As Forster here pronounces, one's Englishness is indelibly imprinted on one's voice; self-consciousness can only accentuate the
characteristic tone. The single escape is in silence, in a fantasy of
cultural cross-dressing that would be a definitive nonverbal act. This
recognition of linguistic complicity has important consequences not

only for a reinterpretation of Forster's Orientalism but for an understanding of the problematics of narrative that *Passage* sets forth. For at the heart of the novel, as at the heart of the Anglo-Indian dilemma, lies a crisis of voice.

Critics have generally acknowledged that the central event of *Passage* is a non-event—a "story" that gives voice to the British fear of contagion by giving free reign to the contagious British voice.[5] When Adela Quested prepares to testify against Dr. Aziz, her defenders claim that "she tells her own story" (170), but the claim echoes from a chamber where all voices sound the same. From the moment Adela enters the public arena, she is supplied with her words, as the prosecutor's leading questions confirm. In fact, one might say, the only "rape" Adela suffers is the appropriation of her voice. Even the charges against Aziz are another person's extrapolations from her disordered state. In her symptoms of hysteria, she presents a text gone awry, and she becomes the victim of those who would read her right. For the British, as for the Indians, this new text only confirms their worst fears; Adela's breakdown is the inevitable consequence of attempted intimacy with the other—a case of cultural transgression with its attendant disease. Adela's vision and recantation transpose the terms of this figure, but they do not challenge its underlying metaphoric base. The source of disturbance turns out to be not contact with the Indian *other* but with the British *same*. Adela recovers her voice, then, only to discover that it was never uniquely hers to claim. As her name suggests, Adela's text is already written; she is quested before she even begins her quest. The attempt to "see India" produces only an exposé of the self.

What is interesting for my purposes is the way a classic anxiety about contamination (the unspeakable fear of interracial sex) is displaced onto an anxiety about the integrity of voice. For I would like to suggest that Adela's narrative can be read as an analogue for the situation of Forster's text—a text generated by fears of narrative/cultural contagion, that has at its heart an unspoken anxiety about originality, authority, and the author's privileged voice.[6] Read in the context of Forster's earlier novels, what is striking about *Passage* is the absence of the distinctly discernible Forsterian voice: urbane, ironic, assured. What we have in its stead is a narrative gone mad—a shifting, slippery, unplaceable voice that seems to take its timbre from whatever voice it happens to be near. The resulting disturbances to the novel's surface articulate what might be called narrative hysteria: the breakdown or fragmentation of the narrative voice. The voice does not disappear, as several critics have claimed, but it persists, like the novel's celebrated echo, in distorted refractions of an original utterance that can never be reclaimed.

In one of the most extended treatments of the subject, Barbara Rosecrance argues for the ultimate cohesiveness of the narrative: "In *A Passage to India*, Forster's voice is finally at one with the implications of his vision, and a contradiction no longer exists between ideology and presentation." Forster, she argues, "has created a voice that is controlling, from the opening phrase of the first chapter" to the novel's end.[7] I propose to make precisely the opposite claim: that it is the uncontrollability of the narrative, the dis-order of narrative speech, that gives us the text we read. Narrative interest, I will argue, resides in the space between ideology and presentation. This space is a condition of colonial discourse, what Paul Scott was to call the "unmapped area of dangerous fallibility between a policy and its pursuit" in his colonial novel *The Jewel in the Crown*.[8] The space is also the focus of reader response. When Adela Quested slips out of character—first to press, then to retract, her charges against Aziz—she becomes an object of interest and interpretation. Similarly, when the narrative seems to slip out of its own voice, the text opens before us its capacity to be repeatedly re-read.

Slippage, for the novel as for Adela, means adoption of a characteristically English voice. But in the case of the novel, it is difficult to distinguish verbal infiltration from the self-conscious adoption by the narrative of British imperialist tones. For even deliberate mimicry has its drawbacks: the potential confusion of voices, the difficulty of bracketing the mimicked part. As the English woman's monitory tale suggests ("If our children stop in India they get to talk *chit chit*"), mimicry is difficult to control. Imitation that begins as an assertion of difference—a sign of conscious superiority—can become an involuntary reflex.

In an analysis of mimicry as it operates on the colonial subject, Homi Bhabha writes, "colonial mimicry is the desire for a reformed recognizable Other, as *a subject of difference that is almost the same, but not quite*. Which is to say, that the discourse of mimicry is constructed around *an ambivalence*; in order to be effective, mimicry must continually produce its slippage, its excess, its difference."[9] For the colonial power, then, seeking to remake the native as a mirror image of itself, the marks of difference offer welcome testimony of the colonialist's superior stance. But for Forster, attempting to mimic his compatriots (the "almost the same, but not quite"), the process works in the opposite way. The inevitable slippage in his discourse reveals not the desired proof of his difference from the colonial oppressors, but the traces of what in him is the same. As with Adela Quested, Forster's attempt at "seeing India" returns only his own gaze.

Forster frequently referred to *Passage* as "my Indian novel," and its "Indianness" has been the subject of much critical concern.[10] I propose, however, to read the statement with the emphasis on the ambiguities of "my"—to read the novel's representation of the problematics of identity (different but same), and to read its areas of dangerous fallibility where, in the discourse of mimicry, criticism and complicity, differentiation and appropriation uneasily meet. Such an enterprise does not attempt to give a balanced reading of Forster. Rather, it is to read deliberately at a slant, to uncover a pattern of significance in what often goes unnoticed but is nonetheless marked. If this approach overemphasizes the disruptive elements of the narrative, it is to give play to one of the novel's "modernist" effects. For readers have generally noticed something unsettling in Forster's novel, what I would call a silent protest against the novel's dominant voice: a resistance to its own unity, a dislocation of its own speech.[11]

This dislocation takes the form of a drama of appropriation played out in the narrating act, as the narrative slips in and out of the voices it projects. While mimicry produces its contagious effects, efforts at narrative demarcation yield only a space of overlapping boundaries and undecidable tones. The novel thus comes to question the status of voice as something distinctly one's own. In particular, the narrative repeatedly demonstrates the voice's subjection to cultural constraints. My argument begins, then, with a reading of key passages in Forster's nonfictional Indian texts, because in these autobiographical writings the relation between culture and narrative is more immediately clear. In documenting Forster's "lapses" into the British cultural stance, I do not mean to cite him as an unusual or egregious case; nor do I mean to reduce him to a British stereotype. Rather, I mean to read him as a preeminent example of the ways we are all implicated in and by the conditions of our discourse.

Such a position takes issue with the prevailing liberal humanist views in Forster studies—views that perhaps find their fullest realization in this recent Indian response: "Forster, in the greatness of his imagination, accepted the muddle and the squalor, and whatever else India offered, with sympathy and love and all humility of heart. With his passion for human contacts, lack of haughtiness, openness to new experience, politeness and generosity, all rooted in his own culture and humanism, he transcended national, racial and psychological barriers that stood in the way of so many of those new to India."[12] Without disputing Forster's comparative achievement in embracing Indian ways, I would challenge the absolute and transcendent terms of this author's praise. To dispense with such terms, as Benita Parry has recently argued, is to enable a richer reading of the text: "Forster's reputation as the archetypal practitioner of the domestic, liberal-humanist, realist English novel, has inhibited contemporary readers from engaging with *A Passage to India* as a text which disrupts its own conventional forms and dissects its own informing ideology."[13]

The strategies that inform Foster's cultural discourse, as well as much of its specific content, find their way into the narrative of *Passage*, though often in defused or deflected form. Consequently, the second stage of my argument, focusing more directly on the novel itself, considers the question of narrative appropriation in largely aesthetic terms. It concerns itself with those moments in the novel where the narrative voice is most difficult to place and where slippage between voices threatens the coherence of the novel's form. The final section of the argument attempts to bring together the novel's cultural and aesthetic critiques. Through a consideration of the novel's presentation of Hinduism, it demonstrates the relation between narrative autonomy and integrity and the recognition of a culturally determined voice. Focusing on the novel's most problematic area of representation, it offers "contagion" as the narrative's generative source. The novel's problematic relationship to its voices becomes then not so much a constraint as an enabling force. For in the narrative's resistance to and enactment of verbal infiltration, the text assumes its distinctive voice.

*   *   *

Land of petty treacheries . . . .
—E. M. Forster, *The Hill of Devi*

In a recent issue of *Critical Inquiry*, dedicated to "'Race,' Writing, and Difference," Abdul JanMohamed distinguishes between varieties of fictional colonialist discourse. "In the final analysis," he claims, Forster's "success in comprehending or appreciating alterity will depend on his ability to bracket the values and bases of his culture."[14] For JanMohamed, Forster, in this respect, achieves considerable success: "Although his statements verge at times on the stereotypic/archetypic colonialist generalizations . . . Forster does not present us with stereotypes." Yet what JanMohamed, implicitly pointing to Forster's masculinist stance, calls Forster's "firm" and "merciless" satire of "the cruder 'imaginary' forms of colonialist racism" often masks the more subtle forms of Forster's race-bound terms. In *Passage*, and more vociferously in the Indian diaries and letters, one frequently hears the residual Orientalist tones: "It's so typical of the Oriental" (*HD*, 16); "Like most Orientals" (*Passage*, 142); "I finish up in Saeed's court—such a funny little affair" (*HD*, 221); "I have ended with a visit typically Oriental" (*HD*, 228).

Even when Forster consciously and deliberately brackets his cultural prejudices, there is considerable seepage across the bracketing lines. In his preface to *The Hill of Devi*, a text compiled largely of letters home from his Indian visits, Forster wrote, "In editing I have had to cut out a good deal of 'How I wish you were all here!' or 'Aren't Indians quaint!' I did not really think the Indians quaint, and my deepest wish was to be alone with them" (*HD*, 3). Yet a brief glimpse at the printed letters immediately reveals how much of the sentiment was left in; in almost the very first letter, we read: "Unversed though I am in politics, I must really give you some account of this amazing little State, which can have no parallel, except in a Gilbert and Sullivan opera" (*HD*, 6).[15] And in one of the first sections of narrative commentary, Forster records his sense of differentiation along racial lines. Playing "that typically British game 'Characters'" in the midst of India, Forster notes the marks of cultural difference that disrupt the field of play: "The Rajah wanted to mark all our characters as high as possible provided Malcolm came out highest, but was puzzled because one of the qualities for which one could be marked was Passion. 'Is not Passion bad?' he inquired anxiously" (*HD*, 11).

As Forster continues his commentary, he indulges in a second, unacknowledged game of "Characters," giving the Rajah only the highest marks, but he speaks his praise from a patronizing position marked by diminutives that celebrate precisely those qualities that make the Rajah quaint: "His clever merry little face peeped out of a huge turban: he was charming, he was lovable, it was impossible to resist him or India" (*HD*, 11–12). The condescension that infiltrates the speech of Forster, the commentator, finds a more direct outlet in the authoritative tones of a diary entry written at the time. But in quoting that entry in *The Hill of Devi*, Forster clearly separates out its tones: "All the same," Forster continues, "I find a stern little entry: 'Land of petty treacheries, of reptiles moving about too cautious to strike each other. No line between the insolent and the servile in social intercourse. In every remark and gesture, does not the Indian prince either decrease his own "izzat" or that of his interlocutor? Is there ever civility with manliness here? And is foreign conquest or national character to blame?'" (*HD*, 12).[16]

What seems most disturbing to Forster in the Indian character is the absence of distinguishing markers in the tones of verbal discourse ("No line between . . ."). What is striking in his own discourse is his insistence on a visible dividing line between his two modes of thought, between his present commentary and his earlier response. His self-deflating observation, "I find a stern little entry," appears as something he is compelled to include in the interest of truth. But this formulation leaves the authority of the entry vague. It is as if he himself did not write it; it is merely something he found. It is an entry without origin, a voice that is never explicitly owned. Calling attention to the conflicting voices he harbors, then, Forster contains the disruptive potential he unveils.

Curiously, a version of these same "stern" sentiments appears in *Passage* in a forum that is doubly displaced—in the mouth of Ronny Heaslop who mouths others' words: "But whether the native swaggers or cringes, there's always something behind every remark he makes, always something, and if nothing else he's trying to increase his izzat—in plain Anglo-Saxon, to score. Of course there are exceptions" (33). Ronny, the narrative informs us, mimics the current club response: "When he said 'of course there are exceptions' he was quoting Mr. Turton, while 'increasing the izzat' was Major Callendar's own" (33–34). Thus when Ronny subsequently takes credit for similar ideas, "Them's my sentiments" (50), there is a disturbing slipperiness about the "my."

That Forster should give these words to Ronny might at first seem surprising, but in the novelistic distribution of "Characters," Forster mixes his deck of cards and redistributes the scores.[17] It would seem that the distance of quotation, even ironic self-quotation as in the diary entry cited in *The Hill of Devi*, allows the necessary dissociation of voice. By detecting the second-hand allusion—by distinguishing the initial appeal of India from the "corrected" British response— Forster preserves the illusion of a "first" uncontaminated voice. In the case of Ronny, he suggests the possibility of an "original" response to India different from the club-prescribed lines. And in his own case, he gives primacy to his *later*, more indulgent response. By invoking a clearly discreditable position ("Land of petty treacheries"), and essentially de-authorizing those earlier words, Forster leaves unchallenged the conventional assumptions underlying his more creditable stance (". . . it was impossible to resist him or India"). His narrative deflections thus allow him to satirize the tyranny of British discourse while simultaneously inviting us to and preventing us from looking closely at its source, from attending to the "Land of petty treacheries" that occupies his voice.

In *Passage*, such narrative deflections abound, in particular where questions of authority are at stake. When, for example, Aziz soars off on a treacherous flight of fantasy, imagining himself a benevolent ruler dispensing justice from the halls of Fielding's house, the narrative deflates Aziz in a condescending way: "His face grew very tender—the tenderness of one incapable of administration, and unable to grasp that if the poor criminal is let off he will again rob the poor widow" (71). The voice could be that of any British official— speaking of the Indian as of a child, and carefully spelling out its every word. But does the voice represent an act of narrative patronage or is it calculated mimicry? Is it a case of slippage into or exposé of the superior British tones: the confident assurance in the legalistic Western mind? Again, Forster's Indian experience offers a gloss on these lines. Describing a fantasy of power provoked by a vision of a vast Indian expanse, Forster offers his own shorthand comments on the response of his Indian friend: "S. all for ruling, though not knowing what it means: Indians do little work after adolescence" (*HD*, 225).

In the fictional account, the affectionate indulgence of the narrator masks the cruder racial theme. But the subsequent silencing of Aziz—anticipating both his own and Adela's later silencing at the hands of the colonial regime—testifies to the threat he poses to narrative control. Aziz's discourse becomes frantic as he senses his loss of social ground; he attempts to dominate all the conversational slots. And in an effort to maintain narrative authority, he begins to improvise in a reckless way, inventing a legend about emperors who so loved water they made it run uphill. The narrator seems compelled to offer a petty correction: "He was wrong about the water, which no Emperor, however skilful, can cause to gravitate uphill; a depression of some depth together with the whole of Chandrapore lay between the mosque and Fielding's house" (71–72). The voice here seems clearly identifiable as the narrator's, but it resonates nonetheless with logic, precision, and pedantry—characteristic British tones. It is the voice of those who can calibrate a continent but cannot see its heart. It is a voice the narrative adopts from time to time to describe the caves, only to reveal in the caves' resistance to representation the sterility of such a discursive mode.[18] But it is a voice—however dispensable and however modulated by ironic overtones—that allows the narrative to reassert control. Its deployment here, moreover, suggests the further threat Aziz poses as a potential locus for narrative identification with the Other.

If the narrative, then, authorizes itself at the expense of Aziz, it does so in part by mimicking the frantic logic of Aziz's improvisations. For in the very next sentence, the narrative displaces its British voice by representing, in the persons of others, the modulations of its tones: "Ronny would have pulled him up, Turton would have wanted to pull him up, but restrained himself. Fielding did not even want to pull him up; he had dulled his craving for verbal truth and cared chiefly for truth of mood. As for Miss Quested, she accepted everything Aziz said as true verbally" (72). Aziz *is* pulled up, but the

catalog of possible responses obscures the original source of the re-
buff: the narrative voice itself. For the narrative interjection, informed
by the demands of verbal truth ("He was wrong"), preempts and
appropriates Aziz's infectious energy. In the transpositions the passage effects, however, the narrative substitutes the unvoiced judgments of an array of characters for its own articulated response, and it
substitutes the British for the Indians as the objects of coercive representation, of the narrative's "knowing" voice. But its assumption of
the "Indian" position does not really work. For in rejecting British
values without relinquishing the forms of its dominant discourse, the
narrative demonstrates that there is no "other" place to stand. Irony
provides only an illusion of difference—a verbal sleight of hand—for
the narrative is defined by the gamut of British responses it outlines.
It is absorbed by the very voices it attempts to keep under hand.

In a rare admission, Forster once acknowledged similar constraints upon his own discourse. Writing to Malcolm Darling of his
experiences in Egypt, he observed: "I came inclined to be pleased and
quite free from racial prejudice, but in 10 months I've acquired an
instinctive dislike to the Arab voice, the Arab figure, the Arab way of
looking or walking or pump shitting [sic] or eating or laughing or
anything—exactly the emotion that I censured in the Anglo-Indian
towards the natives." The admission posits a contaminating, but inescapable, cultural influence—the petty treacheries that infiltrate from
within. Unable to restrain these discreditable feelings, Forster can
only withhold his endorsement of such "acquired" instincts: "Any
how I better understand the Anglo-Indian irritation though I'm glad
to say I'm as far as ever from respecting it! It's damnable and disgrace-
ful and it's in me."[19]

As Forster's experience suggests, and the novel confirms, one
cannot bracket culture; one can only draw the lines within which one
resides. The belief that one can do otherwise may be the subtlest
imperialist ploy. Forster's 1920 essay, "Notes on the English Character," marks the limits of such a stance. Assuming a typically English
persona—in good public speaking fashion he begins with a cliché and
a joke—Forster dissects the informing traits of his countrymen and he
interrogates himself.[20] To illustrate one aspect of the English character, he recounts a personal anecdote, told presumably at his own
expense: "Once upon a time (this is an anecdote) I went for week's
holiday on the Continent with an Indian friend" (AH, 5). Having

found himself the advocate of proportion and emotional restraint, Forster describes his friend's attack on his materialism: "Do you measure out your emotions as if they were potatoes?" And Forster, after some consideration, replies, "Yes, I do; and what's more I think I ought to. A small occasion demands a little emotion, just as a large occasion demands a great one!" (*AH*, 6).

Forster implies here that his English character betrays him into this pettiness: "I spoke as a member of a prudent middle-class nation, always anxious to meet my liabilities." Speaking as his culture dictates, he submerges his personal identity in that of the group. But by the end of the essay he reveals the act as a pose: "In the above anecdote, I have figured as a typical Englishman. I will now descend from that dizzy and somewhat unfamiliar height, and return to my business of note-taking" (*AH*, 7). Forster suggests that his entire performance was an act of mimicry; and I use the term here in the specific sense Luce Irigaray, speaking in another context, intends: the deliberate assumption of the culturally available role. Mimicry, as Irigaray understands it, attempts to "make 'visible,' by an effect of playful repetition, what was supposed to remain invisible": the operative logic of the dominant discourse.[21] Here, dispensing with the direct commentary of the first part of the essay (his critique of the public school mentality), Forster attempts to enact, and thereby expose, the central features of that code. But it is crucial to Irigaray that one does not simply become reabsorbed by the mimicked part; one must also remain "elsewhere," outside the given discourse.

For Forster, however, this last element is absent, and the subversive power of mimicry is allayed. His voice, on the one hand, seems insufficiently distinguished from the voice he imitates. On the other hand, his self-conscious articulation of his acting—the double distancing of the opening ("Once upon a time [this is an anecdote]") and the insistent distancing of the close ("I will now descend . . .")—subsume the performance in a coherent, controlling voice. His need to "call" the act, to provide markers that label and gloss his plot, reappropriates the "alternative" voice, transforming mimicry into a mere masquerade.[22] The role Forster returns to, moreover, "notetaker," is not outside the character he disclaims. Fielding, for example, describes Adela in almost those words: "She goes on and on as if she's at a lecture—trying ever so hard to understand India and life, and occasionally taking a note" (119). Forster does not succeed, then, in dismantling the English character; he offers only a role reversal *within* its operative terms.

Even on his own terms, Forster's ironic stance demands that his words be doubly read: first as his personal utterance; then as appropriated discourse. But a double reading of the passage reads doubly at Forster's expense, exposing Forster's own treacherous double-crossings. For the passage attempts to reduce a complex problem of cultural complicity to a perspectival trick—a narrative virtuoso effect. The trick turns on the fact that two contradictory narrative "moods" (inside/outside) occupy a single "voice," come under the single heading "I."[23] This complicity, however, destroys the illusion of mutually exclusive realms upon which Forster's cultural exemption depends. For the text cannot be read without some crossings between the two "I's". Only by abdicating authority—by literally removing the narrative "I"—can Forster stand outside his compromised discourse. The episode thus insinuates itself into *Passage* as an argument between Fielding and Aziz, transcribed, almost verbatim, in the novel's dialogue.

> "Your emotions never seem in proportion to their objects, Aziz."
> "Is emotion a sack of potatoes, so much the pound, to be measured out? Am I a machine? I shall be told I can use up my emotions by using them, next."
> "I should have thought you would. It sounds common sense. You can't eat your cake and have it, even in the world of the spirit." (254)

Re-presenting his voice in the novel, Forster succeeds in displacing himself. But turning this voice inside out, he betrays its corruptibility—its susceptibility to the petty treacheries that corrode from within as well as without.

*   *   *

> No, no, this is going too far.
> —E. M. Forster, *A Passage to India*

It sounds common sense that one cannot both assert a thing and deny it and have both speech acts stand. Yet some of Forster's most characteristic verbal signatures show a marked predilection for going too far, for exceeding rational possibilities. Writing of the I.C.S. hostility toward "the educated native (barrister type)," Forster remarked, "Granting the type is unreliable and egoistic, and granting that a type with these defects can possess no virtues, it yet seems so unwise to snub it continually, and so (to use a word I never use) ungentlemanly" (*HD*, 193). Forster, it would seem, concedes too much. For having implicitly identified himself with the British prejudicial position, having granted its most damning stereotypes, he attempts a deliberate dissociation from the shared British response. But Forster can dissociate himself only by borrowing from the rejected discourse, only by adopting its moral terms ("ungentlemanly," "unwise"). Since he depends upon a common language to voice his critique, he is implicated, parenthetical disclaimers aside, by the very act that would set him apart. In *Passage* such implicated utterances constitute a sizable subtext; and it is the effect of the novel, if not its intent, to reveal that one cannot *use* a word—even a word one never uses—without absorbing some of its taint.

Forster's acrobatic evasions, as they appear in his nonfictional works, disturb without finally dislocating his discourse. They leave largely unchallenged the coherence of his texts. But the self-referential nature of the novel calls attention to its representational balancing acts. And when such ventriloquistic effects enter the novel, they threaten the logic of narrative in a more insistent way—crossing the carefully preserved borders of race and gender and dismantling the novel's diegetic frame. For these moments figure problematic positions of cultural identity. When, for example, the narrative assumes the affable voice of an intrusive nineteenth-century narrator, the moment unsettles the surrounding text: "Visions are supposed to entail profundity, but—Wait till you get one, dear reader!" (208). The coy, melodramatic accents signal irony, but it is difficult to determine the target of the ironic effect: the characters who have or fail to have visions, the "dear" reader, or the author/narrator himself.

A conventional usage—the narrator's direct address to the reader—covers an attack on conventional expectations that cuts in contradictory ways. But the voice is as hard to place as the tone. "The abyss also may be petty, the serpent of eternity made of maggots" (208), the narrative continues in what seems a straightforward exposure of the visionary mystique. Yet in its context, the passage marks a surrender to an unenlightened state: "the twilight of the double vision." Dismissing the visionary experience, moreover, may be even more conventional than giving it too much heed; it is the attitude of the "typical Englishman" whose critique differs only in the choice of words. How, then, should such a passage be read? The problem only escalates when one considers that the warning, "Wait till you get one, dear reader!" issues forth from a passage in which the narration adopts the outlook, even the voice of Mrs. Moore. Her voice and the narrator's (conventionally coded as male) blend across the semipermeable barrier of the dividing punctuation mark: "The abyss also may be petty, the serpent of eternity made of maggots; her constant thought was: 'Less attention should be paid to my future daughter-in-law and more to me, there is no sorrow like my sorrow . . .'" (208–9).

The sentence hinges on Mrs. Moore's consciousness, and the pettiness projected in the first part becomes in the second a tangible effect of her quoted thought. Her sentiments infect or are infected by the narrative discourse, and either way, it is tempting to credit her with the entire response. Yet to have Mrs. Moore address the reader is, by all the laws of narrative logic, to create an unreadable text. At the same time, to give the narrative autonomy—to insist on the authenticity of its voice—is to recognize narration as a self-canceling event. For in this scenario, narrative retraction undermines narrative assertion, while projection precludes the presence of a stable voice. The narrative's manipulation of verbal postures and positions makes it impossible to pin down. At its moment of greatest intrusiveness, the narrative remains effectually mute.

At one point in *Howards End*, the narrator breaks off his narration to claim responsibility for divulging the thoughts of a character: "If you think this ridiculous, remember that it is not Margaret who is telling you about it . . . ."[24] In *Passage*, the narrative takes a reverse tack; when the narrator enters as a personage, he seems to argue along these lines: If you think this ridiculous, remember I'm not the one who is telling you about it, it's Mrs. Moore. And if not Mrs. Moore, the narrative has a host of other characters in stock. Where the narrator of *Howards End* could sacrifice himself to expand our sympathy for his characters, the narrative of *Passage* protects its own voice at the characters' expense. But the question remains whether *Passage*'s frenetic dissemination of voices finally leaves the narrative without a voice.

This pattern of progressive displacement can perhaps be seen most clearly in an extended narrative commentary at the end of chapter 4, a commentary that calls into question ideas of inclusion, origin, authority, and voice. As the narrative lens scans the reaches of Chandrapore, tracing the effects of Mr. Turton's invitation cards, it projects, in what seems conventional omniscient narration, a vision of the existence that lies outside its self-defined range: "And there were circles even beyond these—people who wore nothing but a loincloth, people who wore not even that, and spent their lives in knocking two sticks together before a scarlet doll—humanity grading and drifting beyond the educated vision, until no earthly invitation can embrace it" (37). The context allows no ambiguity about the source of the observation, but in the very next sentence, where a new paragraph starts, the narrative begins to shift and grade. The slippage, marked by the doubled "perhaps," culminates in a complete disavowal of voice: "All invitations must proceed from heaven perhaps; perhaps it is futile for men to initiate their own unity, they do but widen the gulfs between them by the attempt. So at all events thought old Mr. Graysford and young Mr. Sorley, the devoted missionaries who lived out beyond the slaughterhouses, always travelled third on the railways, and never came up to the club" (37). The narrative, in exemplary British fashion, "places" the missionaries, confining them to a conventional stereotype; and it simultaneously displaces itself. For the distancing mechanisms it enacts here sever it from its initiating words.[25]

The move signals a retreat from metaphysical depths. The narrative takes back through its disclaimers the vision of reality it initially projects. But it takes it back in such a way that the initial vision is never quite erased, much the way, in a different context, Adela's withdrawal of the charges against Aziz leaves the accusation intact. P. N. Furbank, Forster's biographer, tells of Forster's "habit, when correcting himself in a letter, of deliberately leaving the cancelled words visible."[26] Forster finds narrative analogues for this trait, with mimicry standing as a preeminent mode of what might be called "barred discourse." The narrative speaks through and against its

chosen parts. In the above instance, for example, the narrative, having focused on the missionaries, moves in and out of their voice:
"Consider, with all reverence, the monkeys. May there not be a man-
sion for the monkeys also? Old Mr. Graysford said No, but young Mr.
Sorley, who was advanced, said Yes; he saw no reason why monkeys
should not have their collateral share of bliss . . ." (38). Ironically, the
opening gambit, which borrows heavily from the missionary tones,
cannot logically be considered their voice. But as with the missionaries, who borrow from the bible ("In our Father's house are many
mansions"), it is difficult to determine where implied quotation ends.

Essentially, the narrative treats the missionaries the way they
treat their biblical source: as an occasion for speculative excursions, a
silent partner in a dialogue of sorts. In both cases, the originating
authority lacks control over the subsequent discourse. As narrative
hysteria sets in, the text gets out of hand: "And oranges, cactuses,
crystals and mud? and the bacteria inside Mr. Sorley? No, no, this is
going too far. We must exclude someone from our gathering, or we
shall be left with nothing" (38). Confronted with the need for limits to
their openness, the missionaries, the narrative suggests, will pull
themselves up short. But the missionaries may not be the only practitioners of narrative largesse. The entire passage of commentary can
be seen as gratuitous, a circuitous path that leaves the progress of the
novel behind. The passage does not return to its point of origin (the
initial statement about receding circles and heavenly invitations) because the narrative, too, has gone too far. By enacting the process it
describes, the passage forces us to consider the narrative consequences of being left positionless, of being "left with nothing." Like
Adela at the novel's end, the narrative has nothing to espouse. It is
only with the break provided by a new chapter that the narrative can
regain its direction and authoritative tones.

Forster once remarked a proclivity in his Indian letters "to turn
remote and rare matters into suburban jokes" (*HD*, 3). The passage
here has much the same effect but without a comparable audience to
blame. In mocking the missionaries, the narrative excludes itself from
the spiritual domain and implicates itself in the discourse with which
it sports. For if narrative utterance can slip into indirect discourse,
assuming a character's voice, the process can work the other way.
The protest that concludes the passage—"No, no, this is going too

far"—may mark a narrative recognition of a disturbing loss of control. The impersonator and the impersonated may share the same sentiments when they speak in the same tones.

Such ambiguities make the text, despite its easy urbanity, peculiarly difficult to read. Urbanity itself contributes to the difficulty, making the novel's surface a shifting rhetorical screen. And the problem is exacerbated by the fact that the narrative deflections work in opposite thematic ways. For if the narrative uses Mrs. Moore to voice the fear that the abyss might be petty, it uses Mr. Sorley and Mr. Graysford to trivialize the possibility of its being profound. What the examples do share is the narrative's penetration by the voices it seeks to imitate and the narrative's restless stance. When Mr. Sorley finds the discourse ranging out of control, he becomes "uneasy" and "apt to change the conversation" (38). In comparable situations, the narrative changes voice—whether it be to adopt the voice of a character or to change its own perspective and tones.[*]

In the chapter following the missionary digression, the narrative takes up the interrupted speculative discourse, venturing where even the missionaries fear to tread: "Some kites hovered overhead, impartial, over the kites passed the mass of a vulture, and with an impartiality exceeding all, the sky, not deeply coloured but translucent, poured light from its whole circumference. It seemed unlikely that the series stopped here. Beyond the sky must not there be something that overarches all the skies, more impartial even than they? Beyond which again . . ." (39–40). The passage pursues precisely the questions of inclusiveness that provoked the previous chapter's ironic excursion but without the comically deflating tones. If anything, the passage assumes a high literary mode—prose aspiring to poetry in its dawning comprehension of an all-inclusive whole. But the meditation is aborted as violently as if a voice had again cried out, "No, no . . . ." It trails off uncompleted, interrupted by a single-sentence paragraph that signals an abrupt shift in narrative mood: "They spoke of *Cousin Kate*." When Godbole discourses on good and evil in the wake of the catastrophe of the caves, he undermines the eloquence of his oratory, or so the narrative informs us, by a gratuitous shift to an untimely social mode: "And in the same breath, as if to cancel any beauty his words might have contained, he added, 'But did you have time to visit any of the interesting Marabar antiquities?'" (178). Here the disruptive narrative transition has the same self-canceling—and self-liberating—effect: an effect that appears in the narrative every time the principle of receding circles is introduced.[27]

The transitional sentence targets the British ("They") and their importation of bad taste (*Cousin Kate*); it suggests that their trivial conversation drowns out the voice of mystery that the narrative would have us hear. But it is the narrative itself that speaks the offending line, just as it is the narrative that judges Godbole's digressive turn. Like Fielding after a discussion with Godbole, the narrative retreats to "solid ground" (178), retreats from the embrace of otherness. In fact, the ironic sentence works both ways. It rebukes the British for their spiritual paucity, but, as if to cancel any beauty its words might have contained, it rebukes the preceding narrative for its pretensions to beauty and mystical excess. Whichever way one reads the line, its effect is the same: to bring the mechanisms of narration to the surface by calling attention to the frantic shifts in narrative mode.

These passages of indeterminacy strain the cohesiveness of the narrative, and they call into question the principles of authority upon which such narratives rest: originality, omniscience, integrity of voice. The narrative's appropriation of and by its voices suggests that speech can only echo what has already been said. Even irony is no escape, for an echo, by definition, is a repetition in distorted form—irony's characteristic shape. At the beginning of the novel's climactic chapter, before introducing the "extraordinary" incident at the caves, the narrative interjects: "Most of life is so dull that there is nothing to be said about it, and the books and talk that would describe it as interesting are obliged to exaggerate, in the hope of justifying their own existence" (132).[28] But the novel cannot escape its own exaggerations or the exaggerations introduced by conventional literary forms. The very existence of the novel implies some justificatory excess, for a completely unembellished work would not be read. With regard to the caves, not only is the novelistic treatment of them melodramatic, but Forster himself admits to tampering with his source. Furbank records Forster's confession that the caves were "not all that remarkable" until they got into his book.[29] The idea of a completely original, uncontaminated utterance turns out to be as much an aesthetic fantasy as a cultural myth. But it is a fantasy with a tenacious hold. It should not be surprising then that in the treatment of Hinduism, where culture and aesthetics meet and contagion defines the novelistic discourse, the narrative most clearly shows its seams.

*   *   *

... "voluntary surrender to infection" better expresses my state.
—E. M. Forster, Letter to Goldsworthy Lowes Dickinson

Critics have failed to agree about either the ideological status or aesthetic success of the Hindu materials Forster includes at the novel's end. The continuing controversy testifies to the canonical status of the indeterminacy—or at least undecidability—of the narrative stance.[30] The representation of the Hindu ceremony, it would seem, attracts diverse readings precisely because it offers no stable guide to help us read. A voice never easy to place here becomes slippery in the extreme. Describing the ceremony, the narrative reports, ". . . they did not one thing which the non-Hindu would feel dramatically correct; this approaching triumph of India was a muddle (as we call it), a frustration of reason and form" (284–85). The voice seems simultaneously inside and outside its own discourse, problematically tied to and severed from the non-Hindu "we." The syntax of the sentence would exempt the narrative from the judgments it pronounces by giving them another source. It is not the *narrative* that voices these objections; it is the typical non-Hindu who would do so. "Muddle" is not even the narrative's word; the inclusive power of "we" is belied by its parenthetical position—a position that keeps the voice speaking and the designated speaker apart. But the logic of cultural identity would collapse these voices into one, including the narrative in the exclusive groups it defines. The statement thus seems subjective and objective at the same time, asserting on one level of narration what, on another level, it implicitly denies.

What is curious about the passage is that it voices its critique on aesthetic terms. The dramatic improprieties of the ceremony implicate art in the general muddle of the world. In the *Hill of Devi* description of the ceremony, Forster concludes one section with a characteristically deflectionary move: "I don't think one ought to be irritated with Idolatry . . . . But it is natural that Missionaries, who think these ceremonies wrong as well as inartistic, should lose their tempers" (*HD*, 64). Forster would exempt himself from moral judgments, as if

"Idolatry" were not a value-laden term, but he is quite open about his objections on artistic grounds. For him, aesthetic irreconcilability proves an insurpassable barrier to a culture he might otherwise embrace: "There is no dignity, no taste, no form, and though I am dressed as a Hindu I shall never become one" (*HD*, 64). A pose of aesthetic supremacy dooms Forster to a position outside. What Forster does not seem to acknowledge is that between cultural (racial and moral) and aesthetic judgments there is a treacherous blurring of terms.

In *Passage* a similar aesthetic distrust of Hinduism underwrites an indulgent flaunting of its non-Western ways. As the description of the ceremony continues, the narrative succumbs to the reigning spirit of misrule: "Where was the God Himself, in whose honour the congregation had gathered? Indistinguishable in the jumble of His own altar, huddled out of sight amid images of inferior descent, smothered under rose-leaves, overhung by oleographs, outblazed by golden tablets representing the Rajah's ancestors, and entirely obscured, when the wind blew, by the tattered foliage of a banana" (285). The passage offers no explicit judgments, but it betrays a certain unease in its calculated excess. In *The Hill of Devi*, Forster introduces his description of the Hindu ceremony with an explanatory note designed to highlight what his facetious treatment might otherwise conceal: "The following letters on the Gokul Ashtami Festival are the most important of my letters home, for they describe (if too facetiously) rites in which an European can seldom have shared" (*HD*, 60). In *Passage*, no equivalent commentary glosses the religious event. But elements of the facetious continue to intrude, keeping the narrative from entering fully into what it describes. Unable to resist the comic effect, the narrative finally lands itself outside: "The inscriptions which the poets of the State had composed were hung where they could not be read, or had twitched their drawing-pins out of the stucco, and one of them (composed in English to indicate His universality) consisted, by an unfortunate slip of the draughtsman, of the words, 'God si Love'" (285). In the narrative rendition of the setting, the exuberant energy of the ritual is diminished, subjected to the exposure of an orthographic mistake. Like Ronny, who cannot ignore the absence of Aziz's collar stud, the narrative cannot let pass unnoticed the breach of appropriate form. Corrupting influences, it seems to argue, must be countered where English practices are at stake.

The ceremonial ritual, moreover, that the passage describes encroaches on narrative terrain. For the passage as a whole projects the disappearance of the author from the work he creates. "Indistinguishable," "huddled out of sight," "overhung," "outblazed," at times "entirely obscured," the originary source of creation remains an invisible presence, denied even privilege of place. And as the conclusion of the passage suggests, authority is even further compromised once a text leaves its author's hands. It becomes subject to uncontrollable forces of reception and transmission, any of which can render it unreadable; the text, the passage even suggests, can dismantle itself, dislodge itself from its moorings by twitching out its drawing pins. In such a context, the narrative's insistence on the draughtsman's error marks more than just another unfortunate slip. "God si Love," the narrative repeats. "Is this the first message of India?" (285). The voice is that of the Britisher in exile, with its supercilious manner and condescending tone. It speaks for the authority Hinduism denies. But having voiced its resistance, it is absorbed by the surrounding tones.

The novel's Hindu passages focus anxieties that penetrate the entire text: concerns about boundaries, hierarchies, distinctions, identity, autonomy, and voice. In its disorderly order and nonauthoritarian stance, Hinduism represents the potential place of otherness the narrative constantly seeks; but in its abandonment of all boundaries, its indifference to all authority, it poses the greatest threat to the novel as a form of privileged discourse. As a counterstructure that interrogates the novel's logic, Hinduism stands as a system in which narrative authority has no place; as an area of novelistic representation, it remains opaque—a space the narrative can neither see through nor around. The Hindu festival thus becomes the novel's limit text. It is the thing that must be included to complete the novel's pattern ("It was architecturally necessary," Forster once explained);[31] but it is the thing that must be excluded if the narrative is to maintain its omniscient voice.

Omniscience, finally, constitutes the novel's battleground. It provides the vantage from which the narrative speaks, and, in particular, the superior position on which its irony depends. It offers the narrative a place outside the characters from which to pass judgment and an authoritative base for its claims. Yet it is its very pretense to stand outside its domain—literally above the characters and plot—that implicates the narrative in what it critiques: the colonialist stance. In spite of all its maneuverings, the narrative can never fully escape the characteristic imperialist parts: showman and God. It is betrayed by its position and convicted by its tones. Forster himself sensed this danger, although he did not put it in political terms. In a letter written during the time he was working on *Passage*, he wrote: "If you can pretend you can get inside one character, why not pretend it about all the characters? I see why. The illusion of life may vanish, and the creator degenerate into the showman."[32]

As readers have invariably noticed, however, at crucial points in *Passage*, narrative omniscience seems to lapse. There are marked silences and ellipses, most notably surrounding the novel's central mystery: What happens in the caves? The only "explanation" the narrative offers is of some unknown contagious effect.[33] Forster himself professed not to know: "In the cave it is *either* a man, *or* the supernatural, *or* an illusion." But this disclaimer may be less a mark of narrative limitation than the ultimate dramatization of authority and control. As Forster admitted, his uncertainty constituted a deliberate choice: "This isn't a philosophy of aesthetics. *It's a particular trick I felt justified in trying because my theme was India.* It sprang straight from my subject matter. I wouldn't have attempted it in other countries, which though they contain mysteries or muddles, manage to draw rings round them. Without the trick I doubt whether I could have got the spiritual reverberation going. I call it 'trick': but 'voluntary surrender to infection' better expresses my state."[34]

Forster's terms are telling here—for the operation of the "Hindu" section of the novel and for the narrative as a whole. For the "Temple's" critical "impurity," I would suggest, is a function of the recognition it intuits of contagion and contamination as the generative sources of narrative. That "voluntary surrender to infection" might "explain" Adela's experience as well as Forster's technique is not coincidental. For as I have tried to suggest, the novel stages a crisis in narrative voice in terms of violation and transgression, a crisis that, like Adela's, calls up the rhetorical machinery of rape while refusing the fixity of its meaning. Turning a trick on the voice it withholds, the novel sets another voice—another reverberation—in motion.

The voluntary surrender Forster acknowledges here—surrender to the infectious spirit of India—circumscribes a problematic aesthetic position. Moreover, it masks surrender of another kind and infection from another voice: from the novel's troubled and troubling British accents. The alternatives testify to the erosion of the novel's independent ground. Between the insidious accents of Anglo-India and the contagious cacophony of the Hindu state, there are no islands of free speech, as all of the characters learn. In the end, those who would stand outside culture and experiment in intimacy are absorbed by their culture's prevailing discourse. And the narrative is not exempt. The novel ends in abdication; silence replaces surrender as the narrative is dethroned: "But the horses didn't want it—they swerved apart; the earth didn't want it, sending up rocks through which the riders must pass single file; the temples, the tank, the jail, the palace, the birds, the carrion, the Guest House, that came into view as they issued from the gap and saw Mau beneath: they didn't want it, they said in their hundred voices, 'No, not yet,' and the sky said, 'No, not there'" (322). As personalized presence, the narrative neither asserts nor denies. In this last passage, it takes on the tones of the horses, the earth, the temples, the birds, the sky. In the hundreds of voices that declare against the possibility of English-Indian friendship, the one that remains silent is the narrative's own, for the narrative no longer professes to a voice with distinctive features and tones.

Toward the end of the novel, the narrative presents Aziz's new-formed thought: "This pose of 'seeing India' which had seduced him to Miss Quested at Chandrapore was only a form of ruling India . . ." (306). The narrative, one might argue, is seduced by a similar pose— seduced *to* Miss Quested, to the position she occupies in the novel as the unintentional seducer of those she would understand. For narrative "seeing" is also a form of rule. And like Adela, the narrative plays out the conflict of cultures on the body of its text, collapsing the functions of violator and violated. Having set a dramatic machinery in motion, it too recants; having "failed to locate" the unity it desires, it offers, in conclusion, only a depersonalized version of Adela's words of triumphant defeat: "I cannot be sure" (229). Like Adela, the narrative can no longer trust the integrity of its own words. For in a novel generated by contagion and its attendant fears, narrative purity cannot survive; the narrative cannot escape infiltration from what it tells. Art cannot remain inviolate.

   In his cultivated irreverence for all forms of social and political

authority—for all forms of constraint—Forster was fond of preserving art as a place apart. He would willingly sacrifice his country and
his god, he claimed, but not the deity he erected in their place.[35]
When Forster speaks of art, we hear his most sanctimonious tones.
Art, he asserted, "is the one orderly product which our muddling
race has produced" (*Two Cheers*, 90). It is the one material object free
from the external contamination that infects the social and political
realms: "All the others have been pressed into shape from outside,
and when their mould is removed they collapse." But Forster's aesthetic philosophy represents an ideal state; he proclaimed this credo
("Art for Art's Sake") long after he had ceased writing novels. In
practice, as *Passage* repeatedly reveals, art cannot remain exempt. It is
infected by the culture that produces it, muddled by the crossings of
its terms. Politics and society repeatedly invade the discourse of art,
appropriating its voice and coloring its words. If the novel finally
maintains its own internal order, it consists partly in exposing the
"external" forces within it that constantly threaten its collapse.

Forster himself was not unaware of these external constraints
upon the artist, as his lifelong fight against censorship reveals. His
own homosexuality, moreover, placed him curiously inside and outside his culture's dominant voice. The untenableness of such a position, it has been argued, forced his novelistic silence after the publication of *Passage* in 1924. A diary entry from 1911, frequently cited in
arguments of this sort, speaks to the strangle hold on his voice; explaining his inability to write, Forster notes, "Weariness of the only
subject that I both can and may treat—the love of men for women &
vice versa."[36] But the entry acknowledges additional incursions on
his independence—the tyranny of literary conventions that decree
"Passion & money . . . the two main springs of action" and the un-
favorable material conditions under which he works ("Inattention to
health"; "Depressing & enervating surroundings"). Speaking person-
ally, Forster thus admits the contingent status of his voice.

Passage, however, gives such contingency a deeper, more disturbing cast. It suggests that the novelist "may" write only what he
"can," that his voice is manufactured for him and maintained in a
state of contestation. He can "say" only what the conditions of artistic
production make possible, and those conditions are largely culturally
based, represented in social and political terms. The novel's explora-

tion of voices thus testifies, at least implicitly, to the status of voice as a cultural construct. For Forster, the plot of the narrative voice's absorption, silently demonstrated at almost every turn, may be the novel's most unsettling part. The dismantling of the narrative embraces collapse. Without necessarily realizing it, then, Forster may have written himself out—out of the only place from which he felt comfortable writing: the sanctuary of art. *A Passage to India* reveals the closed world of the novel to be a cultural and aesthetic myth; but in forfeiting that illusion, Forster uncovers the open space of the text—a text whose violations demand a vigilant engagement.

Virginia Woolf

Chapter 5

On Not Speaking Out

Is this the way texts write themselves/are written now? Without
quite knowing what censorship they are evading?
—Luce Irigaray, *This Sex Which Is Not One*

After reading *A Passage to India*, Virginia Woolf recorded in her diary
her reservations about Forster's artistic approach: "Morgan is too restrained in his new book perhaps. I mean, what's the use of facts at
our time of life? Why build these careful cocoons [?]: why not say
straight out—yes, but what?"[1] Beneath the characteristic circumven-
tions (the inevitable "perhaps" that withholds commitment; the inconclusive parting shot) and transposed onto the corpus of a man,
Woolf here poses the question(s) her own practice enacts. Positioning
herself as a proponent of straight talking, Woolf inscribes the conditions that nullify the virtues of speaking out.

Elsewhere, when Woolf broaches this subject, she records a similar double response. In a later diary entry, for example, she chides
herself for her own cocoon constructing—her instinct to put up
screens: "But all this is a great mistake. These screens shut me out.
Have no screens, for screens are made out of our own integument; &
get at the thing itself, which has nothing whatever in common with a
screen." At the same time, although not without qualifications, she
affirms the protective purposes screens serve: "The screen making
habit, though, is so universal, that probably it preserves our sanity. If
we had not this device for shutting people off from our sympathies,
we might, perhaps, dissolve utterly."[2] And in the entry in which she
questions Forster's reserve, Woolf defends, almost in the same

breath, her own self-protective retreat: "I met Sydney Waterlow last night, & was monolithic on purpose,—a bad thing to be; but I feared gushing & depths, & intended to keep myself free" (*Diary* 2:304). Both entries record a deep ambivalence toward the frank confrontation with what Woolf variously calls the truth, reality, the soul, life itself, the central thing.

For Woolf, I would suggest, the head-on approach to reality represented what might be called the masculine point of view—the view, for example, of her brother-in-law Clive Bell: "Clive is a great source of pleasure to me, for one thing because he says outright what I spend my life in concealing." Not surprisingly, however, Woolf's approval is riddled with doubts, as her self-contradictory remarks make clear: "Never was there anyone so petty, conceited, open and good at bottom of heart."[3] Even when not attributed to male speakers, Woolf associates this outspoken position with masculine authority. She links it, for instance, to the masculine figure of Ethel Smyth: ". . . if Ethel can be so downright and plainspoken and on the spot, I need not fear instant dismemberment by wild horses."[4] And in the case of Alix Sargent-Florence, Woolf invokes the anonymous (male) arbiters of truth: "Meanwhile Alix is setting up a photographic studio, the point of which is that a million candles flash in your face, and thus absolute truth is obtained—no sentimental evasions—what they call facing facts."[5] As her own disclaimer implies ("what *they* call . . ."), the perspective Woolf outlines is one she does not share; she is not one of "them." Like the narrator of "The Mark on the Wall," a text in which the gender implications of resistance are more fully revealed, Woolf prefers not to name a fact even if it stares her in the eye.[6]

Woolf extends this judgment to questions of literary authority, privileging "feminine" cultivation over "masculine" energy. As she wrote of *Ulysses*, a book she saw as a monument to aggressive masculinity, "When one can have the cooked flesh, why have the raw?" (*Diary* 2:189). Extolling the arts of concealment, Woolf finds herself aligned with the classic virtues of femininity. So, in "A Sketch of the Past," she acknowledges the appeal of the reticent Victorian mode: "It is useful; it has its beauty, for it is founded upon restraint, sympathy, unselfishness—all civilised qualities. It is helpful in making something seemly and human out of raw odds and ends." As in her comments on Forster, Woolf betrays only a qualified desire to condemn: "But the Victorian manner is perhaps—I am not sure—a disadvantage in writing."[7]

For Woolf, the practice had its compensations as well: "On the other hand, this surface manner allows one to say a great many things which would be inaudible if one marched straight up and spoke out." Specifically, she writes in her diary of the difficulties of describing the soul: "And the truth is, one can't write directly about the soul. Looked at, it vanishes: but look at the ceiling, at Grizzle, at the cheaper beasts in the Zoo which are exposed to walkers in Regents Park, & the soul slips in." Yet indirection does not simply function as an alternative (and superior) economy, the type of unproblematic feminine aesthetic some critics would like it to be. For having found the soul in her roundabout way, "It slipped in this afternoon," Woolf discovers that she has forgotten what she wanted to say about it: "I will write that I said, staring at the bison: answering L. absentmindedly; but what was I going to write?" (*Diary* 3:62). Sidetracked by her own metaphor—diverted by the explication of her own circuitous paths—Woolf remains as speechless, as inaudible, as if she had attempted to confront the soul head-on.

In Woolf, moreover, the ideology of direction (speaking out) never ceases to exert its sway. Colluding in conventional definitions, Woolf posits the "true poet" as one who "would have committed himself," avoiding the snares of "verbal felicities" and mere ingenuity.[8] In her own private hierarchy, she maintains the category of "great writers," writers who are marked by a quality of directness and simplicity: "And what it comes to is that the great are very simple . . . for all that they are more to the point than ordinary people; go to the heart of things directly" (*Diary* 3:214). Over and over, her diary entries record her attempts to cast herself in this mold: as one who presents the "true reality," explores the profoundest sources of experience, probes life's darkest depths. Thus she writes of *Mrs. Dalloway*: "Nevertheless, I think it most important in this book to go for the central things, even though they don't submit, as they should however, to beautification in language" (*Diary* 2:249). Woolf's articulation betrays the tensions of a divided loyalty: her attempt to submit to an internalized imperative ("I think it most important") that conflicts with her own faith in verbal felicities ("they don't submit, as they should"). Moreover, Woolf herself does not submit to her self-defined role. After elaborating the nature of her undertaking—defining the central things ("I want to give life & death, sanity & insanity; I want to criticise the social system, & to show it at work, at its most intense")—Woolf adds, "But here I may be posing" (248).

Although the comments on *Mrs. Dalloway* have received considerable critical attention, the final statement has not. Yet Woolf's entire artistic practice is deeply implicated in this potential masquerade—a pose that is and is not acknowledged, a statement that says and does not say what it means. Her retrospective reading of *To the Lighthouse*, for example, pursues a similar strategy. Writing of that novel, Woolf once claimed: "I suppose that I did for myself what psycho-analysts do for their patients. I expressed some very long felt and deeply felt emotion. And in expressing it I explained it and then laid it to rest."[9] Characteristically, however, she feels compelled to add: "But what is the meaning of 'explained' it?" The addendum calls into question the substance of the initial claim; it opens the possibility that Woolf's expressed psychological probing might be a mere act, a possibility reinforced by her presumed nonchalance: "Perhaps one of these days I shall hit on the reason; and if so, I will give it." As in the earlier example, Woolf's profession remains poised between competing interpretive possibilities: a diversionary tactic that evades discomforting truths or a relentless questioning that challenges easy certitudes.

Seen in this context, Woolf's comments on Forster repeat a central critical impasse. She cannot get beyond the question she poses, "Why not say straight out—yes, but what?", in part because she cannot get beyond the pose the question reveals. As is so often the case in Woolf, the questioning impulse disguises what the question might otherwise reveal—that the search for an answer is not her real intent. The questions replace, even become, their own response, subverting the line of direct attack. Here, the question Woolf implants in her question—"yes, but what?"—locates the source of her dilemma: What does one want to confront? And how does one put it in words? But it does so at the expense of the larger question that con-

tains it—Should one make the attempt at all? And to that question—
"Why not say straight out?"—Woolf could never give an unqualified
assent. Her second question, however, diverts attention from the
first; it seems to answer the primary question, and to answer it simultaneously in an affirmative and negative way. For the "yes" suggests
the procedure is worth pursuing, while the "but what?" hints at an
impossibility in the task. Woolf thus manages to endorse the en-
deavor of speaking out, while obviating the necessity of putting such
speech to the test. Her question thus conceals the potentially negative
response it is likely to call forth, conceals the extent to which Woolf's
desire for forthrightness may be less than forthright.

For Woolf has her reasons for not wanting to speak out. And not
the least of these is her suspicion, well documented in her diary, of
her unfitness for the task, an unfitness that might be seen as gender
defined. "I daresay its true, however, that I haven't that 'reality' gift,"
she writes in one entry.[10] "One must write from deep feeling," she
quotes Dostoevsky, and then adds, "And do I? Or do I fabricate with
words, loving them as I do?" Answer it as she might, the question
recurs, "Have I the power of conveying the true reality?" (*Diary*
2:248). Committed to that task, Woolf can never quite dismiss the
possibility that the true reality yields itself to direct attack. She cannot
silence the question, "Why not say straight out?" but neither can she
answer it as she—or perhaps others—would like. Foregrounding her
second question, her artistic solutions entail an aesthetic of deferral
that enables her to keep this question at bay.

This aesthetic poses the problem of Woolf's work as one of posi-
tionality: from what position does she speak? But the question does
not resolve itself into interpretive stability, for Woolf's fictions are
generated from a place of covered speech. Her practice repeatedly
masks what it unveils, interrogates what it asserts, cancels what it
inscribes. Refusing finally to endorse or reject the dominant literary
modes, Woolf's art proliferates prohibitions without admitting the
provenance of the censoring authority. It replicates the censoring
practice without the underpinning belief—a kind of self-censorship
without origin or end. Speaking *through*, *between*, and *around* the subjects it sets itself, Woolf's fiction fills its spaces with self-canceling
effects. Rejecting silence as it does direct speech, it makes its re-

sistance the site of verbal prolixity. In not speaking out, paradoxically, it finds its own distinctive speech.

*   *   *

> [Psychoanalysis] can cure women only by contaminating them,
> by forcing them to "collaborate," to espouse the viewpoint of the
> other, of men, who are supposed to possess truth. The
> psychoanalytic solution restores speech to woman only the
> better to rob her of it, the better to subordinate it to that of the
> master.
>   —Sarah Kofman, *The Enigma of Woman*

The story I have pieced together from fragments of Woolf's letters
and diaries emerges more clearly in her representation of her own
aesthetic philosophy. "Mr. Bennett and Mrs. Brown," Woolf's well-
known literary manifesto, focuses the issues at hand. With Mrs.
Brown as her subject, Woolf puts the problem thus: Why not say
something directly about Mrs. Brown? The answer comes up the
same: Yes, but what? For in trying to show what she means by "character in itself," Woolf's narrator discovers "the hideous perils that
beset you directly you try to describe it in words."[11] "Mr. Bennett and
Mrs. Brown" has generally been read as a transparent proclamation
of a new artistic mode, the formulation of a modernist aesthetic practice. Seen in this light, the essay's aesthetic values seem clear; but
read in terms of its performative structures, the essay brings to the
surface the political stakes aesthetics often conceal. For Woolf stages
her drama to reveal a classic gender paradigm: the silent woman as
spectacle, subject of the masculine gaze.[12]

  Although Woolf claims that Mrs. Brown "is, *of course*, the spirit
we live by, life itself" (119, emphasis mine), she engenders this spirit
in woman's name. And she defines her project as giving voice to Mrs.
Brown, for in her eyes the male triumvirate (Bennett, Galsworthy,
Wells) has robbed Mrs. Brown of speech.[13] In the case of Bennett, she
accuses him, in his own writings, of performing this scenario quite
literally—of blocking out the voices of women. Describing her experience of *Hilda Lessways*, she observes: "But we cannot hear her
mother's voice, or Hilda's voice; we can only hear Mr. Bennett's voice
telling us facts about rents and freeholds and copyholds and fines"
(109). The charge extends to all three writers' treatments of the fictive

Mrs. Brown. Speaking for, over, around, and through Mrs. Brown—using Mrs. Brown as a prop—these writers, Woolf claims, have abandoned the woman herself. Woolf even goes so far as to accuse them of fraud, of trying to "palm off" on a credulous public "an image of Mrs. Brown, which has no likeness to that surprising apparition whatsoever" (118). Mrs. Brown becomes for them, Woolf argues, merely the occasion of their own interested discourse.

These accusations construct Woolf's persona in an opposite guise: the agent of the human soul, the disinterested advocate of truth. The situation is "of course" more complex. For Mrs. Brown is, quite literally, an "apparition"—a figure Woolf constructs out of air. And the words in which the male writers betray her are ones Woolf puts in their mouths. Woolf thus attempts to better her adversaries by adopting their own terms: speaking for them speaking for Mrs. Brown.[14] She herself thus speaks from the classic position of masculine authority—and this despite the "feminine" disclaimer with which she introduces her "true" fantasy: "So, if you will allow me, instead of analysing and abstracting, I will tell you a simple story which, however pointless, has the merit of being true" (97).[15]

Woolf's "story" of Mrs. Brown, moreover, participates, at least initially, in the masculine proprietary mode. It casts Mrs. Brown in classic feminine postures (seductress and prey) at the very moment her gender is defined. In the second paragraph of her essay, Woolf articulates an experience "[m]ost novelists" share: "Some Brown, Smith, or Jones comes before them and says in the most seductive and charming way in the world, 'Come and catch me if you can'" (94). It is at the end of this paragraph that Woolf first uses the feminine pronoun to refer to her phantom; thereafter, she has become "Mrs." Brown.[16]

In addition, the story establishes Woolf as the arbiter of human identity. Taking an anonymous woman she knows nothing about, Woolf confers on her a name ("Mrs. Brown") and the "facts" of her life. Bound to "Mrs. Brown" by a shared gender identity, Woolf assumes the privilege of class to adopt a knowing stance. Mrs. Brown proves readable by virtue of being "a woman of a certain type."[17] Woolf's account of her presumes narrative tractability, for it rapidly accommodates Mrs. Brown to a series of literary and cultural clichés: "I felt that she had nobody to support her; that she had to make up her mind for herself; that, having been deserted, or left a widow, years ago, she had led an anxious, harried life, bringing up an only son, perhaps, who, as likely as not, was by this time beginning to go to the bad" (98). In one version of her life, Mrs. Brown emerges as a quaint Dickensian caricature: "I thought of her in a seaside house, among queer ornaments: sea-urchins, models of ships in glass cases. Her husband's medals were on the mantlepiece. She popped in and out of the room, perching on the edges of chairs, picking meals out of saucers, indulging in long, silent stares" (101). In another, she figures as the center of a melodramatic cabal, involving "secret, perhaps sinister business," a "dreadful revelation," a "heroic decision," and ultimately "tragic" collapse. Woolf thus "restores" Mrs. Brown to speech only to reinscribe her the more firmly in conventional master plots.

Stories like "An Unwritten Novel" and "The Shooting Party" repeat these configurations, with their specular subjects similarly marked by gender and class: "Milly Masters, the house-keeper" or "poor" Minnie Marsh ("some such name as that").[18] For the narrators of these stories, social position determines their subjects' narrative slots: "Tethered to the shores of the world, none of the crimes, sorrows, rhapsodies, or insanities for poor Minnie Marsh; never late for luncheon; never caught in a storm without a mackintosh; never utterly unconscious of the cheapness of eggs. So she reaches home—scrapes her boots."[19] Yet both these stories register a profound sense of discomfort—even transgression—in such narrative acts. They render the violence of projection in the abrupt toppling of the narrator ("Well, my world's done for! What do I stand on? What do I know?"[20]) or the violent destruction of the object of her gaze: "The old woman staggered backwards. She fell against the mantlepiece. Her stick striking wildly, struck the shield above the fireplace. She fell with a thud upon the ashes. The shield of the Rashleighs crashed from the wall."[21] "Mr. Bennett and Mrs. Brown" remains, however, more circumspect about the status of the narrator's specular and speculative acts. Only in the margins of the story does Woolf hint at violation, "As I sat down I had the strange and uncomfortable feeling that I was interrupting a conversation between two people who were already sitting there"; and only there does she suggest the self-interest that underwrites her own narrative "account": "All this shot through my mind as I sat down, being uncomfortable, like most people, at travelling with fellow passengers unless I have somehow or other accounted for them" (97–98).

"Mr. Bennett and Mrs. Brown" anticipates a central concern of Woolf's own modernist project: constituting woman as speaking subject—a project that often takes the form of "making woman speak." The essay, moreover, captures the problematic position such a task entails. For how does one authorize speech without participating in the violence of traditional authority? As the essay suggests, conferring speech on the soul bears disturbing affinities to coercing it, to what *Mrs. Dalloway* names society's ultimate crime, "forcing the soul." In addition, as Woolf's fiction repeatedly reveals, the construction of woman's voice does not resolve the problem of originality; for the question remains, whose words does "she" utter and in whose voice does "she" speak? In Woolf's works, feminine subjectivity occupies a verbal ground where appropriation and empowerment meet. In "Mr. Bennett and Mrs. Brown," Woolf's narrator plays out the possibilities of at least one version of the enterprise of putting woman into speech. Taking up the unknown woman—making her a celebrated cause—Woolf speaks *for* Mrs. Brown. But she does so in both senses of the word: speaking in her favor and speaking in her stead. The result is that Woolf, like her male predecessors, sacrifices "the woman" to establish her aesthetic authority. In this light, "Mr. Bennett and Mrs. Brown" can be seen to reveal the limits of "feminist" advocacy.

Framing Bennett, Galsworthy, and Wells, Woolf's narrative deserts Mrs. Brown not once but repeatedly—in each succeeding story it tells. Spiritualized in the "authorial" versions, materialized in the "attributed" accounts, the absent body of Mrs. Brown grounds Woolf's fantasia on literary sensibilities. But the rhetoric of the text works to obscure the complicitous conditions of Woolf's artistic agency. Blaming the representatives of established literary modes, Woolf distances herself from their apostasy. She positions herself outside their lapsed speech. "To tell you the truth, I was also strongly tempted to manufacture a three-volume novel about the old lady's son, and his adventures crossing the Atlantic, and her daughter, and how she kept a milliner's shop in Westminster, the past life of Smith himself, and his house at Sheffield," she admits, implying, at least, that she resists: "But if I had done that I should have escaped the appalling effort of saying what I meant" (111–12). When Woolf does admit failure, it takes the form of a carefully orchestrated parable of the fall into literary materiality: "I admit that I shirked that arduous undertaking. I let my Mrs. Brown slip through my fingers. I have told you nothing whatever about her" (112). The failure is laid at her predecessors' door: "But that is partly the great Edwardians' fault." Woolf's "lapse" merely demonstrates the Edwardians' failure to bequeath her adequate literary means: "That is what I mean by saying that the Edwardian tools are the wrong ones for us to use" (112).

Enacting her own failure ("I have told you nothing whatever about her")—and overplaying her lines—Woolf makes enactment the most effective form of disguise. For her admissions notwithstanding, the essay maintains Mrs. Brown as the marker of difference that defines Woolf's "modern" aesthetic philosophy. While accusing the British public of colluding in the great Edwardian fraud, Woolf invites their complicity in her own sleight of hand. She entreats her audience's silence toward the fact before their eyes: the absence in body of the "real" Mrs. Brown. And she does so largely by calling attention to her own artistic feats—by recourse to modernist self-referentiality. Pulling the curtain to reveal her essay's rhetorical machinery, Woolf invites her audience to see and not to see: "But now, if you will allow me to pull my own anecdote to pieces, you will see how keenly I felt the lack of a convention, and how serious a matter it is when the tools of one generation are useless for the next" (111).

This moment returns us to the problematic posture that marked the essay's start: the pose of femininity. For as the passage reveals, Woolf's anecdote turns out to be neither "simple," "pointless," nor "true." And it functions not to replace the classic masculine activities, "analysing and abstracting," but to give them material upon which to act. As for Mrs. Brown, she is not what she seems—or at least not what Woolf would have us believe. She is not so much "life itself" as "life constructed," "life written about." "She" is a text to be dismembered: picked apart, reassembled, put to use. Absent herself, "Mrs. Brown" upholds Woolf's artistic autonomy. Her silence constitutes the *condition* of Woolf's speech.

Woolf's desertion of Mrs. Brown is, then, no incidental consequence of a sincere quest for the soul's truth. The quest, rather, reveals itself a pose, for Woolf's spirited polemic requires Mrs.

Brown's visible invisibility: now you see her—now you don't. In this context, the essay's closing oration proves particularly difficult to read. For it reinstates Mrs. Brown as subject by adopting the very position the essay has deconstructed as proprietary or naive: belief in the full presence of Mrs. Brown as autonomous identity. Declaiming against the "division between reader and writer, this humility on your part, these professional airs and graces on ours" (118), Woolf tells her audience what and how to believe: "Your part is to insist that writers shall come down off their plinths and pedestals, and describe beautifully if possible, truthfully at any rate, our Mrs. Brown." Woolf appropriates both audience and object, serving up "my Mrs. Brown" (112) as a collective fiction, the subject of communal belief: "our Mrs. Brown" (118). Mounting plinth and pedestal, assuming the most professional graces and airs, Woolf brings her essay to a resounding close: "For I will make one final and surpassingly rash prediction— we are trembling on the verge of one of the great ages of English literature. But it can only be reached if we are determined never, never to desert Mrs. Brown" (119).

Making Mrs. Brown the battle cry of literary modernism, Woolf reaffirms modernism's masculine modes, returning in her conclusion to the most formulaic echoes of "traditional" literary authority. For what resounds in the passage are the echoes of masculine authority: the pompous flourishes, the appeal to a grandiose literary history, the invocation of the woman as the grounding of the text. What resounds as well is what masculine discourse seeks to repress: the only story Mrs. Brown can tell—a story of the sequential stiflings of the woman in the interest of giving her speech, of the violence to her person perpetrated in her name. Woolf thus fixes both her modernism and her feminism in the condition of paradox. Reaffirming her commitment "never to desert Mrs. Brown," Woolf repeats her original pretense, speaking for a position that would render her own practice obsolete. In speaking out for Mrs. Brown, Woolf simultaneously undermines and exposes the *difference* of her own speech.

*   *   *

This same doubleness surrounds other polemical passages in Woolf's work, and in particular, her outspoken silence on the subject of sexuality. Speaking the silence rather than speaking the thing, Woolf veils the sexual body under guise of an attack on modesty. We see this in *Orlando*'s celebrated sex change scene, where the narrative mimics the discourses of conventional morality: "And now again obscurity descends, and would indeed that it were deeper! Would, we almost have it in our hearts to exclaim, that it were so deep that we could see nothing whatever through its opacity! Would that we might here take the pen and write Finis to our work! Would that we might spare the reader what is to come and say to him in so many words, Orlando died and was buried."[22] Retreating from this darkness in the interest of "Truth, Candour, and Honesty," the narrative "spares" the reader by exposing its sparing. It defers its admission of stark realities with its orchestrated pageant of "Our Ladies," Purity, Chastity, and Modesty; and it muffles Orlando's naked body in the pompous sounds of Truth's trumpet pealings. When the narrative dispenses with this subject, "But let other pens treat of sex and sexuality; we quit such odious subjects as soon as we can" (139), the line reads with uncertain irony. For the text represents the embodiment of Orlando's sex and sexuality as a "pause in the narrative" (138): an occasion "to make certain statements," an opportunity for editorial commentary.

A similar practice governs the narrative in the "Time Passes" section of *To the Lighthouse*. Describing the groping and penetrating airs that approach the Ramsay's bedroom door, the narrative assumes the voice of conventionality to cover its own retreat from the secrets of that room: "But here surely, they must cease. Whatever else may perish and disappear, what lies here is steadfast. Here one might say to those sliding lights, those fumbling airs that breathe and bend over the bed itself, here you can neither touch nor destroy."[23] When the narrative does part the curtain on the bedroom sanctuary, it reveals only the self-embrace of the lighthouse beam: a sexual act without a body or even a human agency.

In *A Room of One's Own*, we see traces of such practices in the "Chloe liked Olivia" tease. Breaking off her reading of Mary Carmichael's *Life's Adventure* to attack male prudery and lasciviousness, the narrator re-marks the noted ellipsis as a lacuna in her own text: ". . . I turned the page and read . . . I am sorry to break off so abruptly. Are there no men present? Do you promise me that behind that red curtain over there the figure of Sir Chartres Biron is not concealed? We are all women, you assure me? Then I may tell you that the very next words I read were these—'Chloe liked Olivia . . . .'"[24] Exploiting the anticlimax of its finish, the passage exposes its horror as nonexistent: "nothing to see." But as my own word play suggests, the passage invokes even as it undermines the specter of the woman's sexualized body. It provokes the lesbian reading it elides—the very reading it purportedly critiques: "Do not start. Do not blush. Let us admit in the privacy of our own society that these things sometimes happen. Sometimes women do like women" (86). Deploying euphemism and innuendo masterfully, the passage implicates the reader in its voyeuristic performance. Both saying and not saying what it means, it invites interminable speculation on the question, "Does she or doesn't she . . . ?"[25]

The ghost of Mrs. Brown that haunts these passages materializes most dramatically in the invocation of Shakespeare's sister at the close of *A Room of One's Own*—a narrative sequence that replicates the textual strategies of "Mr. Bennett and Mrs. Brown" and echoes the earlier essay's impassioned tones and theme. Once more the subject is a woman's body, "the dead poet who was Shakespeare's sister [who] will put on the body which she has so often laid down" (118), and women's speech, "the courage to write exactly what we think" (117–18). Once more, her audience's loyalty is sought to give life to a fictional entity. And once more, the act of speaking out is problematized by the conditions of that speech.[26] Stepping out from her persona, dismantling the fictional "I" ("Here, then, Mary Beton ceases to speak"), Woolf presumes to speak in her own voice ("I will end now in my own person" [109]). But her final speech is an ironic concession to conventional authority: "Here I would stop, but the pressure of convention decrees that every speech must end with a peroration. And a peroration addressed to women should have something, you will agree, particularly exalting and ennobling about it" (114). As in "Mr. Bennett and Mrs. Brown," Woolf disclaims such masculine tropes as truth, fact, and authority: "My own suggestion is a little fantastic, I admit; I prefer, therefore, to put it in the form of fiction" (117). But under cover of her "feminine" position, she writes a peroration that is exalting and ennobling to an extreme, inspiring her audience to be, literally, inspiriting: to instill courage in the obscure, to breathe life into the unborn, to transform fiction (Shake-

speare's sister) into reality. Concluding conclusively, Woolf thus de-
stabilizes her own irony. Is this a "nugget of pure truth" her essay has
been made to yield? And if so, should it be discarded with the other
nuggets, accepted as utopian fantasy, or heralded as the skeleton of a
new belief? Such questions are not simply fanciful, for Woolf's narrative position is less certain than her followers would have us believe.
As in "Mr. Bennett and Mrs. Brown," in the end, speaking out and
not speaking out come to the same thing. As Woolf eloquently
demonstrates—demonstrates in part through her very eloquence—
the power of Shakespeare's sister (like that of Mrs. Brown) resides in
her inability to speak.

As a strategy with political and aesthetic implications, "not
speaking out" gestures simultaneously toward speech and silence; it
marks a resistance to the appropriation of one's words that direct
speech inevitably entails—a resistance to complicitous participation
in the dominant discursive modes. But as a resolution to the problem
of voice, the mode of resistance remains incomplete, poised pre-
cariously between subversive mastery and submissive consent. Such
a strategy remains trapped in the conditions of paradox: it can preserve the authenticity of voice only by keeping voice intact—by keeping it unvoiced, relegated to the fictional and hypothetical domain.

*   *   *

How come this privileged relationship with voice?
—Hélène Cixous, "Sorties"

Virginia Woolf occupies a privileged position in feminist literary criticism, particularly as it is practiced in this country. She stands as a
source of inspiration for feminist practice and as an agent conferring
academic legitimacy. She has become the body in whose name feminism erects its monuments and dates its history. Thus Barbara Hill
Rigney appropriates Woolf's words to acknowledge feminist critics'
debt to her: "If, as Woolf wrote, 'Jane Austen should have laid a
wreath upon the grave of Fanny Burney' . . . , then we, too, should
gratefully bestow on Virginia Woolf a similar honour."[27] And Sandra
Gilbert and Susan Gubar read Woolf as the origin of their own monumental enterprise, *The Norton Anthology of Literature by Women*—a project that completes the work of "hundreds," similarly conceived as

responding to Woolf's words. Marking the beginning and end of Gilbert and Gubar's prefatory remarks, Virginia Woolf circumscribes the "female literary inheritance" they unveil: "We began these prefatory remarks with a reference to Virginia Woolf's pioneering essay on women and fiction; we want to acknowledge now our deep intellectual indebtedness to the hundreds of teachers all over the world who have recently responded to Woolf's impassioned explanation that 'we think back through our mothers if we are women' by laboring to recover the female literary inheritance that we have attempted to reconstitute here."[28]

For Gilbert and Gubar, Woolf emerges as voice, the source of impassioned speech; as voice she represents "the mother of us all," a position Sara Ruddick takes literally, "I was taught *To the Lighthouse* in my mother's voice, by a woman I passionately but reluctantly adored."[29] More generally, the feminist recuperation of Woolf has established her value in the recovery of authentic female speech: a voice distinctively her own. Thus Beth Rigel Daugherty reads the accomplishment of "Mr. Bennett and Mrs. Brown: ". . . Woolf effectively exorcised many patriarchal, critical, and inhibiting voices, and she persuaded herself that her own approach, methods, and style were valid, thus gaining confidence, her own identity and voice, a blueprint for the future, and techniques for combining aesthetic and feminist concerns."[30] Similarly, Phyllis Rose reads Woolf's literary biography: "As a young woman, it took her a long time to convince herself that difference of style did not mean inferiority, that she had her own voice, unique, feminine, worth attending to."[31] Reading Woolf's works as charting the progress from silence into speech, critics like these see themselves as simultaneously restoring Woolf's "own" voice by creating the conditions for her renewed popularity.

My own reading of this voice is more circumspect. Woolf, I would suggest, has become feminism's Mrs. Brown: the "fictional" source of our creativity, the heroine of diverse stories of what feminist criticism would like her to be.[32] Her value thus resides not in her "speech" but in her capacity to be "spoken for," to be "appropriated for feminism" as it is variously defined. In the stories she generates, Woolf runs the gamut of feminist parts, from a "guerrilla fighter in a Victorian skirt" storming the gates of Cambridge to steal the secret of masculine authority[33] to a "feminine" revolutionary, deploying specifically feminine tactics: a lack of "explicit 'system'" and an excess of "sympathy."[34] As Toril Moi has demonstrated, the feminists who reject Woolf do so because they have failed to appropriate her, to find her the writer of liberating texts; but for Moi, as for the many feminists who enshrine Woolf, appropriation remains the end: "A feminist criticism that would do both justice and homage to its great mother and sister: this, surely, should be our goal."[35]

With feminist literary criticism now enjoying academic respectability, perhaps we can begin to define a different set of needs. Perhaps we should no longer ask what constitutes Woolf's feminism but what constitutes feminism's "Woolf"? For it would seem an opportune moment to reexamine the questions and implications of Woolf's authority. Can we imagine a feminist criticism that does not make appropriation its object or homage its goal? Can we reconcile homage and critique? As I have tried to suggest in my readings, Woolf makes an imperfect heroine for the story of woman's liberated speech. Her voice is never some transparent marker of full identity. Rather, it is entangled in problematic relations to authority: intention, origin, control, and propriety. It occupies the unstable ground of mimicry. Might a new feminist practice find its story here: in the space Woolf's voice straddles between speech and non-speech; in the interstices between subversion and verbal complicity?

Chapter 6

The Fiction of Voice

In the considerable attention afforded Woolf's narrative strategies, "voice" remains the term most resistant to definitive critical claims. Neither the assertion of a sophisticated instrument for determinability (as in Mitchell Leaska's ambitious study of *To the Lighthouse*) nor a systematic insistence that all Woolf's voices are the same answers to the powerfully unsettling qualities of her novels' vocal strains.[1] Resisting articulation, voice remains the ground upon which all other narrative possibilities are played. What I want to consider, then, is twofold: the narrative strategies that produce the novel's problematic voice(s); and voice, itself, as a narrative strategy to interrogate the terms of novelistic discourse. I locate my argument in *To the Lighthouse* in part because its emotional accessibility disarmingly assures us that voice, as a register of character, is the thing we know: narrative voice distinguishes characters whose psychic dramas we replay. But I also choose *To the Lighthouse* because its long tradition of critical readings provides a focus for my own counterclaims.

In the history of Woolf's reception, her admirers have often made authenticity the crux of their praise. Even Arnold Kettle's highly qualified defense of the novel locates its admirable traits in this place. Referring to "Mr. Bennett and Mrs. Brown," he asks, "In what sense may life be said, in *To the Lighthouse*, not to escape?" Answering himself, he explains, "In the sense, perhaps, that there is nothing

129

secondhand about this novel, that the convention in which it is written permits Virginia Woolf to convey with extraordinary precision a
certain intimate quality of felt life."[2] Applauding the novel's modernist aesthetics, later critics have continued to uphold its subjective
truthfulness: Woolf's "sense of *lived reality*," her "extraordinary understanding of how people's emotions are always fluctuating," her
convincing presentation of what "experience felt like."[3] Recently,
feminist critics have insisted on the gender specificity of the "felt life"
the novel so intimately represents. Heralding the novel's challenge to
masculine ideology (as represented in Mr. Ramsay), they have, for
the most part, consolidated a set of conventional assumptions about
the relationship between voice, experience, and identity. In the interest of locating the essential female center of Woolf's work, these
critics have neutralized the narrative's decentering and destabilizing
effects. "A woman's voice." "An authentic voice." "Her own voice."
"The voice of female experience." "An authentic woman's voice."
Terms such as these dominate the burgeoning Woolf industry, and,
in the current critical climate, it has become almost *de rigueur* to read
the author of *A Room of One's Own* as embodying, in her characters
and in her narrative stance, the paradigm her title seems to invite: a
voice of her own. What I intend to argue, however, is that Woolf's
narrative strategies work *against* precisely this claim. They present
"a voice of one's own" as the central fiction that the narrative deconstructs.

I turn to a familiar passage from *To the Lighthouse* that speaks to
the question just posed: How does one establish one's voice as authentically one's own? The passage, following immediately upon the
"wedge-shaped core of darkness" interlude, is one of many often
cited to argue for the specificity of Mrs. Ramsay's verbal tones.

> Often she found herself sitting and looking, sitting and looking,
> with her work in her hands until she became the thing she
> looked at—that light, for example. And it would lift up on it
> some little phrase or other which had been lying in her mind like
> that—'Children don't forget, children don't forget'—which she
> would repeat and begin adding to it, It will end, it will end, she
> said. It will come, it will come, when suddenly she added, We
> are in the hands of the Lord.

But instantly she was annoyed with herself for saying that. Who had said it? Not she; she had been trapped into saying something she did not mean.[4]

The narrative rendition of Mrs. Ramsay's meditation posits integrity of voice as its disputed terrain. For Mrs. Ramsay, some element of the alien always intrudes, as here, "We are in the hands of the Lord." She can maintain her verbal integrity only, paradoxically, by disengaging herself from her voice, disembodying her words. *She* does not mean what *they* say or, alternatively, *she* does not say the words at all: "Who had said it? Not she . . . ." Yet the question of authenticity this passage raises extends beyond the problematic, "inauthentic" utterance the passage marks. Where in this passage does Mrs. Ramsay begin to "speak" and to what extent can *any* of her words be called her own? For Mrs. Ramsay's "authentic" voice turns out to be constructed of/by a compilation of conventional truths, "'Children don't forget,'" "It will come," "It will end." From the self-quotation of her first utterance, "'Children don't forget'" to the self-surrender of her last, "We are in the hands of the Lord," there is only a brief passage of familiar words, as proprietary repetition gives way to appropriating forms.

An amalgam of quotations, of fictional constructs, of borrowed terms, her voice occupies a predetermined space. Mimicry and silence mark its farthest poles. How different, finally, is such a constructed verbal identity from Mr. Ramsay's more obvious amalgam of scraps of poetry and heroic clichés? And how different is it from the communal identity Mrs. Ramsay posits in which the recited words of Cowper's poetry become the hypostatized representation of a voice of one's own, with the entire dinner party presumably united by the thought that "this were, at last, the natural thing to say, this were their own voice speaking" (167). What does it mean, in such a context, to speak of a voice of one's own?

Voice, Woolf suggests and her narrative strategies confirm, is never a fully individualized act. At its most intense, moreover, it is not a product of the individual will. Mrs. Ramsay, for example, does not so much articulate her words as receive them from some impersonal thing she becomes, "And *it* would lift up on it some little phrase or other which had been lying in *her* mind" (emphasis mine), just as later, for Lily Briscoe, "words" (Mr. Ramsay's words, the words of the poetry he habitually recites) "wrote themselves all over the grey-green walls" (219) of her mind. And for Virginia Woolf, conceiving the novel "in a great, apparently involuntary, rush," her "lips seemed syllabling of their own accord."[5]

Yet for Woolf the fiction of an authentic voice had a powerful hold. Her own comments on her fiction suggest the profound connectedness she found between the successful rendition of voice and narrative origins and ends. "There's no doubt in my mind that I have found out how to begin (at 40) to say something in my own voice; & that interests me so that I feel I can go ahead without praise,"[6] Woolf wrote in 1922 after completing *Jacob's Room*, a novel generally accepted as marking Woolf's shift into experimental narrative modes. And in *To the Lighthouse*, a work so steeped in this newfound voice that for Woolf the term *novel* would no longer do,[7] Woolf set out to record the voices of her parents. A 1925 diary entry notes, "But the centre is father's character, sitting in a boat, reciting We perished, each alone" (*Diary* 3:18–19). The novel's final configuration merely shifts the central voice. The center is mother's character, Woolf might have claimed, sitting at the window, reading aloud "The Fisherman and His Wife."

For Woolf, self-admittedly "obsessed" by "invisible presences," her dead parents remained with her, preeminently, as a continuing voice. Of her father she observed, "His life would have entirely ended mine. . . . I hear his voice, I know this by heart" (*Diary* 3:208), and of her mother she wrote, "Until I was in the forties . . . the presence of my mother obsessed me. I could hear her voice, see her, imagine what she would do or say as I went about my day's doings" (*Moments of Being*, 80). Writing *To the Lighthouse* silenced the voice, exorcised the ghost: "But I wrote the book very quickly; and when it was written, I ceased to be obsessed by my mother. I no longer hear her voice; I do not see her" (*Moments of Being*, 81).

What I would like to suggest, however, is that if Woolf's novel exorcised her ghosts, it did so, not as most critics have alleged, by virtue of the authenticity of its representations, but rather by exploding the very concept of "voice"—of voice as an individuated essence to be suppressed, deployed, or owned. For Woolf's narrative practices, as I will show, deauthorize their speakers, transgress the boundaries of individual utterance, and call into question the figures that mark the voice as whole. Even the fiction of origins Woolf constructs for her novel assigns her parents' voices to a similar intermediary zone. Both her mother and her father are commemorated in moments of recitation, where their intonations may be original but their words are not their own.

With its complex critique of voice, French feminist theory may help illuminate the narrative strategies that mark Woolf's "feminine voice" as something other than her own, for such theories assert the inevitable fictionality of the term.[8] Woman cannot speak in any "authentic" fashion because, as Julia Kristeva insists, "woman" does not exist; "she" is a social construct, a fictitious form.[9] And as Luce Irigaray repeatedly demonstrates, there is no place for her to speak other than within the bounds of masculine discourse.[10] The feminine voice cannot exist, then, as a positive definable entity but rather exists as a shifting, intermediary state, caught between its representations of its own appropriation and its enactment of an "otherness" it can only adumbrate, a "fiction" of what it might become. If it could speak, Hélène Cixous argues, it would overthrow proprietary terms: "Depropriation, depersonalization."[11]

*   *   *

For Woolf the fiction of an authentic voice operates in multivalent ways. The voices she attributes to her characters, even as they strive for individuation, declare their dependence upon orthodox forms of discourse: borrowing tones from more authoritative voices, whether they be those of other characters or those culled from the literary domain.[12] Voice, moreover, as the novel represents it, bears little relation to what one says, for articulated utterance occupies only a small space in the novel's verbal terrain. Instead, the novel posits voice as comprised of the accents and inflections of the inner life: what one, presumably, thinks and feels. Yet as Woolf remarks in "An Unwritten Novel," ". . . when the self speaks to the self, who is speaking?"[13] What we call interior monologue, Alice Jardine suggests, "the fiction of an interior voice," may be "the last rationalization of a culture hooked on transcendance."[14] Divided from itself, this inner voice, in Woolf's novel at least, remains problematically

marked: neither the exclusive territory of character as speaking subject nor of the appropriating narrative voice.

Mr. Ramsay's self-recitation provides a case in point. The scraps
of heroic poetry that distinguish his speech find echoes in the epic
pretensions that inform his fantasy life. Yet the novel renders problematic the personal and proprietary status of both sets of intoned
words. In the first instance, Mr. Ramsay voices the words of well-
known poems, Tennyson's "The Charge of the Light Brigade" and,
later, Cowper's "The Castaway." The quoted lines, cut off from their
author, belong to the public domain; they are Mr. Ramsay's only in a
limited sense of the term, although they have often been read in just
such a light, as a verbal leitmotif—a marker of individual identity.
They first appear in the novel, moreover, cut off from even their
secondary source. Transmitted through the mind of Mrs. Ramsay,
the words are further projected through a disembodied voice—a
voice that intrudes itself upon her consciousness, as if endowed with
volition of its own:

> Suddenly a loud cry, as of a sleep-walker, half roused, something
> about
>
> Stormed at with shot and shell
>
> sung out with the utmost intensity in her ear. . . . (29)

The narrative further redistributes Mr. Ramsay's quoted words. They
enter the narrative taken over by other voices: stored in Lily's private
arsenal, as she watches Mr. Ramsay ride off "to die gloriously she
supposed upon the heights of Balaclava" (29) or appropriated by Mr.
Bankes as the object of an unspoken interchange,

> Now, for instance, when Ramsay bore down on them, shouting,
> gesticulating, Miss Briscoe, he felt certain, understood.
> "Some one had blundered" (31)

or picked up by Mrs. Ramsay as the impetus for her own meditative
flights.[15]

Once spoken, Mr. Ramsay's words depart from his control. They
hang suspended between voices: cut off from their author, taken up

by alien tongues, fragmented, reconstructed, quoted out of context, misquoted, misapplied, put to unintended use, deployed for private ends. They persist, like their sources (the unnamed poems Mr. Ramsay recites) as unmarked citations, deauthorized tones; they turn up in other voices, quotations within quotations, often without even the distinction of a quotation mark. They thus register the novel's blurring of the private/public line: its refusal to distinguish between individual utterance and the communal property of the public domain. Mr. Ramsay's private appropriation of publicly sanctioned poems leads to his public exposure in the privacy of his home: the invasion of his private space. His appropriation of poetic discourse, moreover, does not ensure his proprietary claims; he wields no power over the origins or ends of the words he declaims.

Mrs. Ramsay, for example, recuperates her husband's fragmentary utterances, but in her voice the words blend into each other, dispersing in telegraphic shots; repeated in this manner, they reflect ironically on Mr. Ramsay's plight: "Stormed at by shot and shell, boldly we rode and well, flashed through the valley of death, volleyed and thundered—straight into Lily Briscoe and William Bankes" (49). In Lily's consciousness, Mr. Ramsay's words take on an independent life; reversed in her memory "('Alone' she heard him say, 'Perished' she heard him say)," they inscribe themselves as the key to all mythologies: ". . . the words became symbols, wrote themselves all over the grey-green walls. If only she could put them together, she felt, write them out in some sentence, then she would have got at the truth of things" (219). Even Mr. Ramsay's factual pronouncements, the very first words, for example, he speaks, "But it won't be fine" (10), undergo a transformational mode.[16] They are appropriated first by Mrs. Ramsay to support her counterclaim, "But it may be fine—I expect it will be fine" (11), then by Charles Tansley, who reproduces them as his own, "There'll be no landing at the Lighthouse tomorrow" (15). The same words surface years later in the mind of James: "'It will rain,' he remembered his father saying. 'You won't be able to go to the Lighthouse'" (276). But as James's misquotation implies, the voice of the father he remembers is a voice he partially invents. Like the other characters, James appropriates Mr. Ramsay's voice to his own ends.

Mr. Ramsay's unvoiced articulations also draw from a public

fund—the storehouse of fictional materials that constitute our shared
cultural life. His quest for *R*, the narrative's most extended trope for
his inner life, borrows shamelessly from the poetry he recites. It reconstructs him in heroic guise, the leader of a doomed expedition,
armed with "endurance and justice, foresight, devotion, skill" (54).
Yet if in these fantasies, Mr. Ramsay appropriates the Tennysonian
poetic voice, the predictability of his self-creations reveals *his* appropriation by literary conventions and clichés. The melodramatic models he relies on shape and delimit his discursive possibilities. Each
new articulation adds more of the same, until Mr. Ramsay, quite
literally, finds himself restructured in the image he projects:

> Qualities that would have saved a ship's company exposed on a
> broiling sea with six biscuits and a flask of water. . . . Qualities
> that in a desolate expedition across the icy solitudes of the Polar
> region would have made him the leader, the guide, the coun-
> sellor. . . . Feelings that would not have disgraced a leader who,
> now that the snow has begun to fall and the mountain top is
> covered in mist, knows that he must lay himself down and die
> before morning comes, stole upon him, paling the colour of his
> eyes, giving him, even in the two minutes of his turn on the
> terrace the bleached look of withered old age. (54–55)

The same fictive process dominates the voice in which the narrative projects Mr. Ramsay's most public, even professional, trait: his
relentless pursuit of the truth. In the name of "facts uncompromis-
ing," fictive propensities again assert their sway. Mr. Ramsay's voice
becomes the site of a struggle between competing discursive modes,
with the rhetoric of adventure, in this instance, finally subsuming the
discourse of truth. The ensuing narrative recapitulates Mr. Ramsay's
characteristic tropes: romantic images, heroic adventure plots, stylized syntax, sentimental themes.

> What he said was true. It was always true. He was incapable of
> untruth; never tampered with a fact, never altered a disagreeable
> word to suit the pleasure or convenience of any mortal being,
> least of all of his own children, who, sprung from his loins,
> should be aware from childhood that life is difficult; facts uncom-

promising; and the passage to that fabled land where our bright-
est hopes are extinguished, our frail barks founder in darkness
(here Mr. Ramsay would straighten his back and narrow his little
blue eyes upon the horizon), one that needs, above all, courage,
truth, and the power to endure. (11)

Yet despite their marked similarities, these examples do not
clearly constitute Mr. Ramsay's dinstinctive, if unoriginal, voice. For
the narrative positions these imaginative structures in a contested
verbal zone. In the latter instance, for example, the lines immediately
preceding the passage in question waver between objective narrative
explication ("Such were the extremes of emotion that Mr. Ramsay
excited in his children's breasts by his mere presence" [10]) and subjective projection of James's thoughts. The narrative represents Mr.
Ramsay "grinning sarcastically, not only with the pleasure of disillu-
sioning his son and casting ridicule upon his wife, who was ten
thousand times better in every way than he was (James thought), but
also with some secret conceit at his own accuracy of judgement" (10).
The syntactical markers leave ambiguous exactly where in this formulation James's thoughts begin and end. It thus remains unclear
whose subjective experience the remainder of the passage reveals.
Does the "secret conceit" belong to Mr. Ramsay, James, or the narrative itself? The passage offers no definitive procedures for locating the
boundaries of shifting subjectivities.[17]
   The keyboard metaphor that facilitates Mr. Ramsay's heroic meditations occupies a similar indeterminate place, poised between Mrs.
Ramsay's reconstruction of her husband's similes and the narrative's
gently deflating irony. Yet the passage itself (the celebrated quest for
R) reads as if we are hearing Mr. Ramsay speak. Its positioning,
however, calls into question the power that lies behind this fantasy
retreat. The invocation of Mr. Ramsay's "splendid mind" (53), for
example, laid out like an alphabet from A to Z, coincides with Mrs.
Ramsay's efforts to salvage her husband from his own folly; the conclusion of this metaphorical excursion coincides with a shift in narrative perspective from ironic exposure of Mr. Ramsay's pretensions to
narrative sympathy. The narrative, too, works to free Mr. Ramsay
from blame. The rhetorical questions that conclude the section ("Who
shall blame him?" [57]) mark a shift in controlling literary paradigms

from the two-dimensional heroics of the Tennysonian incantation to the antiheroic resignation of the expressive realist mode. Where then do we locate Mr. Ramsay and who constructs the subjective experience we perceive?

What I have tried to suggest in this treatment of Mr. Ramsay is that such questions cannot be definitively resolved. In this respect, Mr. Ramsay's case is not unique. For the novel constructs all its voices in a similar way: built of conventional materials, occupying shifting ground, bordered by fluid demarcating lines.[18] Mrs. Ramsay, for example, proves no more capable than her husband of fully individualized speech. In neither case can gender confer verbal authenticity. For if Mr. Ramsay's consciousness displays the shallow platitudes of masculine thought, Mrs. Ramsay's inner life articulates itself by borrowing these tropes, quoting masculine authorities at one remove from their source. As I suggested in my introduction, Mrs. Ramsay's voice consists of a compilation of secondhand truths: proverbial wisdom, literary clichés, reconstituted quotations, echoes of authority. Wed to orthodoxy, Mrs. Ramsay characteristically gives play to a phrase or jingle that has "mated itself in her head" (48). Her "originality" resides in giving meaning to the conventionalized utterances her mind stores: the words, for example, of Mr. Ramsay, "Some one had blundered"; the grim warning of "The Fisherman and His Wife"; the tribute of Mr. Carmichael's "Luriana, Lurilee." The voice she projects cannot transcend the formulaic structures that give it life. It reproduces literary and cultural clichés: "People must marry," "They'll never be so happy again," "They'll say that all their lives." Even in her interior monologues, other voices vie for control. In its representation of her consciousness, the narrative conveys the overpowering of Mrs. Ramsay's voice by dominating cultural strains: the voice of her husband; the authority of gender stereotypes. Caught up by these voices, she thinks in conventional ways: "Then he said, Damn you. He said, It must rain. He said, It won't rain; and instantly a Heaven of security opened before her. There was nobody she reverenced more. She was not good enough to tie his shoe strings, she felt" (51).

The voice Mrs. Ramsay reserves for herself, when having shed her attachments, she "could be herself, by herself," proves no more exclusively her own. Here, too, other voices intervene. The "wedge-shaped core of darkness," her private figure for the distilled essence of the self, reconstructs exotic tales of travel culled from fairytale plots and romantic fantasies. The ensuing adventure narrative rehearses conventional traveler's tropes and familiar literary themes: "Her horizon seemed to her limitless. There were all the places she had not seen; the Indian plains; she felt herself pushing aside the thick leather curtain of a church in Rome. This core of darkness could go anywhere, for no one saw it. They could not stop it, she thought, exulting" (96). "[F]ree for the strangest adventures," this self binds itself to "strangeness" as it is conventionally conceived. A kind of magic talisman conferring unlimited power and full authority, the core of darkness invokes the fantastical flying carpets of storybook legends, childhood memory, and fairytale fantasies.

The passage thus hardly seems the triumphant "piercing to the heart of things" critics have generally held it to be.[19] It reveals, more pointedly, the layers of cultural constructs that comprise individual identity—comprise not only the surface selves others know us by (the "childish apparitions" Mrs. Ramsay disclaims) but also the "true" self ("dark," "spreading," and "unfathomably deep") that has, presumably, shed its personality. In a diary entry for 1926, Woolf describes, in strikingly similar terms, an encounter with the "odd immeasurable soul," a plunge into impersonality (*Diary* 3:112). Commenting on "the mystical side of this solitude," Woolf notes, "how it is not oneself but something in the universe that one's left with" (*Diary* 3:113). The narrative resurrects these sentiments in Mrs. Ramsay's mind: "Not as oneself did one find rest ever, in her experience . . . but as a wedge of darkness" (96). The first diary entry, however, remains starkly unadorned: "One goes down into the well & nothing protects one from the assault of truth. Down there I cant write or read; I exist however. I am. Then I ask myself what I am? & get a closer though less flattering answer than I should on the surface—where, to tell the truth, I get more praise than is right" (*Diary* 3:112). Voiced over in Mrs. Ramsay's accents, the encounter admits flattering illusions and reemergent personality. The embellished narrative account uncovers what the diary entry conceals: that the self has no unmediated core, no primary access to "the assault of truth." In Mrs. Ramsay's adventures, the truth exists only as it is fictionally conceived. Her voice cannot free itself of its heritage of literary genealogies. Even when she tries to purge her voice of intrusive tongues, "purifying out of existence that lie, any lie" (97), she immediately reinstates another fictional screen. The depths of her mind harbor the conventional figures of romantic ideology: ". . . there curled up off the floor of the mind, rose from the lake of one's being, a mist, a bride to meet her lover" (98).

Lily Briscoe, though she consciously rejects Mrs. Ramsay's ideological assumptions, voices them in her own discourse. At the dinner party, for example, she succumbs to conventionally sanctioned lines, at the expense, she affirms, of her authenticity. Speaking in the voice of Mrs. Ramsay, and responding to Mrs. Ramsay's unvoiced plea, Lily says what she does not mean: "She had done the usual trick—been nice" (139). But what begins as self-conscious mimicry of Mrs. Ramsay, "'Oh, Mr. Tansley,' she said, 'do take me to the Lighthouse with you. I should so love it'" (130), passes, in its near repetition, for the authentic thing, "'Will you take me, Mr. Tansley'" (138). The second utterance produces the desired effect, for Lily's borrowed accents no longer mark a difference from their source.

Lily's sense of compromised conversation presupposes the possibility of unconstrained private speech: an inner voice of one's own. But as the narrative represents it, Lily's voice draws from the stock figures Mr. and Mrs. Ramsay rely upon. Her private fantasies reproduce their familiar heroic clichés: the leader of the expedition; the traveler in exotic realms. Thus Lily's secret musings translate Mrs. Ramsay into the object of a quest narrative: ". . . she imagined how in the chambers of the mind and heart of the woman who was, physically, touching her, were stood, like the treasures in the tombs of kings, tablets bearing sacred inscriptions, which if one could spell them out, would teach one everything" (79). And her fantasies at the dinner party inscribe Lily as the hero of a classic adventure plot: ". . . in the dawn on the beach she would be the one to pounce on the brooch half-hidden by some stone, and thus herself be included among the sailors and adventurers" (153). Even her moments of intense private anguish articulate themselves in figures drawn from fictional molds. Her probing of experience uncovers the melodramatic imagination that gives her life its adventurous cast: its sense of danger and accomplishment, "leaping from the pinnacle of a tower into the air" (268), plunging "into the waters of annihilation" (269). To the ultimate question of experience, "What does it mean? How do you explain it all?", her mind answers in the language of Arthurian romance: ". . . a little tear would have rent the surface pool. And then? Something would emerge. A hand would be shoved up, a blade would be flashed" (266–67).

More important, perhaps, Lily's voice registers the voices of those she sets herself against. Her oppositional position shapes her discourse as a series of countertexts, dependent upon and reinscribing the very authorities they reject. Thus Lily occupies an uneasy position as the independent heroine feminist criticism would have her be. Even the most sophisticated critiques continue to assign Lily a place outside the dominant ideology. Thus Toril Moi, for example, claims: ". . . *To the Lighthouse* illustrates the destructive nature of a metaphysical belief in strong, immutably fixed gender identities—as represented by Mr and Mrs Ramsay—whereas Lily Briscoe (an artist) represents the subject who deconstructs this opposition, perceives its pernicious influence and tries as far as is possible in a still rigidly patriarchal order to live as her own woman, without regard for the crippling definitions of sexual identity to which society would have her conform."[20] But, as I have tried to suggest, Mr. and Mrs. Ramsay's voices are not so rigidly distinct; verbal cross-dressing unfixes gender identities. Lily's voice, moreover, is constructed by the oppositional system within which she is inscribed. Her refusal to conform does not so much make her "her own woman" as cripple her in her own eyes, reducing her to an "imitation woman": "Surely, she could imitate from recollection the glow, the rhapsody, the self-surrender, she had seen on so many women's faces (on Mrs. Ramsay's for instance)" (224). Failing this, Lily conceives herself as sexually marred: "A woman, she had provoked this horror; a woman, she should have known how to deal with it. It was immensely to her discredit, sexually, to stand there dumb. One said—what did one say?—Oh, Mr. Ramsay! Dear Mr. Ramsay!" (228). Lily's sense of failure reveals her acceptance of the reigning ideology. Attempting to masquerade as a "real woman," Lily feels betrayed by her own mimicry: the difference that marks her imitation as imperfectly aligned; that marks her inability to speak convincingly *as* Mrs. Ramsay. As Cixous would argue, Lily has been "made to see (= not-see) woman on the basis of what man wants to see of her": she sees herself at a distance, the way the dominant culture wants woman to see and be seen.[21]

Rejecting Mrs. Ramsay's idea of woman, Lily identifies herself as *"not* Mrs. Ramsay," implicitly affirming Mrs. Ramsay's terms. Lily's "rebellions" keep Mrs. Ramsay's voice alive as the thing she must struggle against. Thus Lily plays match-breaker to Mrs. Ramsay's matchmaker—imagining, as in her representation of the Rayleys' marriage, the overthrow of Mrs. Ramsay's plans. Compelled to extinguish the flames Mrs. Ramsay sets alight ("one had only to say 'in love' and instantly, as happened now, up rose Paul's fire again"), Lily preserves Mrs. Ramsay as the ultimate standard of appeal. Her story of "The Rayleys," how Paul had a mistress and "went to coffee-houses and played chess" (262), merely reverses Mrs. Ramsay's master plot. It constitutes a type of continuing dialogue with the dead: "She imagined herself telling it to Mrs. Ramsay" (259). Lily's version, moreover, draws equally on romantic conventions and clichés. Like Mrs. Ramsay's account of Mr. Carmichael, "an affair at Oxford with some girl; an early marriage; poverty; going to India; translating a little poetry 'very beautifully, I believe . . .'" (20), the story repeats a formulaic pattern and follows a predictable narrative line.[22]

Similarly, Lily's defiance of the crippling sexual stereotypes men apply, "women can't paint, can't write" (75), makes even her independent identity as artist a product of *their* terms. If she fails, she merely proves women *cannot*, but if she succeeds in showing women *can*, it is, as she herself suggests, by becoming "not woman." Either way, masculine logic continues to apply, as Irigaray suggests, to "define, circumvent, circumscribe." Any identity formed in simple opposition remains caught in the configurations of the dominant ideology, with "its power to *reduce all others to the economy of the Same.*"[23] The voice Lily projects thus reflects the internalized voices of her culture as much in what she explicitly denies as in what she implicitly accepts.

Tempting as it may be, then, to read *To the Lighthouse* as "a novel about the liberation of the poetic voice,"[24] the narrative renders problematic the meaning of liberation in such a context, especially if one locates the poetic voice in a particular character's consciousness. For the narrative points to the recognition of all voices as entangled, imbricated, and constrained. The search for author surrogates, whether Lily or anyone else, glosses over the novel's relentless representation of compromised authority.[25] The repetition across voices of phrases, images, and imaginative constructs reflects the conditions by which voice can be disowned: subsumed by more powerful voices, absorbed into the narrative matrix, reduced to the configurations of prescribed cultural exchange. This practice of appropriation, if sometimes gender specific in the terms of its application, does not spare either sex. Consequently, the novel does not sustain woman's voice (as represented by character, at least) as the answer to the conditions of complicitous discourse. This refusal marks the radical ground of the novel's critique, its understanding that all voices—masculine and feminine alike—constitute fictional constructs. The novel thus confirms what French feminists frequently articulate: one can no more speak *as* woman than *as* man. As Kristeva suggests, "The belief that 'one is a woman' is almost as absurd and obscurantist as the belief that 'one is a man.' "[26]

*   *   *

If we turn from the representation of characters' voices to the voice of the narrative itself, these concerns can be seen in a reverse light. In what Alex Zwerdling calls a "chameleon method of narration," the narrative turns the problems of voice inside out, confronting us with an entity that constantly proclaims its refusal to be marked.[27] As J. Hillis Miller observes, "Exactly who, or what, is the narrator of *To the Lighthouse*? Where is she, he, or it located? What powers does the narrator have?"[28] "[N]owhere and everywhere, located at no identifiable time," the narrator, he adds, "has none of the characteristics of a person except voice and tone" (173). But how do we define this voice? Where the characters present a deceptive illusion of verbal autonomy and localized identity, an illusion unmasked only by deliberately imposing the type of questions Miller asks, the narrative makes these questions the first condition of readerly access. The narrative voice, moreover, not only resists self-identification, it works to destabilize character boundaries, creating a series of ruptures and breaks that disrupt any notions of unitary identity.[29] These breaks, represented as moments of narrative indeterminacy, call into question, even as they assert, the narrative's own authority. For the narrative dissevers voice (that of others as well as its own) from systems of accountability; neither fully present nor fully absent at any given time, it keeps the origin of all voices a debatable ground. It poises its utterances in and between characters, providing no clear signals for settling proprietary claims.

In the misquotations, miscalculations, and trivializations that riddle the text, we have no definitive way to assign responsibility. The novel's subtly subversive discrepancies thus prove all the more unsettling precisely because they cannot be placed. For example, when the the narrative records Macalister's account of the storm, "when ten ships had been driven into the bay" (244), it returns to that moment, only a page later, as it is seen by Cam and James; as the narrative presents them observing their father, another ship slips in: ". . . he questioned Macalister about the eleven ships that had been driven into the bay in a storm" (245). Almost unnoticeable, the discrepancy remains unexplained; like the characterization of Mr. Ramsay that precedes it, "he liked men to work like that, and women to keep house, and sit beside sleeping children indoors, while men were drowned, out there in a storm," its origins are masked by a collaborative overlay comprised of Mr. Ramsay's voice, the voice of his children ("So James could tell, so Cam could tell"), and the voice the narrative projects.

If, then, as Miller suggests, the narrator of *To the Lighthouse* is only a voice, it is not even the sort of voice we think we know, for it lacks the features that make the voice seem whole: intentionality, originality, propriety, exclusiveness, control. Admitting no limits, it speaks for and through all the characters, unbound by the laws of quotation, unaccountable to the reign of fact. Especially when we turn to "Time Passes," the place where that voice is given freest play, we are confronted with a verbal practice that refuses to answer to traditional notions of reliability. It is, as Irigaray might say, a voice which is not one. How many voices, for example, speak? Even putting aside the voice of Mrs. McNab, the narrative registers at least two distinct verbal modes: the factual voice of the bracketed human realm and the lyrical voice of the temporal interlude, the latter itself divided by marked shifts in tone. The narrative's collective consciousness admits, without clearly distinguishing, voices of its own.

Neither unitary nor defined, this voice registers an excess or overbalance often associated with the place of the feminine in contemporary critical discourse. Roland Barthes's comments, for exam

ple, on the unsettling impact of Kristeva's work speak to that voice's
effect: it "changes the place of things," destroying "the *latest precon-
ception*," subverting authority. As Kristeva herself explains, her project situates itself outside our space, knowingly inserting itself along
the borderlines of our discourse.[30] For Woolf, "Time Passes" represented a self-conscious technical experiment, quite literally a detour
that would disrupt the linear movement of the narrative and defer the
installation of the Lightouse as the novel's end. An early diary entry
describes the passage's intrusive and subversive elements: ". . . this
impersonal thing, which I'm dared to do by my friends, the flight of
time, & the consequent break of unity in my design" (*Diary* 3:36).
Irigaray speculates on the need for such strategic commitments:

> Perhaps this is the time to stress *technique* again? To renounce for
> the time being the sovereignty of thought in order to forge *tools*
> which will permit the exploitation of these resources, these unex-
> plored mines. Perhaps for the time being the serene contempla-
> tion of empire must be abandoned in favor of taming those forces
> which, once unleashed, might explode the very concept of em-
> pire. A detour into *strategy, tactics, and practice* is called for, at
> least as long as it takes to gain vision, self-knowledge, self-
> possession, even in one's decenteredness.[31]

In what seems the kind of "detour into strategy" Irigaray writes
about, Woolf knowingly inserts her wedge-shaped core of darkness
("Time Passes") at the parameters of her more conventional novelistic
discourse.

In a strategic speculation, then, mirroring the novel's own, I
would like, in the remainder of this chapter, to consider "Time
Passes" as a narrative tool to uncover the traces in Woolf's writing of
what French theories of discourse suggest, to use "Time Passes" to
reflect on the way French feminism might reopen Woolf's much-read
text. The section can be read, in Irigaray's terms, as the "speculum of
the other woman"—the woman's voice (voice of the "other" woman)
the novel can do no more than adumbrate. In Irigaray's work, the
term *speculum* maintains a double sense: mirror and probe, reflecting
surface and medical/analytical instrument. Situated between the mas-
sive blocks of her own (discursive) texts, the speculative passage

entitled "Speculum" displaces the discourses it connects: the critiques
of Plato and Freud. In *To the Lighthouse*, "Time Passes" works a similar
exploratory project: parting what it joins, creating the very passage it
illuminates. A distorting mirror to the novel's surface text, "Time
Passes" posits an alternative economy to the specularization both
"Window" and "Lighthouse" suggest in their visual entitlements.

Disembodied itself, the voice of this interlude embodies a pulsat-
ing rhythmic life. It offers a fluid, all-encompassing narrative matrix
to oppose the characters' bounded texts. It is a voice marked by
uncensored digressions and lyrical effusiveness. Collective in number
and colloquial in tone, the voice dispenses with the masculine mono-
logic mode. From the beginning, it assumes an interrogative stance,
both in its own articulations ("But what after all is one night?" [192];
"Did Nature supplement what man advanced? Did she complete
what he began?" [201–02]) and in the voices it projects (the voice of
"certain airs" asking, "Will you fade? Will you perish?" [193], of the
"mystic, the visionary, walking the beach," inquiring, "'What am I?'
'What is this?'" [197–98], of Mrs. McNab and Mrs. Bast, "Some said
he was dead; some said she was dead. Which was it?" [210]). Questions replace assertions as the passage's "definitive" stance. Parading
its own uncertainties, "Time Passes" operates by the tentative logic
of *as if*: "Almost one might imagine . . ." (190); "It seemed now as
if . . ." (192); "Almost it would appear . . ." (193). The passage thus
outlines the speculative territory Irigaray sketches out, a space found
in "hyperbolic doubt, in the systematic questioning of everything"
(*Speculum*, 181).

Bypassing the demands of narrative coherence, "Time Passes"
asserts its ruptures, absences, and breaks, refusing to accede to the
strictures of conventional readability. It dispenses with causal links
and other traditional figures of continuity, proclaiming instead its
own poetic promiscuity:

> In those mirrors, the minds of men, in those pools of uneasy
> water, in which clouds for ever turn and shadows form, dreams
> persisted, and it was impossible to resist the strange intimation
> which every gull, flower, tree, man and woman, and the white
> earth itself seemed to declare (but if questioned at once to with-
> draw) that good triumphs, happiness prevails, order rules; or to

resist the extraordinary stimulus to range hither and thither in search of some absolute good, some crystal of intensity, remote from the known pleasures and familiar virtues, something alien to the processes of domestic life, single, hard, bright, like a diamond in the sand, which would render the possessor secure. (198–99)

Indulging its own meditations, the passage proves hard to track; as the length of the sentence increases, it seems to get out of hand, until one is left with a confused sense of what exactly the passage asserts or denies. Against the law of sequential logic, it upholds the authority of proximity, unfolding itself through layers of contiguity. Like the "downpouring of immense darkness" (189) it documents, the voice of "Time Passes" insinuates itself into the spaces it transcribes, confounding whatever it comes near. Creeping, questioning, musing, brushing, the narrative sustains itself through touch; it charts its own progress through the random contacts it projects, propelling itself across boundaries of time and space, regenerating itself from the seeds of its own fecundity. In the iterations and reiterations that inform it, in the rhythmic repetitions that underpin the passage's flight, we come close to the fiction of a voice answerable only to its own authority. Like the lighthouse beam, it seems to trace its own pattern, bend to its own image, lovingly caress itself.

In "Sorties," Cixous speculates on the possibility of an unappropriated feminine voice to be found in the space of writing: "If there is a somewhere else that can escape the infernal repetition, it lies in that direction, where *it* writes itself, where *it* dreams, where *it* invents new worlds" (72). In many respects, "Time Passes" seems to intimate such a place—a "dark continent" that cannot be theorized, that insists on its fictionality as its birthright. Irigaray's invocation of "nocturnal wanderings" illuminates "Time Passes's" voice of a ten-year's night: "An abyss that swallows up all persons, all names, even proper names. For in fact all properties (and proprieties) will have to be shed to continue this penetration" (*Speculum*, 194). In the wake of the engulfing voice of "Time Passes," proprieties disappear and proper names retreat into brackets outside the "dominant" voice. The violation of propriety, for example, in the representation of Mrs. Ramsay's death can be seen as the necessary price for the penetration

"Time Passes" effects. The transgressive features of the representation only dramatize most fully a practice endemic to the text.

Irigaray's speculative discourse evokes an "otherness" that can be transcribed, given the constraints of language, only in negative terms: "No voice is hers to call, no hands can fill the open hungry mouth with the food that both nourishes and devours. Abandoned, the soul can barely keep faith. No image, no figure alleviates such mortal absence" (*Speculum*, 195). For Irigaray, such lyrical passages clearly have a theoretical, as for Woolf they have a narrative, intent; they point to a set of strategies they enact. Irigaray's "night walking" could be inserted seamlessly into Woolf's: ". . . and should any sleeper fancying that he might find on the beach an answer to his doubts, a sharer of his solitude, throw off his bedclothes and go down by himself to walk on the sand, no image with semblance of serving and divine promptitude comes readily to hand bringing the night to order and making the world reflect the compass of the soul. The hand dwindles in his hand; the voice bellows in his ear" (193).

As speculum, the "Time Passes" section facilitates the exploration of the novel's recesses; as such it projects not an entirely "other" speech but the novel's under-voice (voice-under?)—literally, the novel's sub-text. In this capacity it highlights the strategic features of the text's larger representation of voice. It points to these features—transgression, repetition, citation, proximity, permeability, unaccountability—as *strategies*, as vehicles of the novel's disconcerting acts. But as speculum, such passages can finally only mirror, and "Time Passes" presents, as the other side of its voice, the prevailing desire for authority and control. Its very "otherness" makes it, in some sense, suspect, for as Irigaray reflects, how does one "speak of the 'other' in a language already systematized by/for the same" (*Speculum*, 139)?[32] Is the very strangeness of "Time Passes" strangeness already appropriated, turned to conventional ends?

The problem here mirrors one implicit in the title of Irigaray's text, *Speculum of the Other Woman*. Are *woman* and *other* merely synonymous terms? Or, if woman is always/already "other," is the *other* woman the woman who is *not* other? The woman who is yet to be theorized: the woman on the other side of the looking glass—the one the masculine economy leaves out. Is the mirror of woman, man? Who or what is being mirrored or explored? Putting such questions aside for the moment, does the speculum *belong* to woman—*her* mirror, *her* instrument? Or does it reflect her? explore her? Is woman the subject or object of the title? Who holds the mirror whose reflection we read? From what position does *Speculum* speak? In the discursive situation Irigaray articulates, neither reader nor text occupies a stable place.

With its own occluded agency, "Time Passes" occupies a similarly problematic plane. If the section represents the narrative's fullest self-expression, it also represents the place where voice is most explicitly disowned. For it is never clear what presence stands behind this ungendered, disembodied voice and whose interests that voice serves. Whose views does it mirror, explore, project? Positioned strategically to disconcert the surrounding text, does it end by reintroducing mastery from the other side? For with all its radical resistance, "Time Passes" repeatedly reveals its complicity in conventional modes of discourse. Its voice deploys familiar literary tropes to remake what it undoes: to personalize the impersonal, to inhabit the emptiness, to aestheticize the abyss.

In *The Waves*, Bernard rehearses his repertoire, self-consciously displaying his stock in trade: "For instance, up that back street a girl stands waiting; for whom? A romantic story. On the wall of that shop is fixed a small crane, and for what reason, I ask, was that crane fixed there? and invent a purple lady swelling, circumambient, hauled from a barouche landau by a perspiring husband sometime in the sixties. A grotesque story."[33] In "Time Passes," the narrative acts, less explicitly, in much the same way, proffering its own casebook of generic clichés: "Sometimes a hand was raised as if to clutch something or ward off something" (190). A horror story. "Then smoothly brushing the walls, they passed on musingly as if asking the red and yellow roses on the wall-paper whether they would fade" (190). A sentimental story. "Were they allies? Were they enemies? How long would they endure?" (190–91). A melodramatic story.

These stylized descriptions participate in culturally coded responses to the unknown. The defamiliarization effected by time's passing is familiarized by its representation as text, its reproduction of recognizable accents and tones. The narrative renders the dehumanized landscape in terms reminiscent of the characters' fantasy lives: "The autumn trees, ravaged as they are, take on the flash of tattered flags kindling in the gloom of cool cathedral caves where gold letters on marble pages describe death in battle and how bones bleach and burn far away in Indian sands" (192). Behind this articulation, one hears the voices that inform Lily's quest for Mrs. Ramsay and Mrs. Ramsay's own romantic travelogue: her adventures as a dark wedge-shaped core. Even the "depths of darkness" the passage imagines take on a fictional cast: "In the ruined room, picnickers would have lit their kettles; lovers sought shelter there, lying on the bare boards; and the shepherd stored his dinner on the bricks, and the tramp slept with his coat round him to ward off the cold" (208). Peopling the abyss, the narrative domesticates darkness in a series of received vignettes.

Similarly, the narrative domesticates Mrs. McNab, the "force" working to forestall the very destruction the narrative projects.[34] "[S]omething not highly conscious; something that leered, something that lurched; something not inspired to go about its work with dignified ritual or solemn chanting" (209), Mrs. McNab nonetheless occupies a comfortable domestic space: ". . . she unwound her ball of memories, sitting in the wicker arm-chair by the nursery fender" (211). While conferring on her mythic powers (to tear the "veil of silence," restore life to the wasteland, vouchsafe answers to the mystics on the shore), the narrative keeps her in her place. Mrs. McNab rends "with hands that had stood in the wash-tub," grinds "with boots that had crunched the shingle" (196), and she continues, despite her heroic performance, "to drink and gossip as before" (198).

Itself a force working to control the chaos it represents, the narrative exercises its authority on the figure of the char; it subjects Mrs. McNab to a "rescuing" effort, illuminating the obscurity of her existence with flashes of visionary light:

> Visions of joy there must have been at the wash-tub, say with her children (yet two had been base-born and one had deserted her), at the public-house, drinking; turning over scraps in her drawers. Some cleavage of the dark there must have been, some channel in the depths of obscurity through which light enough issued to twist her face grinning in the glass and make her, turning to her job again, mumble out the old music hall song. (197–98)

Like Mrs. Ramsay who dispenses wedge-shape cores of darkness to everyone she knows ("And to everybody there was always this sense of unlimited resources, she supposed" [96]), the narrative fashions even the unwieldy material of Mrs. McNab in its own image, gracing her with saving insight. Subordinating the recalcitrant details of her life (literally, embedding them parenthetically), the narrative appropriates Mrs. McNab's voice, insisting on its own authoritative reconstruction of what *her* experience "must have been."

Manuscript versions of the passage place such assertions in a more doubtful light: "Was it, then, that she had her consolations . . ?"; "Were there then for Mrs. McNab . . . ?"[35] The shift from hesitant questioning betrays the narrative's knowing stance—a position the narrative can never fully elide. Slipping into the gnomic voice of omniscient authority ("For our penitence deserves a glimpse only; our toil respite only" [193]), the narrative invokes the type of figures its practice would seem to undermine: divine goodness parting the curtain to reveal or withhold "the clear words of truth." Similarly, the narrative invokes the human presences it denies: "Listening (had there been any one to listen) from the upper rooms of the empty house only gigantic chaos streaked with lightning could have been heard" (202). Bound to the laws of representation, the narrative grounds its "otherness" in the known, positing hypothetical sleepers who occupy the reader's meaning-hunting place: "And should any sleeper fancying that he might find on the beach an answer to his doubts . . ." (193).[36] By the middle of the section, these night walkers take on a life of their own, their fanciful excursion now an accomplished fact: "At that season those who had gone down to pace the beach and ask of the sea and sky what message they reported or what vision they affirmed had to consider . . . something out of harmony with this jocundity and this serenity" (201).

Retreating into the familiar, echoing conventional forms of authority, the narrative voice thus reveals its complicity in the dominant discursive modes. In doing so, it makes explicit the narrative practices underwriting the novel as a whole: practices built not upon the positive representation of "otherness" but upon the dislocation and displacement of a single system of narrative control. Crossing the line between character and character, and between its own undifferentiated matter and the construct of a particular consciousness on display, the narrative voice keeps unanswerable the question it continuously prompts: Who is speaking at any particular place or time? Read in the context of French feminist theories, "woman's voice" is not the answer to the novel's problems of representation, but the question the novel repeatedly poses.

*   *   *

Alice Jardine has linked the interrogation of the feminine with the defining features of modernism: "We might say that what we generally refer to as modernity is precisely the acutely interior exploration of that abyss: the unprecedented exploration of the mother's body."[37] In *Heart of Darkness* and *A Passage to India*, the narrative defines itself in and against its exploration of the dark passages that might be culturally coded as feminine; in Woolf's "woman's text," the negotiation of these passages remains problematic. Doubly conceived and doubly tracked, voice appears in the space where de-propriation and appropriation meet to reproduce themselves as opposites. The provisional voice of the narrative both resists and complies with the discourses of dominance as it enacts its fiction of autonomy: the fiction of its own independent existence.

As with "Mr. Bennett and Mrs. Brown," the novel affirms not what it represents but what it gestures at: the pre-voiced or unvoiced; the process of resistance. Thus the novel's final emblem—Lily's painting—testifies not to itself but to what it attempts: "She must try to get hold of something that evaded her. It evaded her when she thought of Mrs. Ramsay; it evaded her now when she thought of her picture. Phrases came. Visions came. Beautiful pictures. Beautiful phrases. But what she wished to get hold of was that very jar on the nerves, the thing itself before it has been made anything" (287).[38] "Voiced," Lily's vision becomes another text, subject to appropriation as a communal property: "the past." For time's passage gives experience its fictive form, and hence, its accessibility—something Woolf seemed to recognize in her own revaluation of her novelistic experiment: "The lyric portions of To the L. are collected in the 10 year lapse, & dont interfere with the text so much as usual. I feel as if it fetched its circle pretty completely this time" (*Diary* 3:106–7). Like the middle section of the text, Lily's painting seals off the disruptive potential of visionary indeterminateness. Critics have frequently identified Lily's painting with Woolf's book, noticing the coincidence of their completion in time and methodology: the words that could refer to either project, "I have had my vision"; the line down the middle that seals off both.[39] But what is not contained in either vision is the voice that frames it. Sealing off vision in its final moments, the text leaves voice open-ended. As the novel's incomplete project—the novel's excess—voice remains *the* modern subject; and as Kristeva might say, it is a "subject in process/in question."

Chapter 7

Afterword: Voice-Over

It remains for these concluding remarks to range over the remains of voice this study documents—literally to voice again (over) the problematic articulations these exemplary modernist works record. It seems fitting to end with an appropriation—the technique of voice-over—that situates this discussion on somewhat altered ground, marking the shift, performed in a variety of twentieth-century critical and cultural practices, from an understanding of voice as emblem of organic unity to one as product of a "technology" of identity. Recent work in film theory, for example, has explored the organization of classic cinema's auditory regime, opening to scrutiny the ways the cinematic apparatus constructs the *illusion* of voice's immediacy, self-presence, veracity, and authenticity. As Kaja Silverman argues, "voice-over" figures in cinema's representational practices as a particularly powerful and productive site of discursive authority—authority significantly differentiated sexually.[1] For in the operation of the voice-over strategy, the male voice comes to be identified with metafictional origins outside the diegesis, while the female voice remains insistently fixed in a diegetic context. In this schema, purity of voice (a privilege dependent upon dissociation from the body, and hence accorded only to male speakers) becomes the measure of the voice-over's (constructed) authority.

Re-voiced in the anachronistic terms of cinematic practice, the voices of early modernist narratives articulate themselves differently.

155

For if the voices we "hear" in the cinema are not what they seem, how much more unstable the *written* voices of modernist fiction with their own elaborate mechanisms for projecting representational transparency. Read in the light of cinematic strategies, the unidentified narrator of *Heart of Darkness*, aligned with a Marlow who assumes a position of increasing invisibility, renders the impression of a doubled voice-over narrative regime; and read in the light of Silverman's argument, we can see yet another way this narrative practice participates in a markedly *male* fantasy. In fact, what film theory might most help us see is the sexual politics implicit in the enunciating agency—in the voice that speaks (or speaks over) the fictional world the modernist novel constructs. For what it reveals is that such voices are never culturally innocent or objective. From this vantage, we might re-read the crisis in enunciation staged in Forster's narrative as a contest between hysterical identification with the feminine and assertion of controlling masculine authority; and we might review Woolf's voicing strategies, ranging from the mimicry of male authority in "Mr. Bennett and Mrs. Brown" to the "refusals" of authority in *To the Lighthouse*'s disembodied language of the body, as another gendered representation of modernism's characteristic negotiation between subversion and complicity.

If the application of narrative theory to film literalizes or materializes certain narrative practices, reading back into novels the insights elicited from film studies helps us more clearly to see the invisible apparatus that produces and supports the fictive voice's "naturalness." As a self-conscious inscription of narrative agency, the technique of voice-over simultaneously reveals and disguises the constructedness of its authority, and thus proves particularly useful for articulating the modern novel's own acts of narrative double-voicing. Applied to the practice of novels, it reactivates the contradictions built into modernism's positions of enunciation—the type of contradictions this study has demonstrated. Taken literally, voice-over reveals the fictive pretension to speak above, beyond, or over the embodied text; it points to the voice that lies over—overlays—even modernism's antiauthoritarian efforts.

This study has tried to make visible that "over"-voice and to make visible the contestations that always underwrite such productions of verbal dominance. It has stopped short of pursuing what

Edward Said points to as a future project: "to undertake studies in contemporary alternatives to Orientalism, to ask how one can study cultures and peoples from a libertarian or nonrepressive and non-manipulative, perspective" (24). And it stops short of answering—in any but a negative sense, at least within these texts—the question Gayatri Spivak asks, "Can the Subaltern Speak?"[2] Such projects would entail attention to other texts—certainly texts other than these acknowledged Western literary masterpieces—and more concerted attention to political structures and the non-literary writings of history. My focus here has been more narrowly conceived.

For me, what the term *voice-over* so nicely suggests is the possibility of a voice-specific archaeology: an investigation of the layering of voices that supports the text's verbal surface. To perform this excavation with some degree of thoroughness, I have chosen to look concretely at a limited number of texts. In tracing the stresses and strains of their verbal and vocal graftings, my readings have uncovered the places where "other" voices have been silenced or written over; I have argued that the disruptions and eruptions produced by these sites of struggle distinguish the modernist aesthetic. While my practice discerns a recurring pattern in these texts by which "culture" appropriates the fictive voice of individuality, I remain convinced that the textual performances I isolate are anything but monolithic—and hence of interest in their details and worthy of extended scrutiny. My own perspective has kept me focused on the voicings-over these texts most insistently demonstrate: the ones attendant upon their own conflicted positions both inside and outside their culture's discourses of dominance. I have not seen fit to "correct" their omissions by attempting to make the silenced voices speak; such an act, I believe, would trivialize or distort the powerful operations of cultural hegemony these texts both resist and illustrate. And the effort would reveal little more than my own unacknowledged appropriations.

The works I have chosen, in fact, have been of interest in part precisely because they represent one of the dominant voices of literary modernism. Of course, to support these features of voice as distinctive of modernism more generally and to support the apocalyptic possibilities this study suggests (of voice being finished or over, the end of voice as we know it), one would have to consider other texts. The novels of Joyce and the poetry of Eliot and Pound represent particularly fruitful ground for such inquiry, especially given the complexities of their political implications and of their aesthetic practices and techniques. In their cultivation of difficulty and their showcasing of their gleanings from literary and cultural history, these authors and texts perform their appropriations self-consciously; on the surface, then, at least, they thus remain more distanced from the fiction of original apprehension and verbal authenticity, even as they construct increasingly intricate and complex replications of it. But I have chosen rather to focus here on a particular "liberal" voice—a voice overtly invested in its unique individuality—and to track its complicitous relations to what might be seen as a verbal (or vocal) superstructure. And I have chosen to focus on works whose historical reception has given them a peculiar status as alternatively, and sometimes simultaneously, the popular and elite voice of both their and our cultures.

Within the careers of the authors I address, these studies of voice occupy rather different positions. For Conrad, the "end" of voice I document in *Heart of Darkness* marks the beginning of his established position as a significant writer in English; and at least retrospectively, the narrative of *Heart of Darkness* has come to represent the "voice" we identify as distinctively, and unmistakably, "Conrad." Somewhat paradoxically, the breakdown of voice that novel interrogates seems to have worked for Conrad as an enabling fiction, making possible, for example, the replicable voice of Marlow (*Lord Jim*, *Chance*) as a "believable" identity—so believable that critics continue to debate the self-consistency of this voice across different novels. The marking of voice, moreover, that *Heart of Darkness* initiates returns throughout Conrad's career as a continuing obsession. If nowhere performed with the almost allegorical purity of that early effort, the tracking of voice continues to organize Conrad's fictional output. Witness, for example, the production and reproduction of Marlow's voice in the face of Jim's inarticulateness (*Lord Jim*), and the staging there of the drama of third versus first person narration, oral versus written accounts, voice versus action and gesture; the inaccessibility of voice (differentiated by race, gender, religion, nationality) to the coherent reconstructions of literature or history (*Nostromo*); the infiltration of voices—private, political, and professional—that reproduce the urban, international world of espionage in the sanctuary of the domestic (*The Secret Agent*); the foregrounding of translation in the recovery of voice as it is discriminated along the axes of nation, profession, age, class, and gender (*Under Western Eyes*).

If Conrad's career leads him from the fantasy of pure voice to the mapping of cultural nuances and discriminations, Forster's career follows an opposite trajectory. The assured vocal distinctions that uphold his mannered, domestic comedies (*Where Angels Fear to Tread*, *A Room with a View*, *Howards End*) dissolve in *A Passage to India*'s vexed explorations of verbal autonomy. The uninflected voice becomes the novel's governing fiction and discredited possibility. For as the novel demonstrates repeatedly—if not obsessively—every voice has echoes that resound culturally. The marked change in voice, variously explained, that distinguishes *Passage*'s narrating persona from that of the earlier novels can be understood in precisely the terms that the operation of voice-over activates. For the text reads as if Forster, in his narrative, were attempting to assume the metafictional authority of such a posture (voice-over) without assuming its compulsory cultural trappings: the racial, sexual, and national positions encoded in and organizing its authority. The narrative's persistent mimicry, however, rules such purity out, revealing that there can be no voice "over" the text—inside or outside—uninfected and uninflected by the dominating cultural discourse. For Forster, the end of the fiction of an independent voice—the recognition that all voices are contaminated—marked the end of his novel writing. But the nonfictional essays that close his writing career rearticulate this problematic, voicing a critique of British culture in the cultured accents of Britain's elite power structure.

For Woolf, the fiction of voice defines her mature practice, informing the aesthetic experiments of her later fiction and the political positionings of her polemical writings. A midcareer novel, *To the Lighthouse* confirms the changing shape of Woolf's artistic direction and marks the culmination of one type of multivoiced rendition. For the anatomy of voice that *To the Lighthouse* performs and perfects gives way to *The Waves*'s more radical display of voices in process. In a kind of minimalist performance, *The Waves* reduces its world to voice only, but voice denaturalized into monophonic components that compete and combine to sound unsettling harmonies. If, as Woolf once suggested, the form of *To the Lighthouse* might most fittingly be termed "elegy," what that novel memorializes and ultimately puts to rest may be the naturalized voice itself—the voice whose fictional power the novel both celebrates and contests. Woolf's subsequent fictions assume an apocalyptic element, so that *The Waves* might be seen to represent "voice" after voice—after voice has been exploded as a self-evident concept. And the fragmentation of voice staged in *Between the Acts* brings its discordant enunciation into that novel's more naturalistic representations. If Woolf's last fictional effort thus leaves voice to occupy the margins, those margins, arguably, have now become the center.

Woolf, then, ends this study in part because her career most fully plays out the possibilities of voice and voicing. To the question, "After voice—what?" that this analysis might prompt, Woolf provides the answer, "voice over"—the postmodern voice, voice over again, voice differently. The reconstituted voice—the voice constituted in contradiction—informs Woolf's last published writings, works that foreground the mutual implication of the ideological and the aesthetic. The notorious citations, for example, that structure *Three Guineas* mark Woolf as a kind of early "appropriation artist." And the split in enunciation that defined Woolf's unrealized project for *The Pargiters* speaks through the genre boundaries of *The Years* to propose the novel/essay. These works, like contemporary postmodern productions, make their "own" voice unlocatable: in flux, under construction, a site of appropriation.

If appropriation has become something of a postmodern discovery, it remains the silent condition of modernist articulation. In "speaking" appropriation in modernist texts, I have been implicitly arguing for a reinvention of modernism under postmodern eyes (ears?). I have been arguing for a practice of reading that might cast the contradictions of modernism in a new political and aesthetic light. In investigating voice in these texts, I am trying, to quote Linda Hutcheon's paraphrase of Charles Russell, "to see what permits, shapes, and generates what is 'spoken.'"[3] I would argue that such attention to the conditions of voice changes the way these texts speak to us; it permits them to speak differently. But in voicing these claims, I am myself appropriating some of the terms currently being used to define postmodernist practice. I do so not to insist that the modernists "did it first," but to suggest that "after" modernism (*post*modernism), modernism's "before" is unrecoverable. The reception of these texts redefines their production of meaning, and part of that reception—as with their postmodern successors—has been their openness to (political) appropriations. "After" postmodernism, however, appropriation seems inescapable.

If one of postmodernism's explicit projects has been to expose and critique modernism's regime of visual mastery, this study puts beside that project the interrogation of modernism's voice-production strategies. It marks the unmarked—and unremarked—voices that uphold modernist fictional authority, putting into question modernism's less visible underpinnings. In terms of voice, it exposes the construction of the given and self-evident, the manufacture of the individual and unique. Like other postmodern productions, its study of voice relies on what it critiques: the modernist investment in the individual subject, personal speech, and the specific text. These terms remain central not only as the site of an internalized contest in the modernism this study reconstructs, but as the self-questioning terms of its own critical methodology. In other words, this study participates in the paradoxes of its own position: simultaneously creator and receiver of modernism's postmodern readings. Occupying an uneasy position inside and outside of modernist practice, the critique of modernism produces its aftervoice or echo. Appropriating the voices of modernism, it revoices modernism's most pressing questions.

Notes

Chapter 1

Epigraph from Jürgen Habermas, "Modernity—An Incomplete Project," in *The Anti-Aesthetic: Essays on Postmodern Culture*, ed. Hal Foster (Port Townsend, Wash.: Bay Press, 1983), 6.

1. Fredric Jameson, "Postmodernism and Consumer Society," in Foster, *The Anti-Aesthetic*, 114.
2. Perry Meisel, *The Myth of the Modern: A Study in British Literature and Criticism after 1850* (New Haven: Yale University Press, 1987). Meisel's effort to distinguish the "will to modernity" (modernism's reigning myths) from "the structure of modernism as a whole" (2) has marked affinities with my project. In some ways, I take up an area Meisel puts to the side ("The present study, however, stops short of moving into the study of ideology proper" [3]); my own study presents literary production as more deeply implicated in and less distinct from "ideology proper."
3. Walter J. Ong, "From Mimesis to Irony: The Distancing of Voice," in *The Horizon of Literature*, ed. Paul Hernadi (Lincoln: University of Nebraska Press, 1982), 13.
4. Michel Foucault, "What Is an Author?" in *Textual Strategies: Perspectives in Post-Structuralist Criticism*, ed. Josué V. Harari (Ithaca: Cornell University Press, 1979), 160.
5. See, for example, Ihab Hassan, *The Postmodern Turn: Essays in Postmodern Theory and Culture* (Columbus: Ohio State University Press, 1987). "The assumptions of Modernism elaborated by formalist and mythopoeic critics especially, by the intellectual culture of the first half of the century as a whole, still define the dominant perspective on the study of literature" (30).

6. Albert J. Guerard, "The Conradian Voice," in *Joseph Conrad: A Commemoration*, ed. Norman Sherry (London: Macmillan, 1976), 4.

7. Guerard, "Conradian Voice," 11, 6.

8. Rosalind Kraus, "The Originality of the Avant-Garde: A Postmodernist Repetition," in *Art After Modernism: Rethinking Representation*, ed. Brian Wallis (New York: New Museum of Contemporary Art, 1984). Kraus's discussion of such discourses in the visual arts would seem to have direct bearing on literary practices: "All those terms—singularity, authenticity, uniqueness, originality, original—depend on the originary moment of which this surface is both the empirical and the semiological instance" (22).

9. Douglas Crimp, "On the Museum's Ruins," in Foster, *The Anti-Aesthetic*, 53.

10. See, for example, Homi Bhabha, "Representation and the Colonial Text: A Critical Exploration of Some Forms of Mimeticism," in *The Theory of Reading*, ed. Frank Gloversmith (Sussex: Harvester Press, 1984), 93–122.

11. Rosalind Kraus argues for the determining presence in modernism of the critical terms it seeks to repress: "the ever-present reality of the copy as the *underlying condition of the original*" ("Originality of the Avant-Garde," 22). Other repressed terms include the multiple as opposed to the singular, the fraudulent as opposed to the authentic, the reproducible as opposed to the unique. Meisel's reading of modernism as founded in the paradox of belatedness—in a crisis of originality— also has affinities to the argument presented here.

12. Vincent Pecora, "*Heart of Darkness* and the Phenomenology of Voice," *ELH* 52 (Winter 1985): 993. Pecora summarizes this concern as one with "a voice that speaks and cannot be located, that *is* and *is not* there," what Derrida formulates as "a sign of pure difference (*différance*) that masquerades as presence" (995), but he insists that "the *problem* Derrida elaborates so fully in his work was already recognized as a *problem* by the time of Nietzsche's work, and to some extent had been anticipated in the hesitating and displaced treatment of Schopenhauer's footnote" (995).

13. Foucault, "What Is an Author?" 159.

14. Quoted in Linda Hutcheon, *A Poetics of Postmodernism: History, Theory, Fiction* (New York: Routledge, 1988), 74.

15. Leonard Woolf's control over Virginia Woolf's body and, as her lifetime editor, control over the body of Woolf texts available to us has earned him, in some circles, considerable critical enmity. Some of the implicit issues in his type of editorship have been more generally addressed in Mary Ann Caws's recent essay, "The Conception of Engendering/The Erotics of Editing," in *The Poetics of Gender*, ed. Nancy K. Miller (New York: Columbia University Press, 1986), 42–62. Bell's much acclaimed biography has not been without its detractors; and the sheer number of biographical works to succeed his testifies, in itself, to the challenges and resistance to his singular authority. The aspects of his biography that have occasioned most dissent are his treatment of Woolf's feminism, her sexuality, and her madness. Similar charges have been leveled against the editing practices of Woolf's *Letters* and *Diaries*.

16. Leonard Woolf, Foreword to Mitchell A. Leaska, *Virginia Woolf's Lighthouse: A Study in Critical Method* (New York: Columbia University Press, 1970), 9.

17. Jane Marcus, *Virginia Woolf and the Languages of Patriarchy* (Bloomington: Indiana University Press, 1987), xi. The particular controversy with Bell has also been played out in the pages of *Critical Inquiry*. See Marcus's "Quentin's Bogey," *Critical Inquiry* 11, no. 3 (March 1985): 486–97.

18. Frank Kermode, *The Classic: Literary Images of Permanence and Change* (Cambridge, Mass.: Harvard University Press, 1983), 44.

19. I use the terms *master* and *masterpieces* advisedly to suggest the gender implications of such totalizing critical categories—to suggest what is implicit in the definitions of classic stature. Much feminist counteradulation (the canonization of women writers) and debunking of male authority participates in this same totalizing tendency.

20. In a much quoted remark, Frederick Karl once called for a "moratorium" on further critical studies devoted to Conrad, "a writer about whom very little new remains to be said unless as the result of original scholarship: manuscripts and typescripts, comparative readings of revisions of texts, unpublished letters, hitherto unexamined relationships with other writers or with compelling issues in the period." See, "Conrad Studies," rev. essay, *Studies in the Novel* 9, no. 3 (Fall 1977): 326. The same type of remark could equally be leveled at Forster and Woolf—and with similar results: scholarship on these writers has not significantly abated—if anything it has grown—in the "aftermath" of exhaustive critical treatments.

21. Alan Wilde argues that the "monumentality" of modern literature is largely a construction of critical assessments of modernism: ". . . modernist literature is by now virtually inextricable from the shape modernist criticism has impressed upon it"—the shape of "something monumental" (20); "What is required, I think, is . . . a recognition that the modernists were themselves somewhat less monumental than they are now taken to be" (47). See *Horizons of Assent: Modernism, Postmodernism, and the Ironic Imagination* (Baltimore: Johns Hopkins University Press, 1981).

22. Jonathan Dollimore, "Introduction: Shakespeare, Cultural Materialism and the New Historicism," in *Political Shakespeare: New Essays in Cultural Materialism* (Ithaca: Cornell University Press, 1985), 9.

23. Lionel Trilling, *Beyond Culture: Essays on Literature and Learning* (1955; reprint, New York: Viking Press, 1965), 27.

24. Lionel Trilling, *Sincerity and Authenticity* (New York: Harcourt Brace Jovanovich, 1971), 99.

25. Joseph Conrad, *Heart of Darkness*, rev. ed., ed. Robert Kimbrough (New York: W. W. Norton & Company, 1971), 71.

26. Chinua Achebe, "An Image of Africa," *Research in African Literatures* 9, no. 1 (Spring 1978), 7.

27. In a much quoted comment, Coppola acknowledged the problematic nature of his enterprise: "Remember, in 'Heart of Darkness,' Conrad wrote about how they talked for hours, but he never disclosed what they said. It was a problem; how do

you keep Kurtz alluring after there has been so much anticipation and build up for three-quarters of the picture?" (Quoted in *Cleveland Plain Dealer*, 19 August 1979).

28. By Coppola's own report, the speech was a literal construction—a composite of taped discussions with Brando, typed from the recording, spliced, edited, re-arranged, and rewritten as script over a period of time.

29. Veronica Geng, "Mistah Kurtz—He Dead," *New Yorker*, 3 September 1979, 70.

30. Geng uses the term *cannibalization* in her review (70), suggesting, perhaps unintentionally, an identification of Coppola with Kurtz. This pattern emerges in other reviews that reinscribe the novel's informing mythology, with Coppola as monomaniacal director: Coppola as Kurtz. A *New York Times* review, for example, refers skeptically to the prevalence of "personal movie-making—on the grandiose scale of 'Apocalypse Now'" and, in what reads like a distinct Conradian echo, to the "lack of restraints" on the artist/director (19 August 1979, sec. 2).

31. Quoted in Christopher Hitchens, "Busted Blue: 'A Passage to India,'" *Grand Street* 4, no. 3 (Spring 1985): 215. The comment, appearing in a letter to Bob Buckingham dated June 1947, refers to an offer for movie rights of *A Room with a View*.

32. Noel Annan, "The Unmysterious East," *New York Review of Books*, 17 January 1985. Hitchens reports that after the release of the film, Santha Rama Rau asked "that her name no longer be exploited on the credits" (Hitchens, "Busted Blue," 216).

33. Frank Kermode, "A Passage to Cambridge," *New York Review of Books*, 14 February 1985, 40.

34. Stanley Kauffmann writes, ". . . I think even more firmly that the art in its making transmutes the major elements of the novel into cinematic form, suggests other resonances, and honors Forster. With his view of film, he might not have acknowledged the honor; nonetheless I think it was paid to him." See "Stanley Kauffmann on Films: Fat Part, Lean Criticism," *New Republic*, 10 June 1985, 25. Compare Salman Rushdie: "Forster's lifelong refusal to permit his novel to be filmed begins to look rather sensible. But once a revisionist enterprise gets under way, the mere wishes of a dead novelist provide no obstacle." "Point of View: Outside the Whale," *American Film* 10, no. 4 (1985): 70.

35. Santha Rama Rau, "Remembering E. M. Forster," *Grand Street* 5, no. 4 (Summer 1986): 114.

36. Harlan Kennedy, "I'm a Picture Chap" (interview with David Lean), *Film Comment*, 21, no. 1 (1985): 30. Kennedy uses the phrase "miniaturist of the heart" in his introduction to the interview.

37. Quoted in Rushdie, "Point of View," 16.

38. Hitchens, "Busted Blue," 217. More subtle versions of this sentiment appear throughout the published responses to the film.

39. Quoted in Gerald Clarke, "View from Prospero's Island," *Time*, 12 January 1987, 70.

40. Quoted in Rushdie, "Point of View," 70. From the *Guardian*, 23 January 1984.

41. E. M. Forster, *The Hill of Devi and Other Indian Writings*, Abinger Edition 14 (London: Edward Arnold, 1983), 16, 12.

42. Quoted in Joseph Epstein, "One Cheer for E. M. Forster," *Commentary*, September 1985, 56.

43. Pauline Kael, "Unloos'd Dreams," *New Yorker*, 14 January 1985, 115.

44. See P. N. Furbank, *E. M. Forster: A Life* (New York: Harcourt Brace Jovanovich, 1977), 1:247n.

45. "Madness and Genius in Woolf's Clothing," *Newsweek*, 18 March 1985, 72.

46. John Leonard, "Mother Courage," *New York*, 15 October 1984, 79.

47. Aaron Rosenblatt, *Virginia Woolf for Beginners*, illus. by Naomi Rosenblatt (New York: Writers and Readers, 1987).

48. Jane Marcus, "'Taking the Bull by the Udders': Sexual Difference in Virginia Woolf—a Conspiracy Theory," in *Virginia Woolf and Bloomsbury: A Centenary Celebration*, ed. Jane Marcus (Bloomington: Indiana University Press, 1987), 149–50.

49. Eric Warner, ed., *Virginia Woolf: A Centenary Perspective* (New York: St. Martin's Press, 1984), 4.

50. Ian Watt, *Conrad in the Nineteenth Century* (Berkeley: University of California Press, 1979), 161.

51. Wilde, *Horizons of Assent*, 63.

Chapter 2

Epigraph from *The Collected Letters of Joseph Conrad*, vol. 2, ed. Frederick R. Karl and Laurence Davies (Cambridge: Cambridge University Press, 1986), 60. Conrad to R. B. Cunninghame Graham, 1 May 1898.

1. Joseph Conrad, *Heart of Darkness*, rev. ed., ed. Robert Kimbrough (New York: W. W. Norton & Company, 1971), 21. All future citations refer to page numbers in this edition.

2. The highlighting of this incident in the *Cliff's Notes* attests to its preeminent "teachability."

3. Ian Watt observes, "It is very widely agreed that the scene is treated in a rather strained, melodramatic, and repetitive way, with little of the convincing detail which had generated the evocative power of the earlier major scenes" (241). *Conrad in the Nineteenth Century* (Berkeley: University of California Press, 1979). Watt goes on to articulate the intellectual and philosophical environment against which Marlow's lie should be understood. The essays included in Kimbrough's edition of *Heart of Darkness* provide a useful overview of the traditional readings of and critical controversies surrounding Marlow's lie.

4. In pointing out these affinities, I do not mean to obliterate all distinctions, nor do I mean to ignore the very real differences that separate and oppose Marlow and the manager. But in a narrative centrally concerned with its own distinctiveness, such problematic points of intersection cannot be entirely ignored. While critical practice has extensively explored the affinities between Marlow and Kurtz, it has been less attentive to the other voices that sometimes raid Marlow's discourse: the manager, the accountant, the harlequin, the Intended.

5. While these issues have been the subject of considerable critical scrutiny, they have generally been treated separately and in the interests of arguments that move in

directions very different from the one I am pursuing here. From the vast field of
Conrad scholarship, I isolate a few essays that seem most pertinent to the particular convergences I explore; it will be my practice throughout this chapter to limit
my citations to, for the most part, recent critical studies (studies published in the
last ten years or so), many of which offer useful summaries of and references to the
preceding stages of the debates: Peter Brooks, "An Unreadable Report: Conrad's
Heart of Darkness," in *Reading for the Plot: Design and Intention in Narrative* (New York:
Vintage Books, 1984); James Clifford, "On Ethnographic Self-Fashioning: Conrad
and Malinowski," in *Reconstructing Individualism: Autonomy, Individuality, and the
Self in Western Thought,* ed. Thomas C. Heller, Morton Sosna, and David E. Well-
bery (Stanford: Stanford University Press, 1986), 140–62; Vincent Pecora, "*Heart of
Darkness* and the Phenomenology of Voice," *ELH* 52 (Winter 1985): 993–1015;
Henry Staten, "Conrad's Mortal Word," *Critical Inquiry* 12 (Summer 1986): 720–40.

6. Throughout the chapter I use the term *polygraph* somewhat loosely, conflating in it
a number of different technologies: the traditional polygraph, measuring involuntary physiological responses in blood pressure, pulse rate, and respiration (per-
fected in the 1940s); voice stress analysis, measuring voice modulations, and hence
stress levels in the voice itself (developed in the 1960s); and voice identification
analysis, not concerned with determining lies but with establishing the positive
identity of individuals through their speech. My concern has been to introduce a
vital metaphor for the narrative process as it has engaged the spaces where these
different, but interrelated, methodologies meet; the argument's effectiveness, I
believe, does not depend upon its being fixed to a single, specific technology.

7. The phrase is, of course, Marlow's. His initiation into Africa—the accountant at the
first station, the grove of death, a two-hundred-mile tramp through the jungle with
a caravan of sixty men, a white companion, weighing sixteen stone, uncer-
emoniously dumped by the natives assigned to carry him—quickly recalls to him
the doctor's words: "'It would be interesting for science to watch the mental
changes of individuals, on the spot.' I felt I was becoming scientifically interesting"
(21).

8. Conrad to Edward Garnett, 29 September 1898, *Collected Letters* 2:94, 96. Karl and
Davies note that Cedric Watts sees this event as the genesis of *The Inheritors* (95
n.1).

9. A number of deconstructive readings of the novel explore its deployment of difference and its illustration of the workings of language as a differential system of
representation. These essays touch on several issues of interest to me here and in
the final section of this chapter. See, for example, Perry Meisel, "Decentering *Heart
of Darkness*: Modernism as Metacriticism," in *The Myth of the Modern* (New Haven:
Yale University Press, 1987), 235–46; J. Hillis Miller, "*Heart of Darkness* Revisited,"
in *Conrad Revisited,* ed. Ross C. Murfin (University, Ala.: University of Alabama
Press, 1985), 31–50; Charles Eric Reeves, "A Voice of Unrest: Conrad's Rhetoric of
the Unspeakable," *Texas Studies in Language & Literature* 27 (Fall 1985): 284–310.
Michael Seidel's "Isolation and Narrative Power: A Meditation on Conrad at the
Boundaries," *Criticism* 27 (Winter 1985): 73–95, focuses primarily on *Lord Jim,* but it
offers many astute judgments of and suggestive insights into *Heart of Darkness.*

10. Conrad to William Blackwood, 31 May 1902, *Collected Letters* 2:417.
11. Conrad to Edward Garnett, 22 December 1902, *Collected Letters* 2:468.
12. Edward W. Said traces the complex relations and priorities in Conrad's writings between vision and speech. He argues that "Conrad's primary mode, although he is a writer, is presented as the oral, and his ambition is to move toward the visual." "Conrad: The Presentation of Narrative" in *The World, the Text, and the Critic* (Cambridge, Mass.: Harvard University Press, 1983), 106. My own argument often reads this dynamic conversely—as operating the other way around. Said offers much intelligent insight, however, into the nature of Conrad's textuality (see 90–110).
13. Toward the end of his narrative, Marlow invokes "The shade of the original Kurtz," who "frequented the bedside of the hollow sham" (69). I have appropriated Marlow's term to describe his own relationship to his audience. Marlow's declaration of his abomination of lies is frequently invoked in critical commentaries, but it is not generally read with the emphasis I have given it: the emphasis on his audience's authenticating presence, "*You know* . . . ."
14. The Norton Critical Edition of *Heart of Darkness* (96) uses this term as title for an excerpt from one of its background sources on the Congo, E. D. Morel's *King Leopold's Rule in Africa* (1904). Such documentary accounting—the excerpt consists of a letter describing a photograph of mutilated natives—contrasts sharply with Conrad's stylized and stylistic renderings of atrocities. Patrick Brantlinger notes that in a letter to Roger Casement quoted in Morel's book, Conrad claims not to have even heard of many of the most graphic abuses of humanity practiced in the Congo. See Patrick Brantlinger, "*Heart of Darkness*: Anti-Imperialism, Racism, or Impressionism?" *Criticism* 27 (Fall 1985): 363–85.
15. Peter Brooks reads the novel along these lines, with Marlow's lying account of the story constituting the novel's motive for retelling.
16. Peter Brooks takes his title phrase from a remark Marlow makes to the manager in their climactic disagreement over Kurtz, "'Oh,' said I, 'that fellow—what's his name?—the brickmaker, will make a readable report for you'" (63). The encounter marks Marlow's alliance with those of "unsound method" as opposed to those inhabiting the manager's world of "false ordering, ready made discourse." For Brooks, the emblem of the "unreadable report" organizes the narrative as a whole: "What we really need, Marlow seems to suggest, is an *unreadable* report— something like Kurtz's *Report*, perhaps, with its utterly contradictory messages, or perhaps Marlow's eventual retelling of the whole affair" ("An Unreadable Report," 242).
17. Hélène Cixous, "Sorties: Out and Out: Attacks/Ways Out/Forays," in Hélène Cixous and Catherine Clément, *The Newly Born Woman*, trans. Betsy Wing (Minneapolis: University of Minnesota Press, 1986), 68.
18. The invisibility of gender has also been sustained by its general omission from serious critical treatments of the text. One striking exception is Nina Pelikan Straus's recent essay, "The Exclusion of the Intended from Secret Sharing in Conrad's *Heart of Darkness*," *Novel* 20 (Winter 1987): 123–37. Addressing the problem of the "feminist reader's access to a text like Conrad's *Heart of Darkness*" (123), Straus engages the question of both the novel's and the academic establishment's sexual

politics, the latter seen as represented in published criticism of the text. Though more polemical than my argument (Straus insists, borrowing a phrase from Gayatri Spivak, that the novel is "brutally sexist"), her astute reading of the novel illuminates many of the same issues that interest me. My own reading shares in the project of "exposing" the ideological structures (Straus would say "delusions") "intrinsic to a particular literary work" (131); but I do not agree that "the woman reader has no access to the sense of pleasure or plenitude" (130) of the text. Such is the case only if one continues to define that pleasure traditionally; Straus's tendency toward single-dimensional and absolutist conclusions belies the rich suggestiveness of her own readings. Johanna M. Smith's "'Too Beautiful Altogether': Patriarchal Ideology in *Heart of Darkness*," in *Heart of Darkness: A Case Study in Contemporary Criticism*, ed. Ross C. Murfin (New York: St. Martin's Press, 1989), 179–95, published after this book was accepted for publication, provides a forceful introduction into the novel's treatment of gender issues, including some of those addressed here.

19. As repository of cultural stereotypes—both racial and sexual—the native woman, by virtue of the threat she represents, serves the interests of the dominant ideology. Moreover, presented as preeminent spectacle—to the reader, to Marlow's male listeners, and to the exclusively male audience of Marlow's fellow colonialists—she remains conventionally placed, in both the narrative arena and on the cultural stage.

20. Chinua Achebe, "An Image of Africa," *Research in African Literatures* 9, no. 1 (Spring 1978): 9. This essay, reprinted from *Massachusetts Review* 18 (1977): 782–94, was originally delivered as a lecture at the University of Massachusetts in 1975. Future citations to this work will be noted in the text. For other contributions to the debate, see: Patrick Brantlinger, "*Heart of Darkness*: Anti-Imperialism, Racism, or Impressionism?" *Criticism* 27 (Fall 1985): 363–85; Wilson Harris, "The Frontier on Which *Heart of Darkness* Stands," *Research in African Literatures* 12, no. 1 (Spring 1981): 86–93; C. P. Sarvan, "Racism and the *Heart of Darkness*," *International Fiction Review* 7 (1980): 6–10; Cedric Watts, "'A Bloody Racist': About Achebe's View of Conrad," *Yearbook of English Studies* 13 (1983), 196–209. See also the special issue of *Conradiana*, 14, no. 3 (1982).

21. Watts, "'A Bloody Racist,'" 199.

22. Clifford, "On Ethnographic Self-Fashioning," 148.

23. Conrad to William Blackwood, 31 May 1902, *Collected Letters* 2:418.

24. Conrad to William Blackwood, 13 December 1898, *Collected Letters* 2:130.

25. See Patrick Brantlinger, "Victorians and Africans: The Genealogy of the Myth of the Dark Continent," *Critical Inquiry* 12 (Autumn 1985): 166–203. In an essay on racism already cited (*Criticism* 27 [Fall 1985]), Brantlinger discusses other sources for Conrad's cultural representations in contemporary anti-imperialist propaganda.

26. Brantlinger, "Victorians and Africans," 184.

27. Clifford, "On Ethnographic Self-Fashioning," 157.

28. Preface to "The Nigger of the 'Narcissus,'" in Joseph Conrad, *The Nigger of the "Narcissus"/Typhoon/and Other Stories* (1897; reprint, New York: Penguin, 1963), 13.

29. Aaron Fogel offers an insightful reading of coercive rhetoric as an informing Conradian practice; he defines "forced dialogue" as "a suggestive model for the organizing principle of Conrad's prose craft, or prose poetic." *The Coercion to Speak: Conrad's Poetics of Dialogue* (Cambridge, Mass.: Harvard University Press, 1985), 5. For a reading of *Heart of Darkness*, see especially 17–21.

30. Benita Parry refers to the concept of the redeeming idea as "a conscience clause" Marlow appends to "a project he condemns as conscienceless." *Conrad and Imperialism: Ideological Boundaries and Visionary Frontiers* (London: Macmillan, 1983), 27. Parry offers an instructive reading of "the fiction's insistently dichotomous iconography" (21), of the way "Marlow's two voices" produce "a fiction that exposes and colludes in imperialism's mystifications" (39). She also offers useful notes and a comprehensive bibliography of the extensive scholarship on Conrad's relations to imperialism and, more generally, Conrad's politics. She does not, however, particularly address the issue of imperialism as a *narrative* event—something reflected in Marlow's relationship to his audience.

31. Homi K. Bhabha, "Signs Taken for Wonders: Questions of Ambivalence and Authority under a Tree Outside Delhi, May 1817," *Critical Inquiry* 12 (Autumn 1985): 144–65. "Hybridity" is a central term in Bhabha's argument.

32. The value Marlow places on the fact that Kurtz "could speak English" to him and the investment he betrays in the owner of Towson's book as a fellow Englishman speak to the desire for cultural and linguistic homogeneity, as do the moments of conspiratorial solidarity he invokes in his English audience. Conrad's own investment, at this time, in solidifying his commitment to Englishness has been noted by several critics.

33. Staten, "Conrad's Mortal Word," 724.

34. Staten sees this passage as an "interpretive crux" (723) for his argument, an argument that focuses on Marlow's conflation of moral and affective restraint. His essay offers provocative and complex readings of both this and the earlier passage in terms of Marlow's "ethos of manliness."

35. Bhabha highlights this dynamic as a central feature of the hybridity of the colonialist text.

36. See, for example, Albert J. Guerard, *Conrad the Novelist* (Cambridge, Mass.: Harvard University Press, 1958). Guerard's argument can be summed up by this typical claim: "Substantially and in its central emphasis 'Heart of Darkness' concerns Marlow (projection to whatever great or small degree of a more irrecoverable Conrad) and his journey toward and through certain facets or potentialities of self" (38). This central assumption informs a whole tradition of readings of Conrad whose manifestations surface in widely different ways. Perry Meisel targets Guerard's "canonical" reading as the focus of his counterargument.

37. Pecora makes a similar argument: "Voice thus becomes, in *Heart of Darkness*, much more than an aspect of literary technique, or a noun that refers to human utterance. It becomes an object of scrutiny, the focus for an investigation of identity and presence, and for a phenomenological critique" ("*Heart of Darkness* and the Phenomenology of Voice," 1001).

38. A version of Marlow's fascination with maps appears in Joseph Conrad, *A Personal Record* (1912; reprint, Garden City, N.Y.: Doubleday, Page & Company, 1926), 13. In his "Familiar Preface" to this volume, Conrad writes of the artist, "In that interior world where his thought and his emotions go seeking for the experience of imagined adventures, there are no policemen, no law, no pressure of circumstance or dread of opinion to keep him within bounds" (xxii).

39. In a letter to the Hon. A. E. Bontine, Conrad introduces this bond in reference to her son: ". . . there is between us that subtle and strong bond of the sea—the common experience of aspects of sky and water—of the sensations, emotions and thoughts that are in greater or less degree the companions of men who live upon the ocean." Conrad to the Hon. A. E. Bontine, 16 October 1898, *Collected Letters* 2:104.

40. Conrad to R. B. Cunninghame Graham, 8 February 1899, *Collected Letters* 2:160. Letter translated from the French by Frederick R. Karl and Laurence Davies.

41. Pecora, "*Heart of Darkness* and the Phenomenology of Voice," 998.

42. Joseph Conrad, "*Youth*": *A Narrative and Two Other Stories* (Garden City, N.Y.: Garden City Publishing Company, 1903), xi.

Chapter 3

Epigraph from E. M. Forster, *The Hill of Devi and Other Indian Writings*, ed. Elizabeth Heine, Abinger Edition 14 (London: Edward Arnold, 1983), 298.

1. In the first category (the interrogation of Forster's political adequacy), see for example, Benita Parry, "*A Passage to India*: Epitaph or Manifesto?" in *E. M. Forster: A Human Exploration*, ed. G. K. Das and John Beer (New York: New York University Press, 1979): "Imperialism, the expression as well as the negation of modern Europe's values, inflicted a catastrophic dislocation on the worlds it conquered and colonised, generated new forms of tension within the metropolitan countries and brought the west into a condition of permanent conflict with other civilisations. Yet about this very epitome of the contemporary chaos, the novel is evasive; neither origins nor motives are rendered and the concept of exploitation is notably absent" (131–32). Nirad C. Chaudhuri, "Passage to and from India," reprinted in *Perspectives on E. M. Forster's "A Passage to India,"* ed. V. A. Shahane (New York: Barnes & Noble, 1968), is probably the best-known political critique of the novel from an Indian perspective. The middle position (Forster's representation of something wider than politics) is implicitly and explicitly embodied in the whole tradition of psychological, metaphysical, and aesthetic readings of the novel. See, for example, Wilfred Stone, *The Cave and the Mountain: A Study of E. M. Forster* (Stanford: Stanford University Press, 1966), John Colmer, *E. M. Forster: The Personal Voice* (London: Routledge & Kegan Paul, 1975), James McConkey, *The Novels of E. M. Forster* (Ithaca: Cornell University Press, 1957), Reuben Arthur Brower, *The Fields of Light: An Experiment in Critical Reading* (New York: Oxford University Press, 1951). The

third perspective (historical and political documentation) includes Jeffrey Meyers, *Fiction and the Colonial Experience* (Totowa, N.J.: Rowman & Littlefield, 1973) and more recently, G. K. Das, *"A Passage to India*: A Socio-historical Study," in *A Passage to India: Essays in Interpretation*, ed. John Beer (Houndmills: Macmillan, 1985), and Frances B. Singh, "*A Passage to India*, the National Movement, and Independence," *Twentieth Century Literature* 31, nos. 2–3 (Summer-Fall 1985): 265–78.

2. For considerations of speech and silence in the novel, see: Gillian Beer, "Negation in *A Passage to India*," in Beer, *Passage to India: Essays in Interpretation*, 44–58; David Dowling, "*A Passage to India* through 'The Spaces between the Words,'" *Journal of Narrative Technique* 15, no. 3 (Fall 1985): 256–65; Judith Scherer Herz, "Listening to Language," in Beer, 59–70; Michael Orange, "Language and Silence in *A Passage to India*," in Das and Beer, *Forster: A Human Exploration*, 142–60.

3. James Clifford, "Introduction: Partial Truths," in *Writing Culture: The Poetics and Politics of Ethnography*, ed. James Clifford and George E. Marcus (Berkeley: University of California Press, 1986), 4.

4. Molly B. Tinsley argues that Forster's syntax mirrors its subject, frequently resisting the Western forms of climax and closure; see "Muddle Et Cetera: Syntax in *A Passage to India*," in *E. M. Forster: Centenary Revaluations*, ed. Judith Scherer Herz and Robert K. Martin (Toronto: University of Toronto Press, 1982), 257–66. My own reading emphasizes the narrative's complicity in conventional cultural forms. This argument is pursued in the next chapter.

5. Talal Asad, "The Concept of Cultural Translation in British Social Anthropology," in Clifford and Marcus, *Writing Culture*, 141–64.

6. Dowling suggests that "for Forster's English characters in particular, their received, spoken English is as voiceless as a piece of writing. One's true voice can be heard only on the other side of speech, beyond the containing arch, in a realm probably silent" ("*Passage to India* through 'The Spaces,'" 258). I remain more skeptical about this "true voice." My own argument concerns itself with the political determinants that foreclose this possibility; I include Aziz as a character whose voice is seen to be appropriated and controlled. I do not discuss Godbole, since the novel does not present him as engaged in this common goal of cultural communication and transcendence.

7. Aziz: "'India shall be a nation! No foreigners of any sort! Hindu and Moslem and Sikh and all shall be one! Hurrah! Hurrah for India! Hurrah! Hurrah!'"

    Fielding: "India a nation! What an apotheosis! Last comer to the drab nineteenth-century sisterhood! Waddling in at this hour of the world to take her seat . . . Fielding mocked again." E. M. Forster, *A Passage to India* (New York: Harcourt, Brace & World, 1924), 322. All subsequent quotations in the text refer to page numbers in this edition. The absence of quotation marks around Fielding's contribution to this dialogue is typical of the narrative's blurring of the lines distinguishing its own voicings from that of the characters. See the following chapter for a fuller discussion of this phenomenon.

8. In this chapter, my analysis of the rhetoric of power tends to concentrate on the determinants of race and nationality, although gender concerns frequently inter-

sect with these structurings. For a fascinating discussion of the rhetorical construction of gender—and its deployment in the colonial situation the novel represents—see Brenda R. Silver, "Periphrasis, Power, and Rape in *A Passage to India,*" *Novel* 22 (Fall 1988): 86–105. Silver's essay, published after the submission of this manuscript, addresses some of the concerns of this chapter, although from a somewhat different position of interest.

9. Bikram K. Das argues that in passages such as this, Forster was "trying to represent, in English, how Indians converse among themselves in languages other than English." He was "concerned with showing that when individuals in a homogeneous linguistic group converse in a language which is native to all of them, communication is natural, spontaneous and unhindered." "A Stylistic Analysis of the Speech of the Indian Characters in Forster's *A Passage to India,*" in *Focus on Forster's "A Passage to India": Indian Essays in Criticism,* ed. V. A. Shahane (Bombay: Orient Longman, 1975), 81, 82. But the English sentiments, accents, and intonations clearly reveal the political and linguistic constraints operating on the Indian speech recorded here.

10. Aziz's warning here is echoed in Ronny's conventional colonialist speech: "So you won't go saying he's innocent again, will you? for every servant I've got is a spy" (204). Similarly, in Aziz's thinking before the picnic, Forster reveals the way the Indians come to buy the colonialist line: "'Indians are incapable of responsibility,' said the officials, and Hamidullah sometimes said so too" (132).

11. Edward W. Said, *Orientalism* (New York: Vintage Books, 1978), 7.

12. Jeffrey Meyers identifies this reference (*Fiction and the Colonial Experience,* 41). The citation has further thematic resonances as well. With Mrs. Moore's loss of charity after her experience in the caves, she can only echo hollow words. Literally, she babbles—speaks "in tongues."

13. I play here on Stephen Greenblatt's metaphor for the textual operation of *Othello,* "the improvisation of power." See "Improvisation and Power" in *Literature and Society,* ed. Edward W. Said (Baltimore: Johns Hopkins University Press, 1980). My discussion of Forster's treatment of improvisation builds upon ideas articulated there.

14. Leonard Woolf, *Growing: An Autobiography of the Years 1904–1911* (New York: Harcourt Brace Jovanovich, 1961), 22.

15. Major Callendar, for example, can only interpret Aziz's delayed response to his summons as an indication of natural shiftlessness ("Now do some work for a change") or subtle deceit: "He never realized that the educated Indians visited one another constantly" (54). Forster himself reports being victimized by this mechanism of the imperial mind. Alluding to the division of the State of Dewas, he notes, "The arrangement must have been unique, and an authoritative English lady, who knew India inside out, once told me that it did not and could not exist, and left me with the feeling that I had never been there" (*The Hill of Devi,* 17).

16. George Orwell, *A Collection of Essays* (Garden City, N.Y.: Doubleday, 1957), 159.

17. Woolf, *Growing,* 46. Forster's *Indian Journal* records another variation on this phenomenon. Referring to a well-known work of Kipling's, "The Enlightenment of

Padgett, MP" (1889), Forster observes of his own experience in India, "I am becoming quite a 'Padgett M.P.', being full of good advice to everyone though too wise to administer it except occasionally to Masood" (*The Hill of Devi*, 197).

18. P. N. Furbank and F. J. H. Haskell, "An Interview with E. M. Forster," in *E. M. Forster: A Passage to India*, ed. Malcolm Bradbury (London: Macmillan, 1970), 29.

19. Brenda Silver argues along somewhat similar lines: "Within this latter discourse, both Adela, the Englishwoman, and Aziz, the Indian man, are elided in the English construction of the event through a deliberate act of periphrasis said by the narrator to be the result of the rape. . . . By reversing the figure, however, we can perceive the periphrasis as embedded in the *cause* rather than the *effect* of the rape. For periphrasis, the elision or negation of the individual human being, functions as part of a rhetoric of difference and power that objectifies the other and creates the space for rape to occur" (Silver, "Periphrasis," 91).

20. Orwell, *Essays*, 155.

21. Orwell, *Essays*, 155. As if to confirm Orwell's judgment, E. A. Horne, an Anglo-Indian official, objects particularly to this reference to "official" speech in *A Passage to India*: ". . . speaking 'officially,' whatever that may mean." *E. M. Forster: The Critical Heritage*, ed. Philip Gardner (London: Routledge & Kegan Paul, 1973), 250.

22. Ted E. Boyle argues that Adela's "irrational" and "emotional" testimony marks a repudiation of rationalism. "Adela Quested's Delusion: The Failure of Rationalism in *A Passage to India*," in Shahane, *Perspectives*, 73–75. Frederick Crews makes a similar claim: "Before Adela can be freed from the echo of the Cave she must retreat a little from her simplistic Western notion of cause and effect. She is finally able to retract her charge because she has achieved a 'double relation' to the controversial event" (*E. M. Forster: The Perils of Humanism* [Princeton: Princeton University Press, 1962], 161). I would argue that Adela's "retreat" reinscribes the logic of cause and effect.

23. Ashis Nandy, in an analysis of the psychology of colonialism, discusses the production of "models of 'official' dissent," models that apply to Fielding's situation here: "It is possible today to be anti-colonial in a way which is specified and promoted by the modern world view as 'proper', 'sane' and 'rational.'" Such models, however, serve as subtle and sophisticated means of acculturation, of preserving the colonial hold. Nandy's analysis of the way colonialism "creates a culture in which the ruled are constantly tempted to fight their rulers within the psychological limits set by the latter" also has relevance for Forster's treatment of Indian dissent. See *The Intimate Enemy: Loss and Recovery of Self under Colonialism* (Delhi: Oxford University Press, 1983), xii, 3.

24. In stating this, I am returning to a position pronounced by Frederick Crews, but I am reassessing the possibilities for critique within the limits so defined: "It seems to me, however, that Lionel Trilling comes closest to the truth when he says that *A Passage to India*, rather than telling us what is to be done, simply restates the familiar political and social dilemmas in the light of the total human situation" (Crews, *Forster: The Perils of Humanism*, 142).

25. Paul Scott, "How Well Have They Worn," *Times* (London), 6 January 1966, 15.

26. St. Nihal Singh, "Indians and Anglo-Indians: As Portrayed to Britons," *Modern Review*, September 1924 (in Gardner, *Forster: The Critical Heritage*, 266); E. A. Horne, "An Anglo-Indian View," *New Statesman*, 16 August 1924 (in Gardner, 249–50). Horne's objections reverse a standard English response, as the continuation of his critique confirms: ". . . just as the average Englishman who goes out to India picks up most of what he knows about Indians from other Englishmen."

27. Sylvia Lynd, "A Great Novel at Last," *Time and Tide*, 20 June 1924 (in Gardner, *Forster: The Critical Heritage*, 215).

28. Chaudhuri, "Passage to and from India," 117.

29. E. A. Horne (in Gardner, *Forster: The Critical Heritage*, 248).

30. Lawrence Stallings, Review, *New York World*, 13 August 1924 (in Gardner, *Forster: The Critical Heritage*, 241).

31. Henry W. Nevinson, "India's Coral Strand," *Saturday Review of Literature*, 16 August 1924 (in Gardner, *Forster: The Critical Heritage*, 258).

32. Ralph Wright, Review, *New Statesman*, 21 June 1924 (in Gardner, *Forster: The Critical Heritage*, 224).

33. Forster himself saw the political implications of this stance; after completing the novel, he wrote, "How dreary fair-mindedness is! Having tried to practise it for four hundred pages, I now realize that it is only a British form of unfairness." See *The Hill of Devi*, liii. The implications of this passage are discussed more fully in the following chapter.

34. Rose Macaulay, "Women in the East," *Daily News*, 4 June 1924 (in Gardner, *Forster: The Critical Heritage*, 197). Macaulay goes on to compare Forster's treatment of Indian characters to fictional treatments in earlier works: "they are as alive as his Cambridge undergraduates, his London ladies, his young Italians, his seaside aunts; they are drawn with an equal and a more amazing insight and vision." She then comments on the convincingness of the novel's portrait of "the Ruling Race in India": "A sympathetic picture, too, for Mr. Forster is sympathetic to almost everyone."

35. Shahane, *Focus*, xiii.

36. Rebecca West, "Interpreters of their age," *Saturday Review of Literature*, 16 August 1924 (in Gardner, *Forster: The Critical Heritage*, 254); H. W. Massingham, "The Price of India's Friendship," *New Leader*, 27 June 1924 (in Gardner, 208); S. K. Ratcliffe, Letter, *New Statesman*, 23 August 1924 (in Gardner, 251).

37. Chaudhuri, "Passage to and from India," 115.

38. Cited by K. Natwar-Singh in "Only Connect . . . E. M. Forster and India," in Shahane, *Focus*, 1.

39. Crews, *Forster: The Perils of Humanism*, 167.

40. G. K. Das, *E. M. Forster's India* (London: Macmillan, 1977), xv.

41. John Colmer, "Promise and Withdrawal in *A Passage to India*," in Das and Beer, *Forster: A Human Exploration*, 118. The assumptions Colmer finds most suspect are "that novels make statements and when they touch on political issues they should tell us what to do next" (119). Such responses echo much earlier claims for the privileged, nonpolitical territory of art. See, for example, these contemporary re-

sponses: "*A Passage to India* is much more than a study of racial contrasts and disabilities. It is intensely personal and (if the phrase may be pardoned) intensely cosmic" (in Gardner, *Forster: The Critical Heritage*, 226); "Mr. Forster is too good a novelist, has too finely proportioned a reasoning faculty, to be concerned with 'issues' in his fiction" (in Gardner, 242).

Chapter 4

Epigraph from E. M. Forster, *The Hill of Devi and Other Indian Writings*, ed. Elizabeth Heine, Abinger Edition 14 (London: Edward Arnold, 1983), 119; hereafter referred to in the text as *HD*.

1. The anecdote Forster records expresses sentiments being formulated, concurrently, by the Society for Pure English (established 1913). One society tract refers to the "special peril" facing the English language on account of "this most obnoxious condition, namely, that wherever our countrymen are settled abroad there are alongside of them communities of other-speaking races, who, maintaining amongst themselves their native speech, learn yet enough of ours to imitate it, and establishing among themselves all kinds of blundering corruptions, through habitual intercourse infect therewith the neighbouring English" (Society for Pure English, *Tract XXI*). Quoted in Philip Dodd, "Englishness and the National Culture," in *Englishness: Politics and Culture 1880–1920*, ed. Robert Colls and Philip Dodd (London: Croom Helm, 1986), 15. The language of danger, disease, and degeneration expressed here, though turned to opposite ends in the novel, runs throughout Forster's treatment of purity of voice.
2. Forster to G. L. Ludolf, 27 April 1922, unpublished letter cited in Donald Watt, "E. M. Forster's Quarrel With the God-State," *Philological Quarterly* 60 (1981): 532. Watt also includes the following unpublished response, dating from Forster's stay in Alexandria in 1917: "I had not realised how much out of touch with my own class I had become. Our table manners remain identical but little else" (528).
3. Edward W. Said, *Orientalism* (New York: Vintage Books, 1978).
4. Quoted in the "Editor's Introduction" to *The Hill of Devi*, liii. See also Forster's letter to Edmund Candler (28 June 1924): "I have almost always felt miserable in a Club, and almost always felt happy among Indians, and I want to go back among them. They won't like my book, I know, because they don't like fairness; dislike it fundamentally, and here something in my own heart goes out to them again. God preserve us from cricket in Heaven!" *Selected Letters of E. M. Forster*, ed. Mary Lago and P. N. Furbank (Cambridge, Mass.: Harvard University Press, 1985), 2:62.
5. In *Delusions and Discoveries: Studies on India in the British Imagination 1880–1930* (Berkeley: University of California Press, 1972), Benita Parry documents the centrality of contagion as a plot motif in English writings about India. The "assault" on Adela is thus a modification of a standard theme. But in widening the scope of the term *contagion* and reversing its thrust, Forster upsets its ideological base. In

Passage, variants of the term *contagion* abound: "Nationality was returning, but before it could exert its poison they parted, saluting each other" (58); "The complexion of his mind turned from human to political. He thought no longer, 'Can I get on with people?' but 'Are they stronger than I?' breathing the prevalent miasma" (60); "'Oh, for God's sake—' cried Fielding, his own nerves breaking under the contagion" (162); "He repeated 'Oh no,' like a fool. He couldn't frame other words. He felt that a mass of madness had arisen and tried to overwhelm them all" (163). E. M. Forster, *A Passage to India* (New York: Harcourt, Brace & World, 1924). Future references to the novel will be incorporated in the text. Where no citation is given, parenthetical page numbers refer to this edition of *Passage*.

6. The analogy between Adela's disorder and Forster's text finds a curious adumbration in one contemporary review, where Adela's cactus-ridden body becomes the implicit metaphor for the novel's effect: "*A Passage to India* is a disturbing, uncomfortable book. Its surface is so delicately and finely wrought that it pricks us at a thousand points." L. P. Hartley, Review, *Spectator*, 28 June 1924, in *E. M. Forster: The Critical Heritage*, ed. Philip Gardner (London: Routledge & Kegan Paul, 1973), 227.

7. Barbara Rosecrance, *Forster's Narrative Vision* (Ithaca: Cornell University Press, 1982), 16, 186. Rosecrance is one of the few critics to insist on the pervasiveness of Forster's narrative voice in *Passage*. For another important and extensive study on the subject, see Michael Ragussis, "The Vision of Evil in Fiction: The Narrative Structure of *A Passage to India*," in his *The Subterfuge of Art: Language and the Romantic Tradition* (Baltimore: Johns Hopkins University Press, 1978), 133–71. For additional essays that touch on some of these issues, see Gillian Beer, "Negation in *A Passage to India*," and Judith Scherer Herz, "Listening to Language," both in *A Passage to India: Essays in Interpretation*, ed. John Beer (Houndmills: Macmillan, 1985), 44–58, 59–70.

8. Paul Scott, *The Jewel in the Crown* (1966; reprint, New York: Avon Books, 1979), 190.

9. Homi Bhabha, "Of Mimicry and Man: The Ambivalence of Colonial Discourse," *October* 28 (Spring 1984): 126.

10. V. A. Shahane's collection of essays, *Focus on E. M. Forster's "A Passage to India": Indian Essays in Criticism* (Bombay: Orient Longman, 1975) is obviously a central work in this debate, as is Nirad C. Chaudhuri's "Passage to and from India," reprinted in *Perspectives on E. M. Forster's "A Passage to India*," ed. V. A. Shahane (New York: Barnes & Noble, 1968), 115–20. Robin Jared Lewis, *E. M. Forster's Passages to India* (New York: Columbia University Press, 1979) documents Forster's exposure to India through records of his Indian travels. G. K. Das, "E. M. Forster and Hindu Mythology," in *E. M. Forster: Centenary Revaluations*, ed. Judith Scherer Herz and Robert K. Martin (Toronto: University of Toronto Press, 1982), 244–56, represents one of the most recent contributions to the discussion.

11. A version of Rosecrance's argument was published under the title "*A Passage to India*: The Dominant Voice" in Herz and Martin, *Forster: Centenary Revaluations*, 234–43. Alan Wilde notes some of these modernist effects, although he stresses their implied counterpart: "In fact, the vacillations, the tensions, the contradictions

tradictions are, as I read it, the very meaning of Forster's life's work, which lies not in its unstable resolutions but in the intensity of its desperate search." See *Horizons of Assent: Modernism, Postmodernism, and the Ironic Imagination* (Baltimore: Johns Hopkins University Press, 1981), 53. Wilde's emphasis on irony as the novel's "pervasive and controlling technique" ultimately aligns his argument more with Rosecrance's than with mine. The problematic status of Forster's irony receives fuller treatment in the later sections of this chapter.

12. Ahmed Ali, "E. M. Forster and India," in Herz and Martin, *Forster: Centenary Revaluations*, 280. Judith Herz's introduction suggests the underlying assumptions of the liberal humanist approach that informs the volume as a whole: "The whole of Forster's life—its interior privacy as glimpsed in the letters, journals, the biography, its public expression as recorded in the fiction, the broadcasts, the essays and reviews—becomes the witness to, the validator of his beliefs" (7). The title of another centenary collection, *E. M. Forster: A Human Exploration*, ed. G. K. Das and John Beer (New York: New York University Press, 1979), reflects similar humanistic concerns.

13. Benita Parry, "The Politics of Representation in *A Passage to India*," in Beer, *Passage to India: Essays in Interpretation*, 30.

14. Abdul R. JanMohamed, "The Economy of Manichean Allegory: The Function of Racial Difference in Colonialist Literature," *Critical Inquiry* 12, no. 1 (Autumn 1985): 74.

15. Evelyne Hanquart's defense of Forster's "travelogues" seems to me typical of the prevailing liberal humanist notion of Forster's enlightened open-mindedness: "Through the pleasure, surprise, and genuine amusement, devoid of any condescension, which permeate them, the recipient was led to an imaginary retrospective participation in noteworthy events of this incursion into Oriental life." See "E. M. Forster's Travelogue from the Hill of Devi to the Bayreuth Festival," in Das and Beer, *Forster: A Human Exploration*, 169. What such a formulation does not allow its practitioners to see is that the terms themselves (pleasure, surprise, genuine amusement) position the speaker culturally and politically.

16. Forster's apparent championship of manliness here seems curious given his numerous attacks on this quality of the public school mentality. Ashis Nandy argues for the homology between sexual and political dominance in Western colonial ideology. He cogently analyzes the deployment of a cult of manliness as an instrument of Western domination. See *The Intimate Enemy: Loss and Recovery of Self under Colonialism* (Delhi: Oxford University Press, 1983).

17. Forster also gives Ronny a characteristic feature by which he is initially known in Indian circles, "Red-nose." In his diaries, Forster frequently remarks his own possession of this same prominent attribute. Such crossing of characters and characteristics renders suspect any definitive attribution of a character as authorial spokesman—a project that has attracted many Forster critics.

18. See, for example, "The caves are readily described. A tunnel eight feet long, five feet high, three feet wide, leads to a circular chamber about twenty feet in diameter. This arrangement occurs again and again throughout the group of hills, and this is all, this is a Marabar Cave" (124).

19. Cited in P. N. Furbank, *E. M. Forster: A Life* (New York: Harcourt Brace Jovanovich, 1978), 2:29.
20. The opening line of the essay reads, "I had better let the cat out of the bag at once and record my opinion that the character of the English is essentially middle class." E. M. Forster, "Notes on the English Character," *Abinger Harvest* (1936; reprint, New York: Harcourt, Brace & Co., 1955), 3. Future citations refer to page numbers in this text, hereafter referred to as *AH*.
21. Luce Irigaray, *This Sex Which Is Not One*, trans. Catherine Porter (Ithaca: Cornell University Press, 1985), 76. Irigaray speaks here of the roles available to women in a culture bound by masculine discourse. As a member of the dominant culture mimicking that culture's roles, Forster's position is not quite the same. The situation is even more complicated when one considers that Forster originally wrote the talk as a speech to be delivered to an Indian audience.
22. Irigaray distinguishes between these terms. Masquerade involves simple role-playing in which the player accepts the conditions of the role. Mimicry, on the other hand, constitutes a self-conscious role-playing that serves to uncover the mechanisms by which such roles exploit the role player (i.e., woman).
23. I allude here to Gerard Genette's terminology in his *Narrative Discourse: An Essay in Method*, trans. Jane E. Lewin (Ithaca: Cornell University Press, 1980).
24. E. M. Forster, *Howards End* (New York: Vintage Books, 1921), 13.
25. Alan Wilde's discussion of the passage points to some of its unstable irony: "So in Forster's meditation on unity, carried on through the description of the two well-meaning missionaries, the irony is only superficially at the expense of Mr. Sorley. . . . More fundamental and more unsettling is the awareness that inclusion and exclusion are alike impossible." See "Depths and Surfaces: Dimensions of Fosterian (sic) Irony," *English Literature in Transition* 16 (1973): 262.
26. Furbank, *Forster: A Life* 2:143n.
27. See, for example, "Bland and bald rose the precipices; bland and glutinous the sky that connected the precipices; solid and white, a Brahminy kite flapped between the rocks with a clumsiness that seemed intentional. Before man, with his itch for the seemly, had been born, the planet must have looked thus. The kite flapped away. . . . Before birds, perhaps. . . . And then the hole belched and humanity returned" (146–47).
28. Richard Martin sees Forster speaking here "with almost devastating sincerity." *The Love That Failed: Ideal and Reality in the Writings of E. M. Forster*, Studies in English Literature (The Hague: Mouton, 1974), 163. Alan Wilde sees Forster "speaking in his own person" and expressing a general sense of malaise. *Art and Order: A Study of E. M. Forster* (New York: New York University Press, 1964), 137. But given this passage's position in the novel, the voice proves much more problematic to place. On the one hand, the ensuing incidents—even in that very chapter—are clearly exaggerated. On the other hand, the "mystery" of the caves turns out to be only an echo after all.
29. "He said much later to the author that the caves were 'not all that remarkable' until they got into his book. He improved them" (Furbank, *Forster: A Life* 1:247n).

30. The range of positions can be gauged by these characteristic responses. Reuben Brower sees the Hindu section as an aesthetic failure: "We are embarrassed not because the possibility of mystical experience is to be rejected, but because we cannot believe in it here as part of the fictional experience" ("The Twilight of the Double Vision: Symbol and Irony in *A Passage to India*," in *E. M. Forster: A Passage to India*, ed. Malcolm Bradbury [London: Macmillan, 1970], 128). Frederick Crews sees Hinduism as the novel's "most engaging fable," but something that remains essentially "powerless before the nihilistic message of the Marabar Caves" (Crews, *E. M. Forster: The Perils of Humanism* [Princeton: Princeton University Press, 1962], 154, 155). George H. Thomson views the Hindu festival as the embodiment of Forster's vision of inclusiveness and unity—one of the great moments when the narrative is "rendered archetypal" (*The Fiction of E. M. Forster* [Detroit: Wayne State University Press, 1967], 248).

31. "It was architecturally necessary. I needed a lump, or a Hindu temple if you like—a mountain standing up. It is well placed; and it gathers up some strings" ("An Interview with E. M. Forster," in Bradbury, *Forster: A Passage to India*, 28).

32. Forster to Goldsworthy Lowes Dickinson, 8 May 1922, cited in Furbank, *Forster: A Life* 2:106.

33. In the introduction to the Caves section of the novel, the narrative even attributes the general reputation of the caves to some impersonal contagious effect: "Nothing, nothing attaches to them, and their reputation—for they have one—does not depend upon human speech. It is as if the surrounding plain or the passing birds have taken upon themselves to exclaim 'extraordinary,' and the word has taken root in the air, and been inhaled by mankind" (124).

34. Forster to Goldsworthy Lowes Dickinson, 26 June 1924, cited in E. M. Forster, *A Passage to India*, Abinger Edition 6 (London: Edward Arnold, 1979), xxvi.

35. In "What I Believe," Forster states, "I hate the idea of causes, and if I had to choose between betraying my country and betraying my friend I hope I should have the guts to betray my country." *Two Cheers for Democracy* (London: Edward Arnold, 1951; reprint, 1972), 66 hereafter referred to in the text as *Two Cheers*.

36. Furbank, *Forster: A Life* 1:199.

Chapter 5

Epigraphs from Luce Irigaray, *This Sex Which Is Not One*, trans. Catherine Porter (Ithaca: Cornell University Press, 1985), 28; Sarah Kofman, *The Enigma of Woman: Woman in Freud's Writing*, trans. Catherine Porter (Ithaca: Cornell University Press, 1985), 48; and Hélène Cixous and Catherine Clément, *The Newly Born Woman*, trans. Betsy Wing (Minneapolis: University of Minnesota Press, 1986), 93.

1. *The Diary of Virginia Woolf*, ed. Anne Olivier Bell (New York: Harcourt Brace Jovanovich, 1978), 2:304. Future references to this volume of the *Diary* will be included in the text.

2. *The Diary of Virginia Woolf*, ed. Anne Olivier Bell (New York: Harcourt Brace Jovanovich, 1980), 3:104. Future references to this volume of the *Diary* will be included in the text.

3. *The Letters of Virginia Woolf*, ed. Nigel Nicolson and Joanne Trautmann (New York: Harcourt Brace Jovanovich, 1977), 3:79. Future references to this volume of the *Letters* will be included in the text.

4. *The Letters of Virginia Woolf*, ed. Nigel Nicolson and Joanne Trautmann (New York: Harcourt Brace Jovanovich, 1978), 4:302. Future references to this volume of the *Letters* will be included in the text.

5. *The Letters of Virginia Woolf*, ed. Nigel Nicolson and Joanne Trautmann (New York: Harcourt Brace Jovanovich, 1976), 2:428. Future references to this volume of the *Letters* will be included in the text.

6. Although "The Mark on the Wall" does not explicitly name its speaker as female, gender coding operates on the level of both style and content. The speaker's meditation offers a critique of the hallmarks of masculine thought: logic, precedence, causality, honor, rules, linearity, hierarchy. The masculine intervention of the discourse of "fact" ("Someone is standing over me and saying—'I'm going out to buy a newspaper . . . . All the same, I don't see why we should have a snail on our wall'") closes the story by foreclosing the woman speaker's inconclusive, self-proliferating text. See *The Complete Shorter Fiction of Virginia Woolf*, ed. Susan Dick (San Diego: Harcourt Brace Jovanovich, 1985), 77–83.

7. Virginia Woolf, *Moments of Being: Unpublished Autobiographical Writings*, ed. Jeanne Schulkind (New York: Harcourt Brace Jovanovich, 1976), 129.

8. In a letter to Clive Bell, Virginia Woolf offered these comments on the early writings of Lytton Strachey: "But (you will expect that but, and relish it) there is something of ingenuity that prevents me from approving as warmly as I should; do you know what I mean when I talk of his verbal felicities, which somehow evade, when a true poet, I think, would have committed himself?" (9 August 1908). *The Letters of Virginia Woolf*, ed. Nigel Nicolson and Joanne Trautmann (New York: Harcourt Brace Jovanovich, 1975), 1:344. She records in her diary a similar complaint about Henry James: "He becomes merely excessively ingenious. This, you seem to hear him saying, is the way to do it. Now just when you expect a crisis, the true artist evades it" (*Diary* 2:136).

9. "A Sketch of the Past," in *Moments of Being*, 81.

10. These comments, and the ones above about *Mrs. Dalloway*, occur in the same diary entry in which Woolf notes Arnold Bennett's criticisms of her work—criticisms that many critics see as prompting "Mr. Bennett and Mrs. Brown": "Its a question though of these characters. People like Arnold Bennett, say I cant create, or didn't in J's R, characters that survive" (19 June 1923, *Diary* 2:248).

11. In Virginia Woolf, *The Captain's Death Bed and Other Essays* (New York: Harcourt Brace Jovanovich, 1950), 97. All subsequent references to "Mr. Bennett and Mrs. Brown" will be included in the text.

12. The analysis that follows draws upon the insights of feminist film theory as it has been articulated in the wake of Laura Mulvey's influential essay, "Visual Pleasure

and Narrative Cinema," *Screen* 16, no. 3 (Autumn 1975): 6–18. As will become clear, I intend to use the tools of this feminist theory both to isolate a potential feminist reading of this essay and to interrogate Woolf's own feminism as the essay practices it.

13. In her recent book, *Virginia Woolf: Feminist Destinations* (Oxford: Basil Blackwell, 1988), Rachel Bowlby uses "Mr. Bennett and Mrs. Brown," with its carefully elaborated railway metaphor, to introduce and engage her larger discussion of Woolf's modernism and feminism: "Virginia Woolf's 1924 essay 'Mr Bennett and Mrs Brown' is a kind of literary Clapham Junction for the crossing and potential collision of questions of representation, history and sexual difference" (2). Bowlby's book, which I encountered after the completion of this manuscript, offers an insightful and provocative discussion of some of the issues I address here. Otherwise, only a few critics have considered the gender implications of this staged scene. Beth Rigel Daugherty reads the essay as "a feminist statement, Woolf's declaration of independence" (280). See "The Whole Contention between Mr. Bennett and Mrs. Woolf, Revisited" in *Virginia Woolf: Centennial Essays*, ed. Elaine K. Ginsberg and Laura Moss Gottlieb (Troy, N.Y.: Whiston Publishing Company, 1983), 269–94. Nancy Armstrong sees Woolf's representation of Mrs. Brown as a means of "reasserting the power of female knowledge over and above that which is written by men and of identifying that body of knowledge with the novel." See "Modern Women: Dora and Mrs. Brown" in *Desire and Domestic Fiction* (New York: Oxford University Press, 1987), 246. Makiko Minow-Pinkney sees Woolf's "early declarations of literary identity" as repressing "a potential feminist awareness" by universalizing "the issue into the Oedipal polemic of the generations" (2); but she suggests that the aesthetic project outlined by "Mr. Bennett and Mrs. Brown" may be precisely the one I note and challenge: "[t]o make the woman's voice heard." See *Virginia Woolf and the Problem of the Subject* (New Brunswick: Rutgers University Press, 1987), 2, 7. These critics, however, all see Woolf's modernist aesthetic as essentially compatible with and supportive of her feminism and they define that feminism, with different degrees of investment, in terms of the authentic representation of women's experience and speech; they thus maintain positions opposite to the one I pursue in the development of this argument. To read this essay as feminist in the way I would like to suggest, one would have to redefine the terms of the feminist project, severing it from essentialist notions of authentic femininity.

14. Samuel Hynes comments on Woolf's misquotations of Bennett in her first published version of the essay in *Nation and Athanaeum*, 1 December 1923, in which she comments more directly on his charges against contemporary novelists; his observations offer an interesting sidelight on her practice in the final version of the essay: ". . . Mrs. Woolf was not overscrupulous in controversy, and revised and rearranged Bennett's words to suit her needs" (37–38). See "The Whole Contention between Mr. Bennett and Mrs. Woolf," *Novel* 1 (Fall 1967): 34–44.

15. Woolf does not refuse to play the traditional feminine critical role ("the charming 'lady' critic who aims to placate and flatter"), as Daugherty suggests ("The Whole Contention Revisited," 279); rather she plays with and upon it. In the example

cited (Woolf's notably deferential introduction), the classic gender split (masculine complexity and analysis versus feminine simplicity and pointlessness), the appeal to moral truth, and the exaggerated deference all mark the passage as mimicry: the *pose* of femininity.

16. In the essay's first paragraph, Woolf refers to "the figure of a man, or of a woman, who said, 'My name is Brown. Catch me if you can.' "

17. I do not agree with Jane Marcus, who argues in much of her work that Woolf's revolutionary treatment of class constitutes a central element of Woolf's feminism. Marcus has recently summarized this position: "Unlike many feminist writers Woolf does not privilege gender over class and recognizes that once the woman writer's voice finds its tongue and speaks and writes its own language, other oppressed voices will find their tongues and write the languages of class and race." See *Virginia Woolf and the Languages of Patriarchy* (Bloomington: Indiana University Press, 1987), 13. My own reading here and in the next chapter suggests the problematic nature of "finding one's own tongue"; and here, as elsewhere, I believe, Woolf's class consciousness compromises her feminism. Samuel Hynes reads class bias as the root of what he calls, "The Whole Contention between Mr. Bennett and Mrs. Woolf."

18. Jean Guiguet classifies "An Unwritten Novel," "Moments of Being," "The Lady in the Looking Glass," and "The Shooting Party" as following the same general plan as "Mr. Bennett and Mrs. Brown." He refers to Minnie Marsh as "elder sister to Mrs Brown," arguing that Woolf "undoubtedly" bore this sketch in mind when "elaborating the typical figure on whom she based her theory." Guiguet is concerned with tracing the development of a uniform aesthetic practice and consciousness; he does not consider these essays in terms of issues of gender or class. See *Virginia Woolf and Her Works*, trans. Jean Stewart (London: Hogarth Press, 1965), 332.

19. "An Unwritten Novel," in *The Complete Shorter Fiction of Virginia Woolf*, ed. Susan Dick (San Diego: Harcourt Brace Jovanovich, 1985), 110–11.

20. "An Unwritten Novel," 115.

21. "The Shooting Party," in *The Complete Shorter Fiction*, 254.

22. Virginia Woolf, *Orlando: A Biography* (1928; reprint, New York: Harcourt Brace Jovanovich, 1956), 133–34. Future citations will be incorporated in the text.

23. Virginia Woolf, *To the Lighthouse* (1927; reprint, New York: Harcourt, Brace & World, 1955), 191. A similar type of advance-retreat strategy operates throughout the narrative in other references to sex or sexuality, in, for example, Mrs. Ramsay's unnaming of the thing she names: "Marriage needed—oh, all sorts of qualities (the bill for the greenhouse would be fifty pounds); one—she need not name it—that was essential; the thing she had with her husband. Had they that?" (93).

24. Virginia Woolf, *A Room of One's Own* (New York: Harcourt Brace Jovanovich, 1929), 85–86. Future references to this book will be incorporated in the text.

25. Jane Marcus offers some compelling evidence for the passage's encrypted references to the censorship trial of Radclyffe Hall's "lesbian novel," *The Well of Loneli-*

ness. Marcus's attention to rhetorical strategies and to the historical placement of *A Room of One's Own* in terms of contemporary discourses on sexuality offers richly suggestive possibilities for reading. But her insistence on this passage's "sapphistry" ("Dot dot dot is a female code for lesbian love" [169]) as its ultimate meaning, for example, and on lesbian seduction as the entire book's narrative agency, distorts and oversimplifies Woolf's shifting and self-crossing narrative positions and means. See "Sapphistry: Narration as Lesbian Seduction in *A Room of One's Own*," in *Woolf and the Languages of Patriarchy*, 163–87.

26. Jane Marcus has located a possible source for Shakespeare's sister in William Black's *Judith Shakespeare* (1883), a novel about Shakespeare's daughter, Judith, "the disinherited rebellious younger daughter" (87). See "Liberty, Sorority, Misogyny," reprinted in *Woolf and the Languages of Patriarchy*, 75–95. The existence of such a source complicates and calls into question the celebrated originality of Woolf's "heroine," marking her as another appropriated voice.

27. Barbara Hill Rigney, "'A Wreath Upon the Grave': The Influence of Virginia Woolf on Feminist Critical Theory," in *Criticism and Critical Theory*, ed. Jeremy Hawthorn (London: Edward Arnold, 1984), 81.

28. Sandra M. Gilbert and Susan Gubar, *The Norton Anthology of Literature by Women* (New York: W. W. Norton & Co., 1985), xxxi–xxxii.

29. Sara Ruddick, "New Combinations: Learning from Virginia Woolf," in *Between Women: Biographers, Novelists, Critics, Teachers and Artists Write about Their Work on Women*, ed. Carol Ascher et al. (Boston: Beacon Press, 1984), 139.

30. Daugherty, "The Whole Contention Revisited," 287.

31. Phyllis Rose, *Woman of Letters: A Life of Virginia Woolf* (New York: Oxford University Press, 1978), 256.

32. Bowlby makes a similar point, ". . . it is as if Woolf herself has since become nothing else than the all-purpose 'exemplary' figure of Mrs Brown, source of an endless variety of treatments and mistreatments and calling forth the most diverse and zealous critics and defenders, all eager to put her in her place, high or low, and to save her from those who have put her somewhere else" (*Woolf: Feminist Destinations*, 14).

33. Jane Marcus, "Thinking Back through Our Mothers," in *New Feminist Essays on Virginia Woolf*, ed. Jane Marcus (Lincoln: University of Nebraska Press, 1981), 1.

34. Barbara Currier Bell and Carol Ohmann, "Virginia Woolf's Criticism: A Polemical Preface," in *Feminist Literary Criticism: Explorations in Theory*, ed. Josephine Donovan (Lexington: University Press of Kentucky, 1975), 50. They preface these remarks in this way: "She is not almost defiantly feminine; she is beyond a doubt defiantly feminine. She is in revolt against the established terms and tones of literary study."

35. Toril Moi, *Sexual/Textual Politics: Feminist Literary Theory* (London: Methuen, 1985), 18. I borrow the term "appropriated for feminism" from Moi: "The major drawback of this approach [of Showalter and others] is surely signalled in the fact that it proves incapable of appropriating for feminism the work of the greatest British

woman writer in this century, despite the fact that Woolf was not only a novelist of considerable genius but a declared feminist and dedicated reader of other women's writings" (8–9).

Chapter 6

1. See Mitchell A. Leaska, *Virginia Woolf's Lighthouse: A Study in Critical Method* (New York: Columbia University Press, 1970). For the argument for homogeneity, see James Naremore, *The World Without a Self: Virginia Woolf and the Novel* (New Haven: Yale University Press, 1973): "Everything seems to be refracted through the medium of a prose which tends to blur distinctions" (113); ". . . the whole book is the product of one voice which at times assumes the role of a given character and approximates his patterns of thought" (123). Naremore acknowledges, however, the problematic quality of Woolf's narrative voice: ". . . it seems to become the voice of everyone and no one. It is probably impossible to find a term that would accurately characterize this voice" (75). For other central treatments of voice, see Erich Auerbach, "The Brown Stocking," in *Mimesis*, trans. Willard R. Trask (Princeton: Princeton University Press, 1953), 525–53; James Hafley, "Virginia Woolf's Narrators and the Art of 'Life Itself,'" in *Virginia Woolf: Revaluation and Continuity*, ed. Ralph Freedman (Berkeley: University of California Press, 1980), 29–43; Harvena Richter, *The Inward Voyage* (Princeton: Princeton University Press, 1970), esp. 129–48.
2. Arnold Kettle, *An Introduction to the English Novel* (New York: Harper & Brothers, 1951; reprint, 1960), 2:103.
3. Harvena Richter uses the term *lived reality* to distinguish one of Woolf's defining subjective modes (*Inward Voyage*, vii). The other phrases are taken from James Naremore (*World Without a Self*, 118–19, 148). Naremore specifically cites authenticity: "*To the Lighthouse*, more than any of the classic novels of its historical period, is suffused with the feeling of an authentic love" (134).
4. Virginia Woolf, *To the Lighthouse* (1927; reprint, New York: Harcourt, Brace & World, 1955), 97. Future references to this work will be incorporated in the text.
5. Virginia Woolf, "A Sketch of the Past," in *Moments of Being: Unpublished Autobiographical Writings*, ed. Jeanne Schulkind (New York: Harcourt Brace Jovanovich, 1976), 81. Future references to this work will be incorporated in the text.
6. *The Diary of Virginia Woolf*, ed. Anne Olivier Bell (New York: Harcourt Brace Jovanovich, 1978), 2:186. Future references to this volume of the *Diary* will be included in the text.
7. "(But while I try to write, I am making up 'To the Lighthouse'—the sea is to be heard through it. I have an idea that I will invent a new name for my books to supplant 'novel'. A new ——— by Virginia Woolf. But what? Elegy?)." *The Diary of Virginia Woolf*, ed. Anne Olivier Bell (New York: Harcourt Brace Jovanovich, 1980), 3:34. Future references to this volume of the *Diary* will be included in the text.

8. While "traditional" feminist critics are beginning to gesture toward the insights French feminism might afford to a reading of Woolf, this richly suggestive area has remained largely unexplored. Makiko Minow-Pinkney's recent book, *Virginia Woolf and the Problem of the Subject* (New Brunswick: Rutgers University Press, 1987), advertised as "the only lengthy consideration of Woolf's work in the light of post-structuralist feminist theory," is the obvious exception; her insightful study, however, pursues a more strictly psychoanalytic approach to the novel than the approach I offer here and, I would suggest, represents a more schematic rendering of the text. Gayatri Spivak's "Postscript" to her "Unmaking and Making in *To the Lighthouse*," in *In Other Worlds: Essays in Cultural Politics* (New York: Methuen, 1987) 30–45, introduces Irigaray to open up the possibility of reading Woolf's novel as an allegory of feminine literary production: the production of the womb. The essay originally appeared in *Women and Language in Literature and Society*, ed. Sally McConnell-Ginet et al. (New York: Praeger Publishers, 1980).

9. See for example, Julia Kristeva, "Woman Can Never Be Defined," trans. Marilyn A. August, in *New French Feminisms*, ed. Elaine Marks and Isabelle de Courtivron (New York: Schocken Books, 1981), 137–41. The French title of this interview, "La femme, ce n'est jamais ça," makes the point more forcefully. In a much quoted statement, Kristeva explains, "In 'woman' I see something that cannot be represented, something that is not said, something above and beyond nomenclatures and ideologies" (137).

10. See Luce Irigaray, *This Sex Which Is Not One*, trans. Catherine Porter (Ithaca: Cornell University Press, 1985). This collection of essays elaborates many of the major concerns of Irigaray's earlier *Speculum of the Other Woman*.

11. Hélène Cixous, "Sorties," in Hélène Cixous and Catherine Clément, *The Newly Born Woman*, trans. Betsy Wing (Minneapolis: University of Minnesota Press, 1986), 96.

12. Lucio P. Ruotolo notes a number of examples of such "derivative" speech: the "modest dreams" reflected in Mrs. Ramsay's wedge-shaped core of darkness fantasy; the authenticating power of Mr. Ramsay's reading of Elton's "Luriana Lurilee" or his denigrating reading of women; the sentimental and baroque idiom of "Time Passes." He is not, however, primarily concerned with the type of argument about voice I pursue here; and his final presentation of Lily as "ready in the absence of Mrs. Ramsay to ask questions of her own in a voice of her own" marks his less absolute sense of the operation of such verbal appropriations. See *The Interrupted Moment: A View of Virginia Woolf's Novels* (Stanford: Stanford University Press, 1986), 126, 128, 132–33, 136. Sallie Sears makes a similar argument about the derivative quality of speech in *Between the Acts*. See "Theater of War: Virginia Woolf's *Between the Acts*," in *Virginia Woolf: A Feminist Slant*, ed. Jane Marcus (Lincoln: University of Nebraska Press, 1983), 212–35.

13. *The Complete Shorter Fiction of Virginia Woolf*, ed. Susan Dick (San Diego: Harcourt Brace Jovanovich, 1985), 114.

14. Alice Jardine, "Pre-Texts for the Transatlantic Feminist," *Yale French Studies* 62 (1981): 230.

15. Mary Libertin focuses on some of the issues attendant upon this deployment of quotation in the context of distinctions between direct and indirect discourse and between indirect discourse at the level of character's reported speech and the level of the narrator's relation to the text as utterance. Tracing Mr. Ramsay's recitation in Lily's consciousness, she notes, "It is neither his utterance with his voice nor her utterance with her voice. We hear his 'words' with her voice; but that it is her voice is not definite until the end of the sentence" (172). See "Speech Acts in *To the Lighthouse*," in *Virginia Woolf: Centennial Essays*, ed. Elaine K. Ginsberg and Laura Moss Gottlieb (Troy, N.Y.: Whitston Publishing Company, 1983), 163–85.

16. Minow-Pinkney extends this argument to Mr. Ramsay's practice of philosophy; reading the novel as a deconstruction of the opposition between fiction and philosophy, she argues for its exposure of philosophy's fictional origins and tropes.

17. Although Mitchell Leaska offers a methodology for making such discriminations, the authoritative rhetoric he relies on to enforce his readings betrays the problematic nature of his task. I cite just a few examples from *Virginia Woolf's Lighthouse*: "The second sentence, (11), is *clearly* Mr Bankes'" (52); "When the content itself of a narrator's utterance acts as the signal, the character and tone of his words will *invariably* reinforce the reader's sense of the particular consciousness through which the material is coming" (55); "But if we examine it carefully, we would find at least three clues indicating Mr Ramsay as its source . . . all of which characterize him and thereby establish him *unquestionably* as the *persona*" (56). Despite the clear distinctions Leaska points to, he must frequently underline the evidence for his readers: "I have italicized the omniscient statements" (54).

18. The differential frames within which Mr. Ramsay's (and other) voices are placed can also be understood by exploring the novel's deployment of free indirect discourse. In part, what I want to suggest is that Woolf exploits the possibility of this technique to illustrate and interrogate the way all voices are constructed. In this reading, the representation of voice marks an intersection between Woolf's modernism and feminism. But the problematic aspects of voice identification should suggest the difficulty of reading the novel's characters as transparent markers of gender ideology; my unwillingness to read Mr. Ramsay as simple exponent of masculine thinking (and to read Lily and/or Mrs. Ramsay as feminist/feminine alternatives) marks the greatest distance of this argument from most other readings concerned with gender themes. I have, however, concentrated my analysis on these three voices, since they are the ones most frequently addressed in other arguments about gendered subjectivity.

19. In what clearly seems the orthodox reading of this passage, Jean Guiguet uses this precise phrase, referring to this moment as "the happiest peak to which Virginia Woolf's thought ever attained." See *Virginia Woolf and Her Works*, trans. Jean Stewart (London: Hogarth Press, 1965), 254. James Naremore devotes considerable space to this passage as illustrative of what he sees as Woolf's central theme, "the embrace of the self with the world outside and beyond" (*World Without a Self*, 142).

20. Toril Moi, *Sexual/Textual Politics: Feminist Literary Theory* (London: Methuen, 1985), 13. For other symptomatic readings of Lily as "heroine," see, for example, Jane

Lilienfeld, "'The Deceptiveness of Beauty': Mother Love and Mother Hate in *To the Lighthouse*," *Twentieth Century Literature* 23, no. 3 (Fall 1977): 345–76; Sara Ruddick, "Learning to Live with the Angel in the House," *Women's Studies* 4, nos. 2–3 (1977): 181–200; Phyllis Rose, *Woman of Letters: A Life of Virginia Woolf* (New York: Oxford University Press, 1978).

21. The full quotation reads: "Within his economy, she is the strangeness he likes to appropriate. Moreover, the 'dark continent' trick has been pulled on her; she has been kept at a distance from herself, she has been made to see (= not-see) woman on the basis of what man wants to see of her, which is to say, almost nothing" ("Sorties," 68).

22. Although the narrative attributes Lily's story of the Rayleys to her own invention, critics have almost universally accepted the story as objective reality, often using it to qualify or discredit a sense of Mrs. Ramsay's successfulness as a character (and human being).

23. Luce Irigaray, "The Power of Discourse and the Subordination of the Feminine," in *This Sex Which Is Not One*, 80, 74.

24. Maria DiBattista, *Virginia Woolf's Major Novels: The Fables of Anon* (New Haven: Yale University Press, 1980), 66.

25. Jane Lilienfeld clearly articulates what has become a common critical assumption in readings of the text: "Readers have long known what is now certain, that Lily Briscoe is an artistic surrogate for the author, and that Lily's formal task is analogous to Woolf's" (165). See "Where the Spear Plants Grew: the Ramsays' Marriage in *To the Lighthouse*," in *New Feminist Essays on Virginia Woolf*, ed. Jane Marcus (Lincoln: University of Nebraska Press, 1981), 148–69. Like other readings that take this line, Lilienfeld sees Lily as achieving an "autonomous" identity: "But Lily Briscoe's complex resolution of her love for and dependence on Mrs. Ramsay in Part III is a psychological paradigm for women who seek autonomy" (164). J. Hillis Miller has suggested that Augustus Carmichael may be seen as an author surrogate; see "Mr. Carmichael and Lily Briscoe: The Rhythm of Creativity in *To the Lighthouse*," in *Modernism Reconsidered*, ed. Robert Kiely (Cambridge, Mass.: Harvard University Press, 1983), 167–89. Elizabeth Abel has recently argued for Cam as another author surrogate, complementing Lily's biographical function: "Thus, Woolf's two most explicit textual representatives—Lily and Cam—inherit her competing narrative loyalties. Lily is her vehicle for thinking back through her mother. . . . Cam enables Woolf to dramatise the narrative plight of the daughter who thinks back through her father" (172). See "'Cam the Wicked': Woolf's Portrait of the Artist as Her Father's Daughter," in *Virginia Woolf and Bloomsbury: A Centenary Celebration*, ed. Jane Marcus (Bloomington: Indiana University Press, 1987), 170–94.

26. Kristeva, "Woman Can Never Be Defined," 137. See also, Hélène Cixous: "It is impossible to predict what will become of sexual difference—in another time (in two or three hundred years?). But we must make no mistake: men and women are caught up in a web of age-old cultural determinations that are almost unanalyzable in their complexity. One can no more speak of 'woman' than of 'man' without being trapped within an ideological theater where the proliferation of representa-

tions, images, reflections, myths, identifications, transform, deform, constantly change everyone's Imaginary and invalidate in advance any conceptualization" ("Sorties," 83).

27. Alex Zwerdling, *Virginia Woolf and the Real World* (Berkeley: University of California Press, 1986), 206. Zwerdling clearly does not see the omniscient narrator as a solution to the characters' limited and problematically demarcated subjectivities: "The 'omniscient narrator,' when she does appear, is scarcely more authoritative than her characters and seems to share their confusion. This is why it is so notoriously difficult to determine, in reading a given passage from *To the Lighthouse*, whether and exactly when the character's thoughts give way to the narrator's" (206).

28. Miller, "Mr. Carmichael," 172. Future references to this article will be incorporated in the text.

29. Describing *To the Lighthouse* as a "novel without bound," Joan Lidoff associates such practices with distinctively feminine modalities: "At the heart of this difference is a female sense of fusion, of lack of separation, boundary or division, that permeates everything in the novel: imagery, structure, style, character, plot, tone—and their interpenetrations" (43). Arguing through object-relations theory focused on the mother-child bond, Lidoff presents an image of the text's narrative with certain affinities to the one offered in my argument. But her reliance on a developmental model of psychology and her emphasis on the type of resolution Lily effects mark our divergence of interests. See "Virginia Woolf's Feminine Sentence: The Mother-Daughter World of *To the Lighthouse*," *Literature and Psychology* 32 (1986): 43–59.

30. Julia Kristeva, *Desire in Language: A Semiotic Approach to Literature and Art*, ed. Leon S. Roudiez, trans. Thomas Gora et al. (New York: Columbia University Press, 1980), 25. Barthes's comments are quoted on the back cover.

31. Luce Irigaray, *Speculum of the Other Woman*, trans. Gillian C. Gill (Ithaca: Cornell University Press, 1985), 136.

32. See also, "The Power of Discourse and the Subordination of the Feminine," in *This Sex Which Is Not One*: "This is moreover the danger of every statement, every discussion, *about Speculum*. And, more generally speaking, of every discussion *about* the question of woman. For to speak *of* or *about* woman may always boil down to, or be understood as, a recuperation of the feminine within a logic that maintains it in repression, censorship, nonrecognition" (78).

33. Virginia Woolf, *The Waves* (1931; reprint, New York: Harcourt Brace Jovanovich, 1959), 115.

34. Jane Marcus reads Mrs. McNab's presence in an opposite way, seeing it as positive proof that "Woolf's feminist project is also deeply concerned with class" (13). See "A Rose for Him to Rifle," in *Virginia Woolf and the Languages of Patriarchy* (Bloomington: Indiana University Press, 1987), 1–17. Marcus associates the voice of the charwoman with Kristeva's semiotic. I would argue that if the semiotic is explored, it is not at the level of character but at the level of text. In my reading, the narrative

treatment of Mrs. McNab marks one of the points of retreat from "écriture fémi-nine."

35. *To the Lighthouse: The Original Holograph Draft*, ed. Susan Dick (Toronto: University of Toronto Press, 1982), 215.

36. Maria DiBattista identifies the sleepers with the narrator: "The narrator is the one sleeper 'tempted from his bed to seek an answer,'" (*Woolf's Major Novels*, 95); her reading of the "Time Passes" section astutely argues for the doubleness of the narration—for the ordering impulse that informs even the moments of lyrical excess.

37. Jardine, "Pre-Texts," 223. Her elaboration of this idea suggests its larger, less specific, conceptual reach: "the concept of 'woman' or 'the feminine' as both a metaphor of reading and a topography of writing"; an "overall philosophical fas-cination with what (who) has been left out of Western Thinking/Writing." See also Alice Jardine, *Gynesis: Configurations of Woman and Modernity* (Ithaca: Cornell University Press, 1985).

38. Woolf describes her own artistic enterprise in similar terms: ". . . I shall here write the first pages of the greatest book in the world. This is what the book would be that was made entirely solely & with integrity of one's thoughts. Suppose one could catch them before they became 'works of art.'? Catch them hot & sudden as they rise in the mind—" (*Diary* 3:102).

39. In a much quoted letter to Roger Fry, Woolf once explained, "I meant *nothing* by The Lighthouse. One has to have a central line down the middle of the book to hold the design together." *The Letters of Virginia Woolf*, ed. Nigel Nicolson and Joanne Trautmann (New York: Harcourt Brace Jovanovich, 1977), 3:385. Lily com-pletes her painting by an analogous recognition: "as if she saw it clear for a second, she drew a line there, in the centre. It was done; it was finished" (310).

Chapter 7

1. See Kaja Silverman, *The Acoustic Mirror: The Female Voice in Psychoanalysis and Cinema* (Bloomington: Indiana University Press), 1988.

2. See Gayatri Chakravorty Spivak, "Can the Subaltern Speak?" in *Marxism and the Interpretation of Culture*, ed. Cary Nelson and Lawrence Grossberg (Urbana: University of Illinois Press, 1988), 271–313. Spivak herself pursues the necessarily nega-tive response she finds to this question. Illuminating the dangers of speaking *for* the subaltern, her essay calls attention to the politics of the critic's position and the ways such politics preclude the possibility of the subaltern speaking.

3. Linda Hutcheon, *A Poetics of Postmodernism: History, Theory, Fiction* (New York: Routledge, 1988), 25.

Index

Abel, Elizabeth, 189 n. 25
Achebe, Chinua, 15–16, 24, 39–40, 41
Ali, Ahmed, 89, 179 n. 12
Annan, Noel, 18–19
Apocalypse Now (Coppola), 16–18. *See also* Coppola, Francis Ford
Appropriation: as challenge to authorship, 12, 13; and colonialism, 4; as condition of authorship, 10; discourses of, 3, 4; and enduring value, 12, 13, 24; and feminism, 4, 121, 127–28, 133; in literary criticism, 11–12, 23–25; as modern subject, 4, 7, 160–61; as political, 6, 13, 16; in popular culture, 11, 13–23; as postmodern subject, 4, 160, 161
Armstrong, Nancy, 183 n. 13
Asad, Talal, 64

Barthes, Roland, 144–45
Beer, John, 82
Bell, Anne Olivier, 11
Bell, Barbara Currier, 185 n. 34
Bell, Quentin, 11, 12, 164 n. 15
Bhabha, Homi, 4, 43–44, 87–88
Bowlby, Rachel, 183 n. 13, 185 n. 32

Boyle, Ted E., 175 n. 22
Brooks, Peter, 35–36, 169 nn. 15, 16
Brower, Reuben, 181 n. 30

Chaudhuri, Nirad, 80, 82
Cixous, Hélène, 36, 126, 133, 141, 147,189 n. 21, 189–90 n. 26
Clifford, James, 40, 41–42, 62, 80
Colmer, John, 82–83, 176–77 n. 41
Colonialist discourse: as appropriation, 4, 18; as narrative (in Forster), 72–75; narrative as (in Conrad), 43–44, 46, 48, 50; narrative as (in Forster), 105–6, 107; and power (in Forster), 64–67; theatricality of (in Forster), 65, 71–72, 73, 75
Conrad, Joseph: 2, 3, 5, 6, 8, 9, 10, 11, 13, 158–59; aesthetic philosophy of, 30, 31, 41, 42, 57; and authenticity, 30, 40, 42; critical reception of, 15, 16, 24, 50; and cultural identity, 10, 31, 40, 42, 43, 44, 47, 48, 50; and ethnographic subjectivity, 40–42; and gender, 6, 36–39, 44–50; and indeterminacy of voice, 50–58; and lies, 29–36, 38, 39, 53; and literary pastiche,

193